FEDERAL UNION: THE PIONEERS

Federal Union: The Pioneers

A History of Federal Union

Richard Mayne
Co-editor
Encounter

and

John Pinder, OBE
Visiting Professor
College of Europe, Bruges

with

John C. de V. Roberts
Professor of International Administration
New England College, Arundel

Foreword by Lord Jenkins of Hillhead

St. Martin's Press New York

Scholarly and Reference Division,
St. Martin's Press, Inc., 175 Fifth Avenue,
New York, N.Y. 10010

First published in the United States of America in 1990

Printed in Great Britain

ISBN 0–312–04493–3

Library of Congress Cataloging-in-Publication Data
Mayne, Richard J.
Federal Union: the pioneers: a history of Federal Union/
Richard Mayne and John Pinder with John Roberts; foreword by Lord Jenkins of Hillhead.
p. cm.
Includes bibliographical references.
ISBN 0–312–04493–3
1. European federation. 2. International organization.
3. Federal government—Research—Great Britain. 4. Federal Union (Great Britain) I. Pinder, John. II. Roberts, John (John C. de V.) III. Title.
JN15.M35 1990
321'.04'094—dc20 89–70360
CIP

Contents

Foreword

It is a remarkable thing that Federal Union has been in existence for over fifty years. It is a great deal easier to found a pressure group for an ideological cause – or indeed to found a new political party – than it is to keep it going for half a century. Yet that is exactly what Federal Union has achieved. Why and how?

The explanation, it seems to me, is that while Federal Union has had firm sinews of belief, it has never got itself into an intolerable or exclusive group which could have made it narrowly sectarian. It believed firmly in federalism but it has always been willing to work closely with those who were prepared to sign for part of the journey and it has not pressed them too far about their ultimate views.

Equally it never made them feel like second-class passengers. As a result, many who have worked closely with Federal Union and the Federal Trust and who began carrying light ideological baggage became spontaneously more and more involved in the federalist cause. It has been a remarkably successful recipe for proselytising and advancing the cause of Federal Union.

This ability to be pragmatic has enabled Federal Union to play a major part in the long-running battle for the European cause. Strict federalists might have said it should have been world federalism or nothing. That would have isolated Federal Union and immeasurably weakened the European cause. Without the steady work of Federal Union, I am not at all sure that we should have had the Macmillan government belatedly seeing the light about Europe in 1961 or the Labour Party turning round from its 'thousand-years-of-history' approach and itself applying to join in 1966. I am not at all sure that we would have had the big majority that the Heath government was able to muster in 1971 or the referendum campaign being able to get that massive, nearly two-to-one majority in 1975.

What Federal Union has consistently challenged is the illusion of national sovereignty. I do not think that the need for such battles is over. Britain is now securely in Europe in the sense that no foreseeable government is going to come out of the Community.

But Britain is not wholeheartedly in Europe. It is addicted to semi-detachment and that is a considerable threat even to our narrow national interests, let alone our broader European aspirations. It is almost unbelievable that the government is about to make the same mistake the fourth time running. It is quite extraordinary that a nation should be so incapable of learning. However, this is the sad truth, and it shows that we have more need than ever for Federal Union, with its fifty-year history of gentle persuasion, to teach us imaginative sense.

LORD JENKINS OF HILLHEAD

Acknowledgements

This book was initiated by the History Committee of Federal Union, whose members are:

Ota Adler, CBE (Chairman)
David Barton, MA, FCA
Sheila Barton
John Pinder, OBE
Dr Roy Pryce
Professor John C. de V. Roberts
Douglas Sanders
E. G. Thompson, OBE

Of these, Sheila Barton collected a great deal of taped interview material from Federal Union members: John Roberts collated this and a mass of information from archives and other sources, and drafted much of the first section, particularly the chapter on World Federalism. David Barton contributed the chapter on Atlantic Union. John Pinder wrote most of the other chapters on the post-war period. Richard Mayne shaped the book as a whole, wrote the early chapters, and edited the final text. Without Ota Adler's wise and helping hand the whole project would never have reached fruition.

It would have been impossible to reconstruct the history of the movement, however, without the active and selfless help of countless Federal Unionists. The warmest of thanks are due to them and to all those who, undiscouraged, gave their time and effort to a cause still making the running after more than fifty years.

Introduction

In the last decades of the twentieth century humanity seems to be awakening from old nightmares. The century's early and middle years were burned and scarred by world war and genocide. The scars remain, a fearful reminder of the evil human beings can do. Perhaps we have learned that lesson. The 'cold war' which so long threatened the world with extinction or worse may in its turn have become a forbidding memory. Today, the European Community is a beacon for the whole of Europe, perhaps the embryo of a 'common European home', in Mikhail Gorbachev's phrase, which would be strong enough, capacious enough and adaptable enough to accommodate new recruits or associates, including the eastern half of Germany. But the years of peace since 1945 have also been years of intermittent warfare – in Asia, Africa, Latin America and the Middle East. Can we ever prevent war? Can nations settle their differences by peaceful means?

These questions still are, literally, a matter of life and death. No less vital are their corollaries. What international institutions will really work? How can medium-sized countries hold their own in a world of giant super-powers? What practical steps can be taken towards international law and order? Is 'world government' feasible as a long-term aim?

Gradually and haltingly, piecemeal efforts are being made to supply practical answers. The United Nations and its agencies seek global solutions; in East and West, North and South, regional organisations are tackling specific problems.

Western Europe, scorched by centuries of conflict, is still struggling to shed the legacy of disunity, mistrust, and narrow nationalism inherited from the past. In an unprecedented reassertion of the human spirit, the nations of Eastern Europe are struggling to secure their freedom. In Western Europe, imperfectly, with some reluctance, and against opposition from the extremes of Left and Right, nations already free have been trying for many years to learn from their bitter history by building a 'community' of their once separate nation-states.

So war, 'cold war' and detente have helped foster these political changes; but much of the thinking which underlay them began earlier still. The convictions which matured in World War II and afterwards had their beginnings in the 1930s. They grew, very rapidly, in the year of suspense that followed the Munich agreement of 1938, only to end in war in September 1939. As that year advanced, the fear of war turned into a grim certainty. Some still hoped to avoid it. Others grew resigned and resolute. But everywhere, as prospects darkened, people were casting about for better ways of dealing with international disputes. In Britain, in particular, a small but growing band of men and women came forward with practical proposals. They were too late to forestall World War II: but they were determined that, when that war had been fought and won, their nations should never again tread the perilous path of the 1930s. In books, articles, pamphlets, letters, manifestoes, and public meetings, these pioneers of federal union worked out with surprising prescience many of the ideas, plans, and policies which were to help shape the post-war world. In particular, the work of the Federal Union Research Institute greatly influenced the thinking of federalists on the continent of Europe who made a crucial contribution to building the European Community.

The British pioneers came from all walks of life. There were novelists like Elizabeth Bowen and Ernest Raymond; there were musicians like Ralph Vaughan Williams and Adrian Boult; there were academics like Neville Coghill and E. M. W. Tillyard. Some were already celebrities, such as Commander Stephen King-Hall or Lionel (later Lord) Robbins. Many were unknown. One such was Alec Wallace, who, when he volunteered for the army, had his pay donated to the movement. After his death in a Japanese prison camp, *The Times*, following the instructions he had left with his mother, recorded that he died for the cause of Federal Union.[1]

A few of Federal Union's supporters were professional politicians, later to be both prominent and powerful. One such was Clement Attlee; a second was Harold Wilson; a third, later, was Roy Jenkins. All, whatever their party allegiance, were united in looking beyond the boundaries of the traditional nation-state. The need and the impulse to do so were strengthened by the arrival in Britain of refugees, exiles, and exiled governments from other countries of Europe now occupied and enslaved. With Poles, Czechoslovaks, Frenchmen, Belgians, Norwegians, and many others working and fighting alongside their island allies, World War II became both an international crusade and, as Romain Gary put it in the title of a well-known novel, *Une éducation européenne*.

Nor was its scope confined to Europe. At the time when the United

States Constitution had been drafted, Benjamin Franklin had looked back to the 'Project of good King Henry the 4th', recalling the Duc de Sully's plan for a union of European states.[2] In much the same way, those in Britain who now proposed federal union looked back in their turn to America's *Federalist Papers* and to contemporary thinkers in the United States. Their diagnoses, and the remedies they sought, were as radical and as challenging as those of the Republic's founding fathers.

'Until our reverence for this quite artificial theory of national sovereignty is dispersed there can be no hope of international order.'[3] 'War is inherent in the relations between sovereign states.'[4] 'National sovereignty has been the hidden hand which wrecked the League [of Nations] ideal.'[5] 'Unless we destroy the sovereign state, the sovereign state will destroy us.'[6] 'The remedy is plain: independent sovereignty must be limited.'[7] Even a loose confederation, as attempted at first by the American colonies, was 'little better than anarchy'.[8] Each state 'must surrender the primary prerogative of sovereignty, the right to make war, and with it the ownership of power and of the tools that serve for war. They must agree, that is to say, to form a Federation.'[9]

Then, as now, its advocates had to stress that federation did not mean the submergence of nations in a monolithic Leviathan state. 'Under a federal system, each citizen has a double citizenship: by virtue of birth he is simultaneously a citizen of his state and a citizen of the federal union.'[10] 'The *raison d'être* of union is the preservation of justice and civilization.'[11] To this end, the union would have federal institutions: a legislature of two Houses, similar to the US Congress; an executive responsible to it; and a judiciary to interpret a written constitution and a bill of human rights.[12] The constituent member states would be guaranteed financial self-sufficiency.[13] The nations must be free 'to develop their own culture and institutions'.[14] 'Federation in itself does not prevent the individual member states of the Federation from making such changes in their social system as they desire to make.'[15]

Here, as in other respects, not all those who debated federation were unanimous. Harold Wilson, then a young and little-known economist, argued against another associate of the Federal Research Institute who was already a famous liberal economist, that the 'economic programme as envisaged by Professor von Hayek would mean a denial of the right to practise collectivism'.[16] Lionel Robbins declared: 'There is no reason to suppose that the coming of national socialism all round would diminish the economic causes of war.'[17]

There were similar Left–Right divisions of opinion over relations with Russia, China and India.[18]

The geographical scope of any federal union was likewise open to question. There was general agreement that it should be a federation of democracies: but which? Most of its advocates had in mind a European union centred in the West; most hoped that it would include, among others, Czechoslovakia, Poland, and Finland.[19] For many, the ideal nucleus would be France, Germany, and Britain.[20] For others, it would be a union of the democracies, including the United States.[21] Most advocates of federal union specifically ruled out Russia – partly on account of its dominant size, but mainly because it lacked liberal traditions and institutions.[22] Sir William Beveridge, author of the Plan which laid the foundations of Britain's post-war welfare state, was anxious to include the self-governing British Dominions; but he added: 'Limitation of area is essential; federalism is a strong remedy for a virulent disorder; it is not a healing lotion that can be sprayed over the world.' 'World federation,' he concluded, 'is for the millennium.'[23]

Later, Beveridge retracted that opinion. Clement Attlee, too, spent the last years of his life campaigning for world federal government, and even in 1940 many saw that as their ultimate goal. 'The national sovereign state is justified in so far as it can serve the welfare of all mankind.'[24] But – 'the progress of science and invention has changed the character of war, and its destructiveness is such that if it continues it will destroy society altogether'.[25] 'Federal union, which is the first step beyond the Nation-State towards the World-State, is thus in the direct line of evolutionary advance.'[26] 'A postwar federation of Europe,' wrote one optimistic and forthright lawyer, 'will be merely a step towards world democracy.'[27]

More than forty years on, the historian may give a rueful smile. Forty years hence – who knows? Progress may be fitful; but the aims remain. How clearly and deeply they were articulated in those early days we shall hope to show. How relevant they still are to today's Europe and today's world will become apparent. So, we believe, will our continuing debt to those concerned, sometimes confused, often practical, but always idealistic men and women we have called 'the pioneers'.

1 Against the Tide

For many people in Britain, as elsewhere, the 1930s were a time of frustration and tragic drift. The stock market crash of 1929, the world economic crisis, the growth of protectionism, the slump, unemployment, and the hunger marches were the fateful prelude to a new decade of gradual economic recovery accompanied by steady political decline. Preoccupations at home, each seeking his own salvation, abetted the appeasement of dictatorship abroad. Mussolini already ruled Fascist Italy. Hitler came to power on the ruins of Weimar Germany. The League of Nations, once hailed as a bulwark against aggression, began to reveal its flaws. Sanctions failed to halt Mussolini's invasion of Abyssinia or deter Hitler's reoccupation of the Rhineland. The democracies stood by while Generalissimo Franco established dictatorship in Spain. Nazi Germany annexed Austria. At Munich, Chamberlain and Daladier bought time by betraying Czechoslovakia and handing the Sudetenland to Hitler. It was the last marker but one in the tide race leading to war.

'What can we do?' was a question many asked but few could answer. Some hoped to strengthen the League of Nations. In 1930, David Davies argued the case in *The Problem of the Twentieth Century*:[1] the upshot, in the following year, was 'The New Commonwealth Society', which had Winston Churchill as the President of its British section, and by the end of the decade, branches throughout Western Europe and the English-speaking world. The League of Nations Union also tried, with no more success, to put teeth into the League's talkative, ineffectual jaws. A number of activists organised, and millions answered, a questionnaire on disarmament, the so-called 'Peace Ballot': six-and-three-quarter-million agreed that aggression should be stopped by war. In a notorious, misunderstood debate, the Oxford Union voted not to fight for King and Country. A handful fought for Spain. Millions, and the House of Commons, cheered Chamberlain's 'achievement' at Munich. Everyone longed for what he promised, waving Hitler's empty pledges: 'Peace for our time'.

THE BIRTH OF A PRESSURE GROUP

In July 1938, two months before the Munich agreement, a group of friends gathered over tea in a small office at 44 Gordon Square, London, not far from University College. Their host was a young man in his late twenties named Derek Rawnsley, grandson of the Canon Rawnsley who had written so warmly of the Lake District and who, with Octavia Hill, had founded the National Trust. Lively, husky, and extrovert, Derek Rawnsley had gone from Eton to University College, Oxford, as the first holder of an Exhibition awarded for combining Classics with knowledge of a modern language. He had learned to sail, ski, glide and fly. The story went that, after escorting some emigrant children to Australia, he had delayed his return so long that he could get back in time for the next University term only by flying solo in a rickety old aircraft all the way to Abingdon.

After Oxford, Rawnsley had set up in business at Gordon Square, founding a print firm to supply art reproductions to schools. But he was always restless, eager to try something new. Barbara Wootton said of him: 'He must have had his full share of fun, and he gave more than his full share.'[2] Other friends testified that he had abounding energy, but little political sense. They were always having to bring his grandiose ideas down to earth. Faced by a difficulty, his reaction would be: 'Well, let's do something.'

That afternoon in Gordon Square, Rawnsley and his friends decided, as he put it, that 'their only hope was in the common sense of ordinary people: 99 per cent of decent human beings don't want war. How could they unite to prevent it? And, the time being one for deeds rather than complaints, what could those present do?'[3]

One of Rawnsley's guests was a school and university contemporary who was also a qualified pilot: Charles Kimber, the 26-year-old heir to a baronetcy, and a former colleague of Rawnsley's in an oil company. Although Conservative by background, Kimber was by conviction a conscientious objector. Disappointed by the political record of Baldwin and Chamberlain, he described himself at that time as a 'Macmillanite': Harold Macmillan, the author of *The Middle Way*,[4] was then no longer obeying the Conservative whip in the House of Commons. Two weeks after the Gordon Square meeting, Rawnsley persuaded Kimber to throw up his oil company job and work with him full-time in an effort to 'do something' about preventing war.

At first, both pinned their hopes on a reform of the League of Nations. They knew that many others had had the same idea; and

Kimber spent several weeks surveying the various attempts at reform already made. Then, on 14 September 1938, in the midst of the Czechoslovak crisis, Rawnsley and Kimber held a party for everyone whom they thought might be interested in launching a new movement. The centrepiece was a barrel of beer; but the meeting was more than merely social. Friends, friends of friends, and even relatives contributed to a modest operating fund; minutes were taken; and it was decided to set up an informal organisation, with Charles Kimber as Secretary, and to draft a public statement of its aims. When news of the Munich agreement was announced, Kimber was so disgusted that he was tempted to quit; but his colleagues dissuaded him. In fact, growing disillusion with Chamberlain's alleged 'Peace with Honour' made more and more people anxious and eager for a fresh start.[5]

Kimber, Rawnsley, and their friends made no attempt to align themselves with one political party: they preferred the independent approach favoured by such bodies as the League of Nations Union. Derek Rawnsley suggested that they call themselves 'Pax Union', combining the twin notions of peace and unity, but with a Latin touch to make it international. Others disliked the proposed hybrid title; but they quickly agreed on their objective. What they sought was a democratic European organisation with some degree of power over the nation-states.

One of those present at the debate was a young barrister named Patrick Ransome, who was soon to join Kimber and Rawnsley in founding Federal Union. He had studied under Harold Laski, read international law at Cambridge under Professor Lauterpacht, attended the International Court of Justice in The Hague, and worked for a time at the International Labour Office in Geneva. He was a member of the editorial board of the magazine *Night and Day*, and later was to join the BBC. What made all this remarkable was that he was confined to a wheelchair, having been crippled from birth. A gentle, likeable, rather fastidious man with Liberal sympathies but little taste for party politics, he had found a more congenial role in publishing, writing, and research. Recently, he had written a series of articles on international affairs for *The Morning Post*; and it was these which had led a friend to introduce him to Rawnsley. Now, as the argument about names and aims continued, Patrick Ransome broke in, 'What you mean is federalism', he said.

'SOCIETY IS FEDERAL'

At that time, neither Charles Kimber nor Derek Rawnsley had any clear notion of what 'federalism' meant. The same was true – then as now – of most of their compatriots, even if British administrators, seeing how successfully the North American colonists had devised and applied a federal constitution, might later make federal constitutions for a number of colonies reaching independence. But federal experience and federalist theory, so deeply ingrained in the United States and Switzerland, were and remain foreign to most Britons, whose Constitution – at least in theory – is centralist in the extreme. Even the word 'federal' has been suspect in British eyes. However, it was not always so. Without counting *The Federalist* of Hamilton, Jay and Madison, which although written in America drew its main inspiration from English political thought, there were significant works from the nineteenth century by such authors as Lord Acton, James Bryce, A. V. Dicey, Edward A. Freeman, J. S. Mill, J. R. Seeley, H. Sidgwick and W. T. Stead;[6] and there was interest both in the idea of federations of sovereign states and in the application of federal ideas 'directly to the reorganisation of the British state'.[7] While most of these authors were favourable to the federal idea. Dicey defended the centralist tradition. In his *Introduction to the Study of the Law of the Constitution*, first published in 1885, he included the chilling observation: 'Federalism substitutes litigation for legislation.'[8]

This had not discouraged British proponents of the idea. From 1910 onwards the journal, *The Round Table*, advocated federalising the Empire, which its editor, Philip Kerr (later Lord Lothian), saw as a step to world federation. In 1912 Winston Churchill, persuaded by Lionel Curtis, another of the leaders of *The Round Table* group, argued for a federal United Kingdom; and by 1918 Austen Chamberlain, like his father Joseph before him, and prompted by F. S. Oliver, a friend of Curtis and Kerr and a biographer of Alexander Hamilton, saw federalism as a solution to the Irish problem.[9] On the Left, Bertrand Russell and H. G. Wells were to expound the need for world government, while Norman Angell, H. N. Brailsford, G. D. H. Cole, R. S. Tawney and Leonard Woolf also saw federalism as the solution to 'the problem of war'.[10] From 1917 onwards, the influential political philosopher Harold Laski had espoused the federal idea. In his *Grammar of Politics*, first published in 1925, he declared 'Society is essentially federal in nature . . . authority must be federal also.' Meanwhile in 1929, a 'New Europe Group' had proposed a European federation with a common currency and a common foreign and defence policy, autonomy for the regions and worker participation.[11]

In later writings, Laski made his message even more clear-cut. In 1933, in *The Intelligent Man's Way to Prevent War*, he declared that peace 'cannot be built upon a system of separate sovereign states'.[12] In the 1934 edition of *A Grammar of Politics*, he stressed 'the incompatibility of the Sovereign state with that economic world-order so painfully struggling to be born'.[13] Among other things, he made a series of suggestions for reforming the League of Nations; and his arguments helped convince many people of the need to look beyond the self-interest of the nation-state.

One who needed no convincing was Lord Lothian, a Liberal who had resigned from the National Government in 1932 on the issue of Imperial Preference. After editing *The Round Table*, then being at the centre of politics, in war and peace, as Lloyd George's Private Secretary during the First World War and through the Versailles Conference, he had written extensively on the need for federal government in order to prevent war.[14] In 1935, in the Burge Memorial Lecture, later published as *Pacifism is not Enough (nor Patriotism Either)*,[15] he insisted that war was inherent in an international system based on national sovereignty. Pacifists, he declared, would fail unless they worked for a federal constitution and government with the power to ensure justice in relations between the states.[16]

Soon afterwards, Lionel Robbins proposed a federal remedy for the international economic crisis, in his *Economic Planning and International Order*,[17] published in 1937. He pursued the theme in a series of lectures given in Geneva in the spring of 1939, published as *The Economic Causes of War*.[18] Another book published in 1939, by the historian Ramsay Muir,[19] also showed how British ideas were evolving. As the Chatham House journal *International Affairs* put it:

> The book records the failure of the League of Nations, and sketches the outline of a new world order by which European civilization may yet be saved. It is to be a federation of States which will consent to their sovereignty being limited in three definite respects. First, they must abandon the right to be judges in their own cause and to make war at their own pleasure. Second, they must pursue a common policy of opening the channels of trade.

> And third, they must accept a common regulation of the conditions under which subject people, whether civilized or backward, are to be governed.[20]

LAUNCHING FEDERAL UNION

Federation, then, was already being mooted when Patrick Ransome raised it at Rawnsley's meeting; and the logic of his arguments at length overcame any objection that they were over-ambitious, abstract, or abstruse. A few months later, in January 1939, when the Gordon Square group's first manifesto was printed, it bore the brief, crisp, and open-ended title FEDERAL UNION.

The next step was to seek recruits. Working from Kimber's father's home near Burnham in Buckinghamshire, the group ransacked *Who's Who* for the names and addresses of all those admitting to an interest in world affairs. Lacking a secretary and a typewriter, they had to write every letter by hand. When they took several hundred to the mail-box, the Post Office protested. At last, however, the work was done; and soon, in a trickle and then a flood, the replies began to come in. One early respondent who came to meet Charles Kimber was W. K. Hancock, a constitutional lawyer and Professor of History at Birmingham University. In effect, he was the emissary of a small group at Chatham House, the Royal Institute of International Affairs, which had already been discussing the federalist ideas of Lionel Curtis.

A veteran politician and a Fellow of All Souls, Oxford, Curtis at 67 was a man of extraordinary magnetism whom, as the historian A. L. Rowse put it, 'no millionaire could resist'. 'He believed himself,' Rowse went on, 'intolerably, to be a prophet; what made him tolerable was that he was warm-hearted and lovable.'[21] Curtis had just returned from Australia with his friend Lord Lothian when he received the Federal Union manifesto; and his purpose in sending W. K. Hancock to meet the Gordon Square activists was to see whether they were suitable as potential associates. As Charles Kimber recalled afterwards:

> Curtis himself saw federation as God's will and as a vehicle for extending the Pax Britannica by way of an Imperial federation to which, I suspect under Lothian's influence, he was prepared to admit lesser breeds if they conformed to Anglo-Saxon good

manners. He was tremendously valuable in the early days in giving the movement respectability – or, as he would have said, weight – particularly at Chatham House.[22]

When Professor Hancock reported favourably on his mission, Curtis, Lothian, and Wickham Steed, a former editor of *The Times*, promptly got in touch with the group at Gordon Square, to advise them on drafting a statement of objectives, and to assist them in raising funds. Curtis's preference was for working through a committee of the influential. He helped to form a panel of advisers, consisting of himself, Steed, and Barbara (later Baroness) Wootton, who at that time was Director of Studies for Tutorial Classes at London University and was acting as Secretary to a study group at Chatham House.

Together with Lord Lothian, this advisory panel wrote to friends and likely sympathisers, seeking signatures to a leaflet declaring that national sovereignty had to be overcome and that federation must replace it. Broadly worded as this was, it secured a number of prominent names: the Archbishop of York, the Bishop of Chichester; Lord Astor, Sir Herbert Barker, Sir Montagu Burton, Sir Richard Gregory, Lord Marley, Sir Walter Napier, Sir John Orr, Lady Rhondda; Professor Norman Bentwich, Dr H. Hamilton Fyfe, Lancelot Hogben, Julian Huxley, Ramsay Muir, Lionel Robbins, Seebohm Rowntree, Arnold Toynbee; J. L. Hammond, Storm Jameson, E. McNight Kauffer, Captain B. H. Liddell Hart; Canon C. E. Raven; even J. B. Priestley and Dr Ralph Vaughan Williams. Altogether, there were thirty-five men and women signatories, all eminent in varying degrees. For the time, it was an impressive list.

A WIDER AUDIENCE

Others had taken up the cause independently. Lothian, following the many years he had spent advocating an international order based on federation, had written to *The Times* calling for enforcement of law on the individual as the alternative to war.[23] Richard Law, son of Bonar Law, and a Conservative MP from 1931 to 1954, who was to become Minister of Education and the first Baron Coleraine, had written a series of articles on the subject before getting in touch with Rawnsley and his group. And in the middle of one morning, the telephone rang at Gordon Square to announce Ernest Bevin, one of the country's most prominent trade-union leaders, later to be Minister of Labour in Churchill's wartime coalition and Foreign Secretary in Attlee's Labour government after the war. Bevin was near Gordon Square, he said: might he call in? As Charles Kimber recalled, 'He came stomping across the room and he asked a lot of very searching questions. At the end of it he said: "I will do what I can to get any articles in the Union magazine, and I'll send you the names of anybody who I think might be interested." And he did.'[24] Another left-wing sympathiser was Leonard Woolf, whose study, *The Future of International Government*, published by the Labour Party in 1939, was severely critical of unrestrained national sovereignty.

Meanwhile, Federal Union was seeking wider publicity, partly through notices in the press. In May 1939, at the Friends' (Quaker) Meeting House in London, it held its first public rally. One of the speakers was Professor C. E. M. Joad, Head of the Department of Philosophy and Psychology at Birkbeck College, University of London, and later to become a celebrity on the BBC's 'Brains Trust' radio programme. But the main attraction at the meeting was Barbara Wootton, overcoming her 'strong distaste for international politics'.[25] In her view, federation was a step towards world government, the only way to put an end to war. Not all the movement's founders were so sanguine: but her conviction, strongly held and powerfully argued, won many converts.

Within a few weeks, the movement had published two further pamphlets: one, entitled *Federal Union and the League of Nations*, by Richard Law, and the other *The Ending of Armageddon*, by Lord Lothian. Since Lothian had meanwhile been nominated His Britannic Majesty's Ambassador in Washington, his paper carried a disclaimer pointing out that it had been written earlier and in a private capacity.

At the beginning of July, 1939, Federal Union staged a weekend conference for some 300 members at Besant Hall, Baker Street. The speakers included not only C. E. M. Joad, Lionel Curtis, and Wickham Steed, but also the editor of the *New Statesman*, Kingsley Martin, newly recruited by Charles Kimber. Some years later, Curtis recalled having stressed that 'Federal Union should concentrate on the task of getting into the heads of ordinary people the idea that an international federation was the only way to prevent world war.'[26]

Already, in fact, it was beginning to do so. The 300 people at the Besant Hall conference came from all over the country; and later that month a number of local groups or branches, which had sprung up without any formal organisation, sent thirty-seven delegates to a meeting which appointed a provisional National Council.

MIXED MOTIVES

They came from many backgrounds, and they represented several contrasting schools of thought. Some were disillusioned members of the League of Nations Union, which in the mid-1930s had numbered some half-a-million. Some were simple idealists. As Charles Kimber recalled:

> A great volume of correspondence arrived at Gordon Square from what one can only call disciples of Bertrand Russell, H. G. Wells, and Norman Angell, who had preached the evils of national sovereignty and prophesied, like Tennyson before them, world federation. As a result our initial intake included many to whom federation was an ideal, and who were so unworldly that they saw world federation as a contemporary possibility.[27]

Many recruits to Federal Union believed in Atlantic union. Prominent among them was Professor George Catlin, who for years had been pressing for Britain and the United States to form the nucleus of a future world federal government. Ideas of this sort were given a fillip in 1939 by the publication in Britain of Clarence K. Streit's book *Union Now*.[28] In the United States, this had had considerable success, and groups had been formed across the country to publicise Streit's ideas. His analysis of the world's ills and his advocacy of federal solutions were powerfully eloquent. What he proposed, essentially, was a nucleus of fifteen democratic countries, linked in a federal union; his book discussed how this might be organised, and what difficulties and technical problems would be involved.

In Britain, the organisers of Federal Union first heard of Streit's work from Harold Butler, former head of the International Labour Office. Eagerly, they wrote to the author, who answered that he would be very pleased if they subscribed to his ideas. On closer inspection, they had their doubts. If a start was to be made on some form of union, it seemed to them more hopeful to begin with Britain and her European neighbours, together perhaps with the Commonwealth: the United States were too isolationist, self-sufficient, and overwhelmingly powerful.

Nevertheless, the British publishers of *Union Now* allowed Federal Union to insert postcards in the UK edition, giving the organisation's London address and inviting inquiries. One of those whom Streit's message converted to a belief in federalism was Douglas Sanders, a

Quaker who became a leading figure in the movement for more than forty years. He recognised, as he told Charles Kimber, 'that you are not Streit and you've got something different to say'[29] – in effect, as Kimber wrote later, that the idea of being federated with the USA 'seemed to the three of us who started Federal Union quite unrealistic and, to Patrick (Ransome) and myself certainly, undesirable' – at least until Britain had been united with Europe.[30] Sanders himself gradually came round to this view; but others did not. In Kimber's words, the *Union Now* postcards brought into the movement 'an enormous number of people who were really disciples of Streit and for whom he was the law'.[31] Later, this was to cause problems.

The final strand in Federal Union's growing membership comprised those in whose thinking Britain and Europe came first. For some of them, this included the Dominions; continental Europe was the essential focus – the origin of so many wars, including World War I, the victim of Hitlerite aggression, and the likely theatre of the war that was looming ahead. Exiles from Germany, Austria, and now Czechoslovakia swelled the numbers of those in Britain who were agonisingly concerned with Europe's future. The circle soon widened to include not only academics, but also diplomats, businessmen, trade unionists, and practical politicians.

Some were attracted – and others rather disturbed – by the ideas of Count Richard Coudenhove-Kalergi, for fifteen years or more the leading apostle of 'Paneuropa'. In June 1939 he spoke at Chatham House. France, he declared, 'is waiting till other States associate themselves to its great task of uniting Europe'. He stressed the need for Britain to act. 'Everything depends on this country. If Great Britain has the European vision and the courage to fight for it, our generation will see the United States of Europe.'[32]

A few weeks later, on 26 July 1939, the Director of Studies at Chatham House, the historian Arnold Toynbee, set out in a striking unpublished memorandum his 'First Thoughts on a Peace Settlement'. 'We must aim', he wrote, 'at a political union (a full and permanent federation not just a limited and temporary alliance) between Great Britain and France.' He continued: 'If we accept the establishing of a world-dominating democratic federal super-state as our concrete peace aim, then the logical thing for us to aim at would be to try to expand our Anglo-French nucleus into a federal state embracing all the already democratic states in Western Europe and overseas.'[33]

THE GATHERING STORM

By the end of July 1939, Federal Union was expanding fast. Its subscription income had risen to more than £1300 – at that time a sizeable sum. Around the small core of permanent staff, up to twenty volunteers were helping to handle the growing volume of mail. Membership had doubled to more than 2000, with a score of local branches organising meetings and debates. A newsletter was at the press. An international committee had been formed, with contacts in France, Belgium, the Netherlands, and Switzerland.

And yet, as the summer advanced, everyone knew that time was running out. It was during these last weeks of sunshine and growing uneasiness that a young recruit to Federal Union, the headmaster of Dartington Hall School in Devon, W. B. Curry, wrote one last passionate appeal for unity as Europe drifted inescapably towards war. His book was called *The Case for Federal Union*.[34] It had the movement's blessing, if not an official *imprimatur*. Subtitled 'A New International Order', it was published within a few weeks as a Penguin Special. It reached an immense audience. It still makes cogent reading today.

Curry prefaced his book with two quotations. One was from a letter by the German poet Rainer Maria Rilke, written in the second year of World War I. 'What to write when everything one touches is unspeakable, unrecognizable, when nothing belongs to one, no feeling, no hope . . .' The second was from Bertrand Russell. 'The world has become so intolerably tense, so charged with hatred, so filled with misfortune and pain that men have lost the power of balanced judgement . . . But there is no rational ground for despair: the means of happiness for the human race exist, and it is only necessary that the human race should choose to use them.'[35]

The words were brave: but the days of peace were numbered. 'We realized, of course,' wrote Charles Kimber, 'that short of a miracle we were too late. But at least it was a positive reaction at a time when most people could only hope and could not bring themselves to believe that anything so insane could actually come about and who, instead, persuaded themselves that appeasement would bring the reasonable settlement which the Peace of Versailles had failed to do.'[36]

By now, Hitler was threatening Poland. On 23 August 1939, he concluded the Nazi–Soviet Non-Aggression Pact, leaving him free to pick off his victim nations one by one. Ten days later, the world which Federal Union had hoped to organise for peace was plunged into war.

When W. B. Curry's work appeared, he had to explain 'Why this book is published now':

> It is too late to avert this war, but if we can avoid the mistakes of 1919 we may succeed in averting the next . . . It is not sufficient to defeat Hitler. If victory is to be worth fighting for, we must have better notions of what to do with victory when we get it . . . We shall need a peace settlement different from any other that has ever been made. It must be a settlement that includes the neutrals and the Germans, and tackles the causes of war at their roots.[37]

Even the British government seemed to agree. On 11 September 1939, the Rt Hon. Anthony Eden, then Secretary of State for the Dominions, who had a few months before responded positively to a letter from Lothian about the Federal Union idea,[38] declared:

> For some of us the challenge has come a second time in our generation. There must be no second mistake. Out of the welter of suffering to be endured we must fashion a new world that is something better than a stale reflection of the old, bled white . . .
>
> Can we finally rid Europe of barriers of caste and creed and prejudice?
>
> Can frontiers and faiths, language and commerce serve to unite nations and not divide them? Can we create a true unity in Europe?

History, and Eden's post-war policies, were to give equivocal answers; but Curry was glad to quote the questions in his book. He recalled how, during World War I,

> a few students of public affairs . . . organized themselves to study and advocate the idea of a League of Nations . . . They undoubtedly influenced the course of events . . . The establishment of the League . . . owed something to the advocacy that must, at the time, have seemed to most people voices crying in the wilderness. Is it not possible that advocacy NOW of Federal Union might play the same part in the next few years?[39]

Curry, and his friends and colleagues, were determined to see that it did.

2 At War

When Britain declared war on 3 September 1939, Londoners expected to be bombed. In fact, aerial bombardment was delayed for the long months of the so-called 'phoney war'; but the warning sirens sounded shortly after the broadcast announcement that war had broken out, and schools, firms, ministries and individuals at once put into action the plans to evacuate the capital which they had prepared during the year's uneasy truce since Munich. Gas masks already issued were now carried everywhere; blackout curtains were hastily put up; men and women appeared in uniform; 'Anderson' shelters were erected; street lamps and car headlights were dimmed; everyone prepared for the worst.

EMERGENCY ORGANISATION

Federal Union was no exception. Fearing the threat of air raids on London, Charles Kimber organised its evacuation from Gordon Square to his private house at Lulworth Cove in Dorset. As one of the staff, Margaret Richards, recalled: 'It was like an excursion with a holiday at the other end to most of us. Files now filled a bedroom, and we did the cooking on a rota.'[1] The invasion was not popular with Mrs Kimber. After some weeks without air attacks on London, the office returned to the capital, moving into No. 3 Gower Street. The three founders still retained, however, an office at No. 44 Gordon Square. There space was so restricted that Derek Rawnsley had to be housed in a basement scullery.[2] At that time, the paid and volunteer staff numbered no fewer than eighteen – but was said to be doing the work of forty.

Since 5 September 1939, they had been publishing a small-format weekly called *Federal Union News*. Edited by Kimber, this carried editorials, signed articles, reviews, and readers' letters, as well as practical information and reports on meetings. Paper restrictions limited its circulation to a maximum of 3000; but its readership was greater. On occasion, it forsook its pocket-size format to appear as a broadsheet.

Federal Union's staff and sympathisers were also helping to run a number of outside ventures. Ronald Gillett, a banker member, inspired the establishment of a Federal Union bookshop: it sold, among other things, the Everyman edition of the *Federalist Papers*, Lionel Curtis's *Civitas Dei*, and Clarence Streit's *Union Now*.[3] The runaway best-seller, however, was W. B. Curry's *The Case for Federal Union*.[4] Published just after the outbreak of war, within six months it had sold 100000 copies. In addition to the bookshop, there were also two Federal Union clubs. One, at No. 101 Piccadilly, was founded by Robert Byron, a Fellow of All Souls and the author of *The Road to Oxiana*; the other, further east, was a luncheon club which met for food, drink, and debates every Wednesday at the Old Cock Tavern in Fleet Street, then London's newspaper centre.[5]

The main focus of activity, however, was in public meetings, many of them organised by the branches. These regularly received not only *Federal Union News*, but also notes of topics for debate, including such subjects as free trade, rights of secession, and the possible languages to be used by any future federation.[6] They were also eager for visiting speakers. Some of these found themselves addressing audiences hundreds strong as far afield as Oxford, Manchester, Edinburgh, and Bristol – at times as often as one a day. What had begun as the nucleus of a pressure group was expanding into a countrywide organisation.

Its growth was encouraged by the party-political truce occasioned by the wartime coalition. For obvious reasons, the major political parties – Labour, Conservative, and Liberal – had agreed not to campaign or stand against each other until the end of the war. They could not, however, prevent voters' seeking to express political feelings; and when parliamentary seats periodically fell vacant, independent candidates often did remarkably well. It was a situation exploited in particular by Sir Richard Acland's left-wing movement 'Common Wealth' – whose chairman, the Australian lawyer R. W. G. Mackay, was also a Federal Union activist. In January 1940, Federal Union itself very nearly entered the by-election lists, when one of the Cambridge University seats fell vacant. Federal Union, together with 'many distinguished Cambridge graduates', decided to nominate Patrick Ransome for the constituency, whose voters were some 39000 members of the University. He planned to base his campaign 'on the belief that if the Allies were to offer Federation to Germany, no greater stimulus could be given to the people of Germany to overthrow the present regime'. It was a vain hope; and the proposed election campaign itself came to nothing. Ransome stood down, because the other two candidates Professor

A. V. Hill, Secretary of the Royal Society, and Professor John Ryle, an 'Independent Progressive', were willing to support federal principles. 'I have no doubt,' explained Ryle, 'that an effective union of the democratic states, together with a declaration of rights and greater freedom of international trade, would supply the strongest bulwark against future wars.'[7]

DISTINGUISHED SUPPORTERS

Any new movement with unorthodox ideas is likely to attract eccentrics. Federal Union, no doubt, had its share of the woolly-minded, the crankish, and the politically vague. But what in retrospect may seem surprising is the support it secured from people which a later generation came to call 'The Establishment'.

One such was Sir William Beveridge. As a young man, he had been a social worker at Toynbee Hall, where Beatrice Webb had described him as 'an ugly-mannered but honest, self-devoted, hard-headed young reformer of the practical type'. Brought into the Board of Trade by Winston Churchill before World War I, he had been responsible for setting up the new labour exchanges, and had had a distinguished civil service career, ending as Permanent Secretary in the Ministry of Food in 1919. From 1919 to 1937 he had been Director of the London School of Economics, moving on to become Master of University College, Oxford. This, as it happened, had been Derek Rawnsley's college; and when he was launching Federal Union he had gone to the Master to seek his support. 'I'm too busy to do anything about that now,' Beveridge had answered. 'But if there's a war, come and see me.' When war came, Beveridge was as good as his word. He was to play a key role in Federal Union's academic work.

Other 'establishment' figures who gave the movement their backing included William Temple, the Archbishop of York; H. N. Brailsford; John Middleton Murry; J. B. Priestley; Lord Lytton; Sir Thomas Beecham; Sir John Marriott; Lancelot Hogben, then a Professor at Aberdeen; Friedrich von Hayek, then a Professor at the London School of Economics; E. M. W. Tillyard of Jesus College, Cambridge; and A. L. Goodhart, Professor of Jurisprudence at Oxford. Even Clement Attlee, echoing a Labour Party study group document, included among his Party's peace aims the pithy statement 'Europe must federate or perish'.[8] The Co-operative Party advocated federation. So did some trade unionists. Walter Padley, of the Union of Shop, Distributive and Allied Workers, argued in favour of 'first the Socialist United States of Europe and finally a Socialist World'. In 1941, the TUC's President George Gibson was to tell its Annual Congress: 'I believe firmly in the future federation of nations. But I also believe that pending the creation of a Federal Europe, it is for the English-speaking nations to show the way to the creation and functioning of a federation of Nations by practical demonstration of its policy and of its advantages.'[9] In the same year, the Socialist economist G. D. H. Cole declared that 'Socialist Planning for Europe' was a *sine qua non*. Discussing 'The Shape of the New Europe', he argued that since 'continental capitalism . . . is incapable of being restored to its old authority . . . it will be a disaster if Great Britain "contracts out" of the new Europe'.[10] Cole never joined Federal Union; but his fellow left-winger H. N. Brailsford wrote a cogent pamphlet for it on *The Federal Idea*.[11]

Supporters of Federal Union were not all economists, politicians, trade unionists, or academics. They included the novelists L. A. G Strong and Beatrice Kean Seymour, as well as the science-fiction writer and philosopher Olaf Stapledon, author of *First and Last Men*. A lifelong Socialist and pacifist who had served in the Friends Ambulance Unit in World War I, Stapledon joined Federal Union in 1939. In 1940, he published a two-volume set of reflections entitled *Philosophy and Living*. It appeared as a Pelican book, and was very widely read. Among other things, it affirmed that: 'Western civilization is being undermined by vested economic interests and by absolute national sovereignty'.[12]

The most colourful of Federal Union's recruits has been mentioned already. This was the philosopher and broadcaster C. E. M. Joad. Bearded, bright-eyed, and highly articulate, with a light, precise, slightly pedantic voice, Joad came to represent for many people the expression of cool reason in a world of emotion and violence. Not everyone liked him. At Federal Union's summer schools, he indulged a penchant for nude bathing, often by moonlight, sometimes in the company of female acolytes. Joad's left-wing views alienated some eminent Federal Union supporters, such as Lionel Curtis, while his personality displeased Barbara Wootton. Others, on the contrary, found him sympathetic and even oddly heroic.[13] Originally, he had been a simple pacifist, believing that 'of all things that can happen to a civilized community armed conflict is immeasurably the worst'.[14] The rise of Nazism had convinced him that circumstances could justify the use of force, and he had become a federalist. His clarity of mind, in other spheres verging on cynicism, was here matched by sincerity and deep conviction; and he used his energy and flair for publicity in devoted service to the cause.

CONSCIENCE AND CONTROVERSY

The issue of pacifism had arisen as soon as war had broken out. One of Federal Union's three founder-members, Charles Kimber, was a conscientious objector, although his wife was not. Margaret Richards, who had taught at Dartington Hall and whom its headmaster, W. B. Curry, had persuaded to join Federal Union's staff, described her own very characteristic evolution:

> Like many citizens of my generation, I became an ardent supporter of the League of Nations Union; I canvassed for the Peace Ballot; backed disarmament on the one hand and collective security on the other; was cheered by the notorious Oxford Resolution; argued with my employers (who were Japanese) about their policy in Manchuria, and became indignant when they laughed at my passionate advocacy of respect for the League . . . After Manchuria, Abyssinia; after Abyssinia, the Rhineland; after the Rhineland, the League began to look somewhat like an Anglo-French alliance, and we all had to start thinking again.[15]

Later, when the bombs began to fall on London, Margaret Richards became a fire-watcher, guarding the roof-tops of Gordon Square. She agonised with Barbara Wootton about how to square this with her pacifist convictions.[16]

Many pacifists supported Federal Union as a legitimate compromise between belligerence and passivity – so that, as one put it, when a future generation asked what they had done to build the peace in whose shelter they now lived, they would not be forced to answer: 'Oh, I didn't do anything – I only said I wouldn't fight.'[17]

For some purists, even this was too much: but for most members of Federal Union, it was too little. Derek Rawnsley joined the Royal Air Force; many others spent the war on active service. And a majority of those seeking federal solutions to international problems felt bound to recognise that any federal authority must, in the last resort, be backed by some form of force. Typical of their views was the simile produced by Ota Adler, who had come to Britain from

Czechoslovakia in the decade before the war. 'I don't drive on the left-hand side of the road because I'm afraid of the police; but I know there is a police – I know there's a law. I know it's wrong to break it, but a wrong with an enforcement. It's not enough to be wrong without it.'[18]

Nor was this the only debate unleashed by war. Early in 1940, the Liberal peer and elder statesman Lord Samuel conjectured that the future choice for Europe would lie between some traditional modes of behaviour, such as the balance of power or a concert of Europe, and something newer, such as a League of Nations, Federalism, or a Confederation of States.[19] Professor Gilbert Murray, a fervent supporter of the League of Nations, while pessimistic about a European federation, thought that a federation of France and Germany would be 'an enormous blessing'.[20] Equally sceptical about a federal Europe were two writers otherwise sympathetic to federalism: John Parker, MP, and the Earl of Rosse.[21]

These, however, were mere murmurs of dissent among friends. Some others chose to heap obloquy on Federal Union. W. B. Curry's book was a particular target of attack. Curry, a genial, balding, pipe-smoking man, was no firebrand; but he had a knack of explaining things plainly and simply – too simply, for some of his critics. Harold Nicolson dismissed *The Case for Federal Union* as 'thoughtless'.[22] Geoffrey Vickers felt that an improved nation-state might still be the 'dream awaiting fulfilment' and that federal union was unlikely to be feasible.[23] D. M. Sutherland, former editor of the *Pall Mall Gazette*, denounced Federal Union as 'A Plot to Sabotage the British Empire'.[24] In February 1940, an Irish lady – named coincidentally, 'Lawless' – wrote: 'Kindly send me no more of your *Infamous Communist* Literature.'[25] Sir Waldron Smithers, a right-wing Conservative MP, asked Churchill in November 1941 to agree that it should be suppressed.[26] One local branch of Federal Union attracted the scrutiny of the Local Defence Volunteers (later renamed the Home Guard, later still 'Dad's Army'), who had mistaken its initials for 'BUF' – the British Union of Fascists.[27]

One of Federal Union's early opponents was the communist lawyer D. N. Pritt, QC. Predictably, he followed the Party line. 'Wars will cease only when the capitalist system is abolished.' 'War is impossible between Socialist states' because 'they have nothing to quarrel about'. Above all, he feared that a federation based on the trio of Britain, France, and the United States – Curry's own preference – would primarily be an anti-Soviet bloc.[28] John Strachey too attacked federal union on the grounds that only socialism could 'save the world from periodic inter-imperialist war'.[29]

Nor was Pritt or Strachey Federal Union's most distinguished antagonist. That role, paradoxically, was reserved for H. G. Wells. In his early seventies by the time war broke out, the author of *Kipps* and *Mr Polly* had also long been known as the prophet of internationalism and world government. Curry had acknowledged a debt to him, and quoted him in his book: 'As Mr Wells has put it: "The only way to organise world peace lies through such a federation, and the only way to get that federation is boldly frontwise, in the sight and knowledge of all mankind."'[30] At least one of Wells's disciples had heard of Federal Union in its embryo phase, and had quoted 'Pax Union', as it then still called itself, as aiming for a Federal Parliament as the basis of a reformed League of Nations.[31] Federal Union, for its part, had initially defined its objective in Wellsian and universalist terms: 'To unite all democratic peoples under one government as a first step towards a World State.'[32]

The apparent entente was too good to last. As early as the autumn of 1939, Wells expressed the fear that 'federation would become a magic catchword';[33] and he began to devote some of his still abundant energy to a new and more general campaign. With the backing of the Labour-inclined *Daily Herald*, he and his sympathisers began to canvass proposals for a Universal Declaration of the Rights of Man. A committee was set up to sift ideas from groups and individuals; and Federal Union decided to play an active part. Ritchie Calder, then a Federal Union activist, described the enterprise as 'one of the biggest attempts ever made to sound public opinion on fundamental principles'. It might become, he thought, 'the Magna Carta of federation'.[34]

By the spring of 1940, more than 120 Federal Union groups had submitted reports either to headquarters or direct to the *Daily Herald*.[35] The Rights of Man Committee included a number of Federal Union supporters, notably Barbara Wootton, Sir John Boyd Orr, Francis Williams, and Sir Richard Gregory. But in May 1940, when Sir Richard Acland, the future founder of the Common Wealth party, proposed linking Federal Union and the Rights of Man campaigners with his own embryonic group, H. G. Wells sharply refused. Acland's stage army, he declared, was 'an incoherent combination of progressives, in a movement going nowhere in particular under some foggy "leadership" of your own'.[36]

Federal Union was more persistent in seeking Wells's support. 'I suppose you'd better invite the old fool', said Lionel Curtis; but when Charles Kimber visited Wells at his house in Hanover Terrace, Regent's Park, and was given tea served by a neat maidservant, Wells refused to have any truck with Federal Union.[37] Writing in *Picture Post* on 11 May 1940, he stigmatised 'this Federal Union stuff' as 'the cheapest dope available'.[38] This, Federal Union retorted, was 'woolly-minded nonsense'; but Wells continued to lambast what he called 'the puerility of current Federal Union schemes', while his opponents condemned his 'intellectual dishonesty'.[39] It was a sad coda to a remarkable career. As Wells's biographers put it, 'H.G. had now reached the point where every organization was out of step'.[40]

EXPANSION AND ORGANISATION

Meanwhile, Federal Union itself had been consolidating its ground. On 24–25 February 1940, all the local groups which had a secretary appointed by Head Office sent delegates to a conference in London aimed at approving a democratic constitution for the whole movement. The conference elected a National Council, and unanimously agreed on a statement of Federal Union's aims:

1. To obtain support for a federation* of free peoples under a common government, directly or indirectly elected by and responsible to the peoples for their common affairs, with national self-government for national affairs.
2. That any federation so formed shall be regarded as the first step towards ultimate world federation.
3. Through such a federation to secure peace, based on economic security and civil rights for all.

* Note: the Federation would control foreign policy, armed forces and armaments. It would have substantial powers over tariffs, currency, migration, communications and similar matters. It would also have power to ensure that colonies and dependencies were administered in the interests of the inhabitants and not for the benefit of any particular country.

To this end the present policy of Federal Union is:

1. To work for an Allied statement of Peace Aims challenging the idea of race superiority with a declaration of the rights of man, and the method of aggression with a declaration of readiness to

federate with any people whose government is prepared to recognise these rights.

2. To welcome any steps towards such a federation of the Allies or any other groups of peoples, provided that at the time of its formation the federation is declared open to accession by other nations, including Germany.

In this way, by preparing belligerent and neutral opinion for federation, Federal Union believes it will obtain a response which will shorten the war and ensure a peace with hope for the future.[41]

To coincide with the Delegates' Conference, Federal Union held a public meeting at 8.00 pm on Saturday 24 February in the Queen's Hall – almost the last to be held there, Charles Kimber recalled, 'before it was bombed out of existence'.[42] The demand for tickets was enormous. Two thousand five hundred people crowded in to hear Barbara Wootton and other speakers. One admirer remembered her standing very demurely and replying very simply to the questions. 'Do you really believe all this rubbish?' 'The answer to that is YES.' Questions were followed by a collection: it yielded more than £550.[43]

On 28 February, the provisional steering committee considered Federal Union's own 'Beveridge report', in which Sir William had proposed how Federal Union might develop as an organisation.[44] It duly did so. In March, the National Council voted into office an Executive Committee to supervise day-to-day affairs. Top of the poll came Professor Joad; his colleagues included Barbara Wootton, Lionel Robbins, W. B. Curry, and the distinguished constitutional lawyer W. Ivor Jennings (later Sir William Ivor Jennings and Vice-Chancellor of Cambridge University), whose book on *A Federation for Western Europe* was shortly to be published.[45] The Council also approved an optimistic budget, including five annual salaries which together totalled nearly £2000. Federal Union now had more than 10000 members; by April 1940 there were 253 local branches, co-ordinated by a 'travelling organiser'; and in London alone there were a dozen public meetings in a month.[46] Articles and pamphlets poured from the press.

AN ABORTIVE FEDERATION

That Spring of 1940 was both beautiful and cruel. As the lilacs and the roses of Louis Aragon's poem began to blossom, the Nazi Panzer divisions overran the Netherlands, Belgium, and Northern France. The 'phoney war' was over: battle was engaged at last. By June 1940, France was on the verge of collapse; and just then, in a desperate effort to keep her in the war, the British government – prompted by Jean Monnet – actually proposed what federalists had been urging: political union between the two Allies.

Although, during the process of forming Federal Union, the consensus had been for a federation of free peoples without any suggestion as to which of these peoples might be likely to join, the federalists' thinking had begun to crystallise, in the autumn of 1939, around the project of a European federation centred on Britain and France, to be joined as soon as possible by a democratic, post-war Germany. This was the message with which Curry and Robbins concluded their books. It was the assumption underlying a number of high-level conferences organised by Beveridge and Ransome, bringing together 'the best talent available outside the Government service' to plan the constitutional and economic aspects of a federation.[47] It was also the specific policy laid down by Federal Union's Conference in February 1940, and confirmed by the National Council in March.

This political project was realistic enough to make an extraordinary impact on public opinion. William Temple, the Archbishop of York, said in December 1939 that 'the whole scheme of Federal Union has made a staggeringly effective appeal to the British mind';[48] and by March 1940 Wilson Harris, the Editor of *The Spectator*, unlike the Archbishop an acknowledged sceptic, was writing that 'there is no question about the hold the idea of Federal Union has taken on certain sections of opinion in this country'.[49]

Meanwhile the Foreign Office had been working on a scheme for a relationship between Britain and France after the war which would 'for all intents and purposes make of the two countries a single unit in post-war Europe'[50] and on 1 March 1940 had secured the Prime Minister's approval for the idea. At Chatham House Arnold Toynbee had drafted for the Foreign Office an Act of Perpetual Association between France and the UK, which was approved by Lord Halifax, the Secretary of State for Foreign Affairs, and his Permanent Secretary, Sir Alexander Cadogan. The French Prime Minister Edouard Daladier had endorsed the idea; but its implementation was interrupted when he fell from office. However, Federal Union's onslaught on British public opinion continued, with books by Jennings and Mackay, a pamphlet by Beveridge and a symposium entitled *Federal Union*, in addition to the stream of articles and the intense programme of meetings.[51] *The Times*, *The Guardian*, the *New Statesman* and *Time and Tide* supported the movement's ideas, in each case with a strong editorial commitment.

It was against this background of crumbling defences in France and a remarkably federalist climate of opinion in Britain that Jean Monnet, later to be celebrated as the founder of the European Community, seized the opportunity to launch the idea of Anglo-French union as an immediate goal. Since the beginning of the war, he had been working as an Anglo-French official, co-ordinating Allied war supplies. Now, he decided that co-ordination was not enough. Together with his British colleague Arthur Salter, and with the help of Sir Robert Vansittart, he proposed that: 'There should be a dramatic declaration by the two Governments on the solidarity of the two countries' interests, and on their mutual commitment to restore the devastated areas, making clear also that the two Governments are to merge and form a single Cabinet and to unite the two Parliaments.'[52]

Through Churchill's adviser Desmond Morton, Neville Chamberlain's private secretary Sir Horace Wilson, and David Margesson, the Conservative Chief Whip, Monnet succeeded in getting his plan put to the Cabinet. Chamberlain persuaded Churchill to include it on the Cabinet agenda; and Monnet meanwhile drafted, with Morton, Salter, Vansittart, and Monnet's own assistant René Pleven (later Premier of France), the declaration of indissoluble union which he had proposed. It envisaged, among other things, common citizenship, a customs union, and a single currency. As Monnet recalled later: 'Churchill, who had come to power to defend the very existence of the British Empire, was startled when he read our words.' But his sense of duty, and the urgency of keeping France in the war, overbore his instinctive reluctance. Even that other great nationalist patriot, Charles de Gaulle, who had just arrived in London, reached the same conclusion.

After lengthy debate on the afternoon of Sunday, 16 June 1940, the War Cabinet approved the text. It agreed to propose to the French government that 'France and Britain shall no longer be two nations, but one Franco-British Union', whose constitution would 'provide for joint organs of defence, foreign, financial and economic policies', with a single War Cabinet, with shared responsibility for post-war reconstruction, with associated parliaments and with common citizenship. Churchill wrote subsequently of his surprise when he saw 'the staid, solid, experienced politicians engage themselves so passionately in an immense design'.[53] Perhaps he would have been less surprised if he had been shown *Federal Union News* of 18 May, which had identified three members of Churchill's new Cabinet as supporters of the Federal Union idea: Clement Attlee, the Lord Privy Seal, with his slogan 'Europe must federate or perish'; Ernest Bevin, Minister of Labour, one of the original supporters of Federal Union; and Sir Archibald Sinclair, Air Minister, who had expressed his commitment in an earlier issue of *Federal Union News*. There was also Anthony Eden, then War Minister, who despite his post-war coolness towards European unity had recently spoken warmly of it and had responded positively to Lothian's letter about Federal Union. Other Cabinet members had doubtless been influenced by the flow of ideas – from Federal Union, from heavyweight press editorials and from the 'extraordinarily broad consensus in British politics that the day of the nation state was past and only some form of Federalism could save the world'.[54] Vivid testimony to the evolution of British opinion is given by Churchill's Assistant Private Secretary, Sir John Colville, whose reaction on hearing Archbishop Temple propose European federation in a broadcast soon after the outbreak of war had been: 'What a glorious dream, but how difficult in practice . . .' On hearing the Cabinet's Declaration of Union dictated in his office on 16 June, however, he saw it as a historic document whose effects could be 'more far reaching than anything that has occurred this century – and more permanent'; while on the following day, he was to reflect that 'we had before us the bridge to a new world, the first elements of European or even World Federation'.[55] Unlike several members of the Cabinet, however, and for all his post-war vision of a United States of Europe, Churchill did not appear to share in the 'broad consensus'; but Federal Union's success in creating it must surely have contributed to the enthusiastic acceptance of Monnet's proposal by the Cabinet as a whole.

When the Cabinet had approved the declaration, de Gaulle read it over the telephone to Paul Reynaud, the French Prime Minister, whose government had by this time fled from Paris to Bordeaux. When Reynaud heard it, his face lit up. For a moment, it seemed as if human will-power was about to turn the tide of history. De Gaulle prepared to leave that night for Bordeaux. Churchill planned to meet Reynaud the next day at Concarneau on the South Breton coast. Monnet proposed to travel with him in the same destroyer.

Just as he was about to leave London – 'the Cabinet told us that the trip was off. A message had come from Bordeaux: Reynaud had resigned. When the news came, Churchill was already on the train. He climbed out, he wrote later, "with a heavy heart". That was how we all felt on the evening of so hard a day.' At about 10 o'clock that night, Monnet managed to telephone de Gaulle. 'On arriving at Bordeaux airport, he had learned that Albert Lebrun, the President of France, had appointed Marshal Pétain as Prime Minister. It was all over, said de Gaulle: further effort was useless: he was coming back.'

Monnet was less easily discouraged. He made one last effort to save the situation, flying to Bordeaux in a Sunderland flying-boat big enough, if need be, to bring back almost the whole French Cabinet. But it was too late. Defeatism defeated too many people. Monnet returned to London empty-handed, but with his flying-boat full of refugees.

'So,' he wrote,

> our generation shirked a bold decision that could have changed the course of the war and, what is more, the course of men's minds . . . That is why, looking back, I believe that those days of June 1940 had a profound effect on my idea of international action. All too often I have come up against the limits of mere co-ordination: it makes for discussion, but not decision. In circumstances where union is necessary, it fails to change relations between men and between countries. It is the expression of national power, not a means of transforming it: that way, unity will never be achieved.

Failure, for Monnet, embodied lessons for the future: in this case, the conviction that the nation-state must be transcended. In 1940 it was not the British who 'shirked a bold decision' for a union of nation-states. After the war France was to lead the way in building the European Community, while Britain held back. But the fact that the Anglo-French union so nearly succeeded in 1940 was a proof that federalist ideas need not be academic pipe-dreams. In desperate days, men and women were able to shake off old habits of thought and try new ways to solve age-old problems, looking beyond the traditional barriers that kept nations apart.

EBB TIDE

In retrospect, Monnet's proposal of Anglo-French union marked the flood tide of federalist hopes for practical action during World War

II. It also coincided with the high tide of Federal Union as a would-be mass organisation.

With the Nazis occupying all of continental Western Europe, Britain stood alone. For a few weeks, she seemed to face the danger of invasion. Federal Union decided to send duplicates of all its records down to Dartington, and debated whether or not to evacuate the office again. Potential recruits to the movement now had more immediate preoccupations; and, to keep up the momentum of recruitment, the Executive Committee asked branch secretaries to make a further enrolment effort. It asked new members not only to wear Federal Union's badge but also to make a solemn affirmation: 'I pledge myself to work in all circumstances for the overthrow of Nazism and for the world beyond Hitler – for a Federal Union of the Free.'[56] If it sounded high-flown, it was at a time when many British people had reason to believe that they would soon be fighting the Nazis in Britain itself – perhaps in the armed forces, perhaps as civilian guerrilla warriors, perhaps in underground Resistance groups.

That test never came; but hard times came to Federal Union. Its rapid expansion had been too good to last. There had been no shortage of volunteers for staff positions: one advertisement, for a Public Relations Officer, attracted 279 replies.[57] But government regulations limited civilian employment: and before long the movement faced a more immediate threat. Money was growing short.

In the summer of 1940, when the danger of invasion had abated but the aerial bombardment of Britain had only begun, R. W. G. Mackay began to suspect that all was not well with Federal Union's finances. The Treasurer seemed unforthcoming; but Mackay persisted, and finally secured a full financial statement. When the Executive Committee examined it, there was consternation. The movement was in debt to the tune of several thousand pounds.

The chairman, Barbara Wootton, was flabbergasted. What should be done? Only Mackay could offer any concrete proposals.[58] After much discussion, he agreed to seek an accommodation with the creditors, but on two conditions: first, that he should become chairman of the Executive Committee, with full powers to take any necessary action; second, that these should include authority to dismiss selected members of the staff.[59]

The first step was to make economies. Headquarters staff was drastically reduced: the Public Relations Officer and the Publicity Manager had to go, together with a number of junior employees. An appeal was launched asking members to contribute £1 each: this, it was estimated, should have brought in 'some £12000 to £15000'. But, despite the Executive Committee's 'great confidence . . . that the movement shall, even in these dark days, carry on', the results were disappointing. The first four days of the appeal produced £50; a week later, the fund reached £150, and a week after that, £250. Not until September 1940 did the proceeds reach £1000; and by then bankruptcy seemed to be inevitable.[60] Federal Union's liabilities, moreover, were the personal responsibility of its members, since at that time it had still not been incorporated as a limited company.

On Mackay's advice, it soon took steps to remedy this situation. On 4 January 1941, Federal Union Limited was formed, with seven directors: Curry, Joad, Miss F. L. ('Jo') Josephy, Barbara Wootton, Francis Williams, Dr L. T. M. Gray and Mackay himself.[61] As a company, it had no reserves: a month later, it had a £50 credit balance at one bank, and a £337 overdraft at another. In March 1941, paid-up membership amounted to 1351, rising to 1900 by late April; but the company's debts, for which the former Executive Committee and Council were legally liable, still totalled £1900.[62]

Personal loans came to the rescue. Dr Gray advanced £100 to meet payments to creditors: George Catlin and Ota Adler offered to give £50 apiece if ten more members would do the same.[63] But Federal Union's income still covered only half of its expenditure: it needed to raise more then £1100 before the end of the year.

Meanwhile, there were further upheavals at headquarters. Mackay left to take up government work – although continuing as honorary legal adviser; Dr Gray also resigned, to be replaced as Vice-Chairman by Curry. Mackay's place as chairman was taken by Josephy; and her political position as an aspiring Liberal parliamentary candidate was balanced by two additions: the Labour MP John Parker, later to become Father of the House of Commons, and his Conservative colleague Major Albert Braithwaite, who later became the movement's Hon. Treasurer.[64] A further notable recruit to the board was Henry Usborne, a businessman who after the war was to become a Labour MP.[65] In October 1941, with the agreement of his fellow-directors, he transferred the outstanding debts of Federal Union Ltd to a group of his friends who were also members of the movement. In effect, they offered it a loan facility of up to £5000.[66]

It had been a risky period. At one point, London members of Federal Union had even resorted to selling ice cream on Hampstead Heath, over the August Bank Holiday, to raise £96.[67] But now, with a little help from its friends, and with membership still rising by one or two hundred a month, Federal Union had weathered to storm. By October 1942, the creditors were nearly all paid off, and the loan was steadily being reduced.[68]

The movement had always to be frugal, but financial prudence and stability were assured for a time when Alan Sainsbury became the Hon. Treasurer in August 1943 and remained in that position until after the end of the war. Then Joint General Manager of Sainsbury's, he was later to become Chairman and then President of the company, and an active member of the House of Lords, first as a Labour then as a Social Democrat peer. It was Lord Lothian who had convinced him that peace could not be organised without limitation of sovereignty; and he was introduced to Federal Union itself late in 1938, at a meeting in Bloomsbury addressed by Kimber, Ransome and Rawnsley.[69]

The election of Sainsbury as Hon. Treasurer showed that Federal Union had learned the lesson of Mackay's firm chairmanship. Euphoria was not enough. Expansion must be controlled carefully. Economy had to be the watchword. Organisation was the key to success.

As an organisation, Federal Union had become country-wide. Its basis was thirteen regions, for each of which it still hoped to have a regional organiser. Each region in turn was divided into its parliamentary constituencies, in every one of which the movement hoped to establish a branch. Activities included conferences, study groups, weekend schools, public and informal meetings. The subscription was modest: the minimum was only one shilling a year. For ten shillings and sixpence, the member received *Federal Union News* for one quarter; a guinea would bring this and pamphlets up to 3d each. £1.10s covered a full year's subscription to *Federal Union News* plus all published pamphlets.

Federal Union held its first summer school at Dartington Hall in 1942: for members sent by some of the regional committees it was a week's welcome respite from air-raids.[70] Early in 1943, the movement launched a campaign for signatures to a Manifesto, calling for a 'People's Poll' on federal institutions for the post-war world.[71] This proved largely abortive – although as the fortunes of war changed for the better, Federal Union began to attract still more recruits. By September 1944, the membership figure had reached 4727, many of them Service personnel attracted by a paperback book, *Federate or Perish*, recently published by Federal Union and written by John S. Hoyland, Principal of Woodbrooke, the Quaker College.[72]

A MOVEMENT, NOT A PARTY

In the abnormal world of wartime, with official party politics in abeyance, Federal Union had spent time, money, and effort in trying to become a mass movement. In heartening ways, it had succeeded. But times were hard. Although the National Council now had nine active sub-committees, including a Forces and a Youth section, in 1944 the regional and branch organisations were in decline.[73] Of the thirteen regions, only two were genuinely active, and of the sixty branches only nineteen were still in being. London was the chief focus of activities; and although the prospect of the 1945 General Election led to efforts to mount a political campaign, both funds and personnel were lacking.

By the time the war ended, Derek Rawnsley had been killed. Charles Kimber had resigned as General Secretary and as Honorary Editor of *Federal Union News*; now, he also resigned from the Council.[74] Patrick Ransome and Barbara Wootton had earlier resigned from the Council, and Margaret Richards from the post of Secretary.[75] When the election campaign began, federalist candidates included Miss Josephy (Liberal) and R. W. G. Mackay (Labour): but Federal Union as such did not take part. The big battalions of politics had returned: the professionals had taken over. Old loyalties and habits had reasserted themselves, and Federal Union was in no position to challenge the British party system or 'break the mould'. When its six-strong headquarters staff moved from Gower Street, where its lease had expired, to new and modest premises at No. 20, Buckingham Street, it seemed as if a chapter in its activities had come to an end.[76]

The impression was deceptive. If the hard light of political reality had revealed the limitations of a small, idealistic movement, it also threw into sharp relief the extent to which Federal Union's influence exceeded its actual power. It had helped create the climate of opinion in which the War Cabinet could confidently make its historic offer of union to France. Later it was to play a key role in the thinking of those continental Europeans who helped to found the European Community. More immediately, through the work of the Federal Union Research Institute, federal ideas began to pervade much of the debate about 'peace aims' which had so long occupied the writers, thinkers, and statesmen who were hoping, as the phrase went, 'to build a better world' after the war.

3 Peace Aims

The writer John Middleton Murry, best known now perhaps as the husband, widower, and editor of Katherine Mansfield, was sympathetic to Federal Union, but by no means uncritical. 'As it stands,' he wrote soon after the war began,

> Federal Union is a utopian scheme, and cannot wholly escape the charge of 'pseudo-practical shortsightedness' brought against it by Mr H. G. Wells. That does not mean that it may not be the most promising means of focussing public attention on the necessity for a true international community, and also on the arduous conditions that have to be fulfilled before such a community can be established . . . If the Federal Union movement is going to make it its business fearlessly to explore, and honestly to acknowledge all the practical difficulties which lurk behind its gracious eighteenth-century facade – well and good; it will be engaged in an effort of political education of the first importance.[1]

It did, and it was.

RESEARCH AND EDUCATION

'If there's a war, come and see me.' When war broke out in 1939, Derek Rawnsley had remembered that invitation from Sir William Beveridge, Master of University College, Oxford. Accordingly, Rawnsley had gone back to his old college once again, and met a generous response. In the autumn of 1939, with the help of Patrick Ransome, Beveridge hosted in the Master's Lodgings a conference of economists to consider 'economic aspects of federation'. It was the first major event sponsored by Federal Union's newly formed Research Department. A few months later, in March 1940, this was constituted as the Federal Union Research Institute, with Beveridge as its chairman and Patrick Ransome as Hon. Secretary.[2]

Beveridge was a tremendous worker who infected others with his appetite for work. Under the energetic guidance of Beveridge and Ransome, the Federal Union Research Institute held a series of conferences on the constitutional, economic, and colonial aspects of 'a federation embracing, as a minimum, Britain, France, Germany, the four Scandinavian countries, Belgium and Holland'.[3] Ivor Jennings was fully justified in claiming that the participants included the best talent available outside the government service.[4] On constitutional matters they included Jennings himself, Professor A. L. Goodhart, Professor Joseph Chamberlain (later of Columbia), Lionel Curtis, K. C. Wheare, and Harold Wilson, with Beveridge in the chair. Wilson also attended the economic conferences, which were again chaired by Beveridge, and included Lionel Robbins, James Meade, F. A. von Hayek and Barbara Wootton. The colonial conferences gathered together such specialists as Professor Norman Bentwich, Dr Lucy Mair, Professor W. M. Macmillan, Sir Drummond Shields, Arthur Lewis, and Professor Arnold Plant, with Lord Lugard as a very active corresponding member. Together, the experts broached some of the key issues which were to surface in post-war debates about the United Nations and, later, the European Community: the roles of various institutions, the approach to foreign affairs and defence, the liberalisation of trade, the free movement of people, and the problems of international exchange rates.

The flavour of these early federalist discussions can best be caught by selective quotation:[5]

'We are in the midst,' declared Lord Lothian,

> of the greatest race in armaments ever known, which if it continues can only lead to universal bankruptcy. And everyone feels that another world war, fiercer and more ruthless than the last, may break out at any time, either because it is deliberately provoked or because an accident or a fool may set in motion events which it is beyond the power of statesmanship to control. The real cause of our troubles is that the nations are living in anarchy . . . the consequences of which have been intensified a hundredfold in recent times by the conquest of time and space . . . anarchy cannot be ended by any system of co-operation between sovereign nations but only by the application of the principle of federal union.[6]

'Under a federal system,' wrote Patrick Ransome, 'the democratic principle of responsible government is extended beyond the frontiers of the individual state.'[7] 'Independent sovereignty,' Lionel Robbins thought, 'must be limited. As citizens of the various national states, we may hope to diminish the danger of conflict by opposing policies which tend to evoke it. But this is not enough . . . There must be an international framework of law and order, supported by solid sanctions.'[8]

Dr Joad saw such a development as a natural evolution in human history:

At an early stage in the evolution of human beings, family integrates with family to form a larger whole, the tribe; later tribe joins with tribe to constitute a whole yet larger, the department or province; later province with province to form the Nation-State . . .

The changes in the range and scale and pace of living resulting from the abolition of distance are prodigious. Yet while the circumstances of our lives have changed beyond the imagination of our predecessors, our political structure has remained stationary. The horse and foot mode of travel is outmoded, yet we still live in horse and foot communities. The world is economically a single whole, yet politically it is based upon the assumption that it is a congeries of economically self-sufficient national units.

Across the surface of this world run the frontiers of the Nation-States. Many of these were fixed in the remote past; the most recent date for the most part from the eighteenth century. They represent a mode of living very different from that of today. When a man could travel for several days through the territory of a single State, State frontiers made some sort of sense; today, when he can fly in twenty-four hours across the boundaries of half a dozen States, they make nonsense . . .

As the world shrinks, its member States will be jostled ever more closely together, until the pressure grows so severe that, unless they consent to soften the hard outlines of their separate individualities, they will grind one another to pieces . . .

Human beings are enormously more destructive than they have been before; so much so that, unless they can learn to control the powers with which science has invested them, they may well destroy themselves altogether.[9]

From such general considerations, the debate soon moved to practical matters. 'It is no exaggeration to say,' Lionel Robbins argued, 'that a federation will stand or fall by the adequacy of its economic constitution.'[10] The novelist and playwright J. B. Priestley added that it must have regional roots:

If I thought federalism meant the cosmopolitan touch everywhere, I would certainly oppose it . . . But . . . I cannot see the slightest reason why the delegation of national sovereignty to a federal authority should blot out all regional influences, depending as they do not on political organization but on local climate, landscape, social traditions and the like. Indeed, it is possible that the removal of national barriers, many of which are purely artificial, and the disappearance of cunningly stimulated national feeling, might increase the natural attachment of all sensitive persons to the region in which they live . . .

It might do most of us good to have loyalties at once wider and narrower than the ones we have at present. Wider, because we substitute for the nation a great federation of peoples, with whom we co-operate instead of competing. Narrower, because once we are free of the age-long dog-fight of the nations, once we have no longer to attend to the horrible, cynical spectacle of the powers lying, cheating and arming, we can attend to what is in all truth our own bit of the world, our own hills and dales and woodlands, our own wind and rain, our own folk whom we know by name, the near magical world in which we spent our childhood. . . .[11]

Noting the reluctance of statesmen to delegate sovereignty, Sir John Boyd Orr suggested that 'The psychologist should try to find the reason for this prejudice . . . It is probable that the leaders identify the state with themselves and feel that the loss of its sovereign power would be a loss to their personal power.'[12]

K. C. Wheare (later Sir Cecil Wheare and Vice-Chancellor of Oxford University), Australian by birth and a Fellow of Beveridge's College, already an authority on constitutional law who was to write a classic book on *Federal Government*, saw less sinister reasons:

Federal Government is a thing of which most people in the United Kingdom of Great Britain and Northern Ireland have had no direct, personal experience, and they find it hard, therefore, to understand what it is . . . They are accustomed to a form of government one of the leading characteristics of which is that one single legislature, the King-in-Parliament at Westminster, has authority to make laws for the whole of the United Kingdom on all matters whatsoever; and these laws duly made prevail over rules made by any other body in the Kingdom and are accepted by the courts as valid law and supreme law. The result is that people in this country may doubt whether acts of parliament are good laws, but they cannot doubt that they are good law. In a federation it is otherwise. There, it is possible to doubt not only whether the acts of some legislature in the federation are good laws, but also whether they are good law, and it is possible for a court to declare acts which are almost universally recognized as good laws to be bad law and no law at all. This international obstruction, in a federation, of the will of the elected representatives of the people as expressed in acts of the legislature, appears to us to be a strange device. Why do people adopt such a form of government, and why do they continue to put up with it? . . .

What then is federalism? Its essence consists, I think, in this: that in a federal system, the functions of government are divided in such a way that the relationship between the legislature which has authority over the whole territory and those legislatures which have authority over parts of the territory is not the relationship of superior to subordinates as is the relation of the Parliament at Westminster to the Parliament at Stormont . . . In a federal government there is a division of governmental functions between one authority, usually called the federal government, which has power to regulate certain matters for the whole territory, and a collection of governments usually called state governments, which have power to regulate certain other matters for the component parts of the territory . . .

It is only when a group of territorial communities are prepared to co-operate with each other for the regulation of certain matters but for those matters only, and when they are determined at the same time to remain separate and supreme, each in its own territory, for the regulation of other matters, that federal government is appropriate. Federalism provides for this desire for co-operation in some things coupled with a determination to be separate in others . . .

Since federal government involves a division of functions and since the states forming the federation are anxious that this division should be explicit and guaranteed and that they should not surrender more powers than they know, it is essential for a federal government that there be a written constitution embodying the division of powers, and binding all governmental authorities throughout the federation. From it all state and federal authorities derive their powers and any actions they perform contrary to it are invalid. It must be the supreme law of the land . . .

It is preferable, though not essential to federalism, that the power (to amend the constitution) should be exercised by the federal and state authorities acting in co-operation, as is done in the United States, for example, where amendments may be carried by a two-thirds majority, in both houses of Congress, together with a simple majority in the legislature of three-quarters of the States. In Australia and in Switzerland the people are associated in the amending process through a referendum . . .

In any case of dispute between federal and state governments as to the extent of the powers allocated to them under the constitution, some body other than the federal and state governments must be authorised to adjudicate upon those disputes. It is not accidental therefore, that there exists in the United States, Australia and Canada a body of this kind. The United States has its Supreme Court; Australia has a High Court together with, for some cases, the Judicial Committee of the Privy Council; and Canada has the Judicial Committee of the Privy Council. Switzerland has no institution performing this function and is to this extent imperfectly federal . . .

Finally, if the governmental authorities in a federation are to be really co-ordinated with each other in actual practice as well as in law, it is essential that there should be available to each of them, under its own unfettered control, financial resources sufficient for the performance of the functions assigned to it under the constitution.[13]

Having analysed federal government so exhaustively, Wheare conceded that it was no easy option:

It has usually been hard to establish a federal government. The forces of separatism and individualism which make federalism necessary make any super-state government at all almost impossible. And when a federation has with difficulty come to exist, it is only with difficulty that it continues to exist. Its operation requires great skill and tact. Its success depends upon an enormous patience and an enormous capacity for compromise among the statesmen who work it. Swift and decisive government is impossible. Deep dividing issues must be avoided. Changes can come about only at the pace of the slowest. Federal government is conservative government. Federal government is above all legalistic . . .

It has seemed wise . . . to recall that federalism is a form of government which is not always appropriate or always easy to work. It is fair to recall at the same time that federal government is at least government; it is order, not anarchy, it is peace, not war.[14]

Sir William Beveridge, likewise addressing the delicate balance between state and federal authority, recalled that 'The purpose of federation is not the power of large nations but security for citizens of all nations and for their different cultures.' 'Effective democracy,' he went on, 'is a condition of federation' – for practical, not merely doctrinal reasons. A federal constitution, he suggested would require:

(a) A Federal Legislature of two Houses, one with membership based on population or electorate and chosen directly by the citizens, and one with equal or nearly equal representation of the separate States, whose members might be either elected or nominated by national governments.
(b) A Federal Executive responsible to the Federal Legislature.
(c) A Federal Judicature interpreting a written constitution.
(d) Constitutional guarantees for the maintenance of effective democracy in each of the member States, i.e. for peaceful change of governments and policies in them by free discussion and association and secret voting.[15]

These broad constitutional proposals were elaborated and debated in much greater detail by other participants in the discussions. Ivor Jennings, then Reader in English Law, University of London, at the London School of Economics, and already earning a great reputation as an authority on the British constitution, carried the analysis as far as a draft treaty. He also added some pertinent general points. Discussing the legislature, for example, he maintained: 'It is . . . essential for the successful operation of a federation that representatives should not vote on national lines . . . We . . . must have, if the system is to operate, party organisations cutting across national boundaries.' He pointed out that pressure groups could play a federating role:

> If the temporary revulsion which always arises at the coming of peace could be used to overcome the opposition of interested economic groups, and the moment seized to give economic control to a federation, those groups would perforce have to bring their pressure to bear on the Federation. They would, so to speak, become federalists because they would come to the . . . equivalent of Washington to ask for federal favours.

Finally, he argued that a federal president was much to be desired. 'It is necessary to create a federal patriotism, and for this purpose it is useful to have a figurehead who can become the focus of that patriotism. The President should thus exercise what Walter Bagehot called the "dignified" functions of the Federation.'[16]

A colleague of Jennings's at the LSE, Otto Kahn-Freund, who had been a judge in pre-Nazi Germany and emigrated to Britain after Hitler's rise to power, was alone in proposing a federation governed by a Council of (national) Ministers – rather as in the present-day European Community. 'It is possible,' he pointed out, 'to have a uni-cameral federal unit and a government not responsible to the federal parliament, which is entirely or partly composed of delegates of the member governments. The *Bundesrat* of the Bismarck Constitution is not necessarily bound up with an undemocratic system.'[17]

The economists were no less painstaking than the constitutional lawyers. Reporting on their first Oxford conference, Barbara Wootton wrote:

> It was agreed (a) that the federal control of trade, currency, migration and dependencies would prevent divisions of economic interest from coinciding with national boundaries, and so help to destroy the economic basis of nationalism; (b) that the degree of unification to be proposed depended more on public sentiment than on technical factors, and must be primarily governed by what the public would be ready to accept.

She quoted a Memorandum of Discussion prepared afterwards by one of the participants:

> Complete unification of currency was defined as including:
>
> Federal control of legal tender;
> Federal control of inter-State payments;
> Federal central bank . . .
>
> A minority opinion was in favour of retaining distinct national currencies and regulating their relative value by federal control of exchange rates . . .
>
> Importance was attached to freedom of migration as being, like a common currency, an important symbol of unity . . .
>
> It was agreed that the Federation should have the sole power from the outset of concluding commercial treaties with outside countries.
>
> It was agreed not to urge immediate abolition of all inter-federation tariffs, though the argument was used that sudden abolition of tariffs would cause less dislocation if it was carried out by many countries than if by comparatively few . . .

> It was generally agreed that complete freedom of trade within the Federation was the ideal to be aimed at eventually: subject, however, to minority reservations as to the possibility of tariffs being used in connection with collectivist experiments.[18]

This was a reference to the idea of 'Socialism in one country' of the federation, espoused most notably in the discussions by Harold Wilson. The adoption of a common currency and the abolition of tariffs, he feared, would inhibit what he called 'the Blum experiment' of the pre-war French government in raising wages and labour standards, as well as controlling the trade cycle by means of exchange-rate policy – 'the Swedish experiment'. Wilson conceded, however, that 'a closer economic union must be one of the long-period objectives of the federation': it could be 'a factor making for political unity and the potential cause of a greatly increased standard of life'. Accordingly, he envisaged that 'the gradual reduction of tariffs might be achieved by steps [and] the currency question might be tackled on similar lines.'[19]

Lionel Robbins, while disagreeing with Wilson, proposed that these matters should not be predetermined, but that the federal institutions themselves should be empowered to decide the policies for currency, migration, and trade. He also endorsed the idea of a transition period for the freeing of trade and of migration. In liberalising trade, he emphasised, much more was involved than 'the machinery of tariffs and quotas. State measures of indirect protection such as the illegitimate use of veterinary regulations must be subject to Federal review. Moreover, it is agreed that the Federal function in this respect involves overriding powers in regard to transport regulations.' The Federation must therefore 'have full powers in regard to legislation concerning restraint of trade, company registration, patent law and banking. It would be highly undesirable if the laxity of the law in any particular State in this respect should make it possible for anti-social practices to find refuge from legislative restriction elsewhere.'[20] He could hardly have identified more accurately some of the issues that would be preoccupying the European Community half a century later.

Robbins's fellow-economist James Meade, at that time moving from the staff of the Economic Section of the League of Nations to become Economic Assistant and later Director at the Cabinet Office, was equally prescient about the controversy that would come to surround the Community's project for economic and monetary union. He argued that a common currency would be feasible only if 'wage rates and other costs' were 'flexible within each nation', and if the federal authorities had 'extensive powers over international monetary policies and over public expenditure in the various constituent nations'. If neither were the case, there would have to be flexible exchange rates: 'nevertheless it is equally desirable to eliminate the possibility of unjustifiable exchange depreciations'. To this end, the right to fix national exchange-rates might be vested in the federal authorities.[21]

Robbins took what came to be the other side in the Community's controversy. He recognised:

> that there is a school of thought, especially strong in Great Britain and Scandinavia, which, far from regarding the existence of different monetary systems for existing national areas with disfavour, looks upon it as a positive advantage. The reasons for this attitude are various. But the reason which is relevant here is that it is thought that variations of the rate of exchange are an easier way of maintaining equilibrium with the rest of the world than internal expansions or contractions of credit.

Yet he remained unconvinced:

> The convenience of a system which would eliminate all the tedious business of turning one currency into another, the superiority of a state of affairs in which the disturbances arising from the lack of co-ordination of the monetary policies of the different states would be automatically eliminated by a general unification, seem so obvious that, to the lay mind, it must be difficult to conceive that any other policy could be favoured. And the writer of this essay must himself confess that, on this point, he believes that the lay mind is thoroughly justified. The advantages of a single money are so great that it seems difficult to believe that, once they were firmly established, they would ever seriously be called in question. Would it be seriously suggested that it would be better for England and Scotland to have different currencies or for the different districts of the Federal Reserve System of the United States to have special dollars of their own and independent powers of varying the rate of exchange with other kinds of dollars?[22]

The technical and political debates between 'liberals' and others were never fully resolved. Robbins believed that 'International liberals and international socialists can surely be at one . . . that national ownership of the means of production is not conducive either to international union or to international peace.'[23] But Friedrich von Hayek, contending that planning at federal level would be impossible because the member states' ideals and values would be too divergent for any agreed policies,[24] stung Harold Wilson by his advocacy of 'less government all round'. 'The whole trend of democracy in the last century,' Wilson retorted, 'has been towards closer and closer state control over economic affairs. To tell collectivists that peace can only be assured by methods which will put back the democratic clock a hundred years or more will place them in a cruel dilemma.'[25]

Barbara Wootton faced it with resolution:

> For a socialist to demand, on this account, a boycott of federalist movements is like refusing to ride in a bus because buses can be used to carry people to anti-socialist meetings. Federation itself, like planning and collectivisation, is a neutral instrument. It is the job of the socialist to direct its great possibilities towards his own particular ends . . .
>
> No; socialism and federation are not the true alternatives. The true alternatives which face the socialist are these. He can continue to socialise and plan and equalise within his own particular territory and under his own particular flag, leaving his (still foreign) comrades in equal isolation to do the same. He can shut his eyes to the yawning gap in socialist programmes which the decay of internationalism has torn open . . .
>
> Or he can reject what has proved itself to be only the socialism of the battlefield and of the war cabinet . . . In the graves of France and Flanders and the ruined homes of London he can read the implications of international anarchy in a shrinking world; and he can consign the nation-state to the limbo of out-worn political systems, as he has already consigned the private bank and the workhouse to the limbo of economic anachronisms.[26]

R. W. G. Mackay agreed. 'Objections to a . . . Federation,' he wrote,

> will be raised by a large number of people drawn from the Left-wing elements of the community, on the ground that it will postpone, and not advance, the cause of Socialism for which they work. They will argue that a Federation . . . will be a Federation of

capitalist States, which will mean the further development of imperialism . . .

Federation in itself does not prevent the individual member States of the Federation from making such changes in their social system as they desire to make . . .

In the concluding lines of *Equality*,[27] Professor Tawney writes: 'What confronts us to-day is not merely the old story of the rivalries of ambitious nations, or the too familiar struggles of discordant economic interests. It is the collapse of two great structures of thought and government, which for long held man's allegiance, but which now have broken down. The first is the system of independent national States, each claiming full sovereignty as against every other. The second is an economic system which takes as its premise that every group and individual shall be free to grab what they can get, and hold what they can grab.'

The task of citizenship today is to deal with the first of these two problems, namely the system of independent national States. The solution of the problem of national States must take priority over the solution of any other political question. It is a condition precedent to the solution of any other question.[28]

In other words, as Barbara Wootton put it, 'Political federation is now a necessary condition for ordered political activity of any kind.'[29]

PREPARING FOR PEACE

The public offshoot of these debates, which drew to a close at the end of 1940, was a series of Federal Tracts. The first was *Peace by Federation*, written by Beveridge in February 1940. It was followed by a series published by Macmillan from the spring of 1941 onwards: *Economic Aspects of Federation*, by Lionel Robbins; *The Colonial Problem and the Federal Solution*, by Norman Bentwich; *What Federal Government Is*, by K. C. Wheare; *The Philosophy of Federalism*, by C. E. M. Joad; *Socialism and Federation*, by Barbara Wootton; and *Federation and the Colonies*, by Lord Lugard.

The energetic Miss Josephy, who succeeded Mackay as chairman of the Executive Committee in August 1941, did not set much store by these 'academic' activities, and was moreover worried lest Barbara Wootton's tract might discourage non-Socialists. An effort was therefore made to seek contributions of a more conservative complexion.[30] When the tracts were reissued in 1943 as a book, *Studies in Federal Planning*,[31] edited by Patrick Ransome, the half-dozen additional chapters included one by A. L. Goodhart on 'The Constitution of the United States' and one by George Catlin on 'Anglo-American Union', while these were counter-balanced by one on 'World Government and World Peace' by the left-wing political analyst, Konni Zilliacus. Federalists and sympathisers continued to publish cognate studies throughout the war. One notable contribution to the Federal Union Club's *World Review* was an essay by Sir Thomas Beecham on the post-war prospects for the arts.[32]

In fact, the Federal Union Research Institute had never been academic in any pejorative sense. Some of its adherents took pleasure in its acronym, FURI. And its chairman, Sir William Beveridge, had always been categorical about the aims. In the spring of 1940 he wrote:

> To have before us a clear vision of the better world that we wish to see emerging from our struggle . . . will give us heart to endure to the end the bitter sacrifices that may be necessary for success . . . National sovereignties should be replaced by the application of federalism . . . In no other way can we guarantee that the conflict in which we are now engaged will not be repeated.

These words were part of a preface to a pamphlet[33] drafted by Charles Kimber which first mooted the notion of what came to be called 'winning the peace'.

> We must devise now the foundations of the new order and canvass support for our ideas in this country and in the countries which will have the great responsibility of making the peace.

Those who worked in FURI made a major contribution to that end. Their writings, moreover, were to have great influence on continental thinking about post-war European unification. Federal Union worked hard to distil and popularise the fruits of FURI's debates. In 1941, in wartime Britain, Federal Union established its Peace Aims Committee, comprising Charles Kimber, C. E. M. Joad, Miss Josephy and Konni Zilliacus.[34] Its aim was to persuade public opinion and governments that the forthcoming peace settlement must include certain essential elements. In particular, Charles Kimber stressed:

(1) a Charter of Rights and a Federal Constitution, with direct loyalty from all individual citizens;

(2) joint machinery found essential in wartime should be carried forward into peacetime;
(3) the coming of peace should initiate a world war on want with planning for freedom and plenty led by a world federal government;
(4) (a) political warfare (Britain's propaganda service) should offer a Democratic Union, World Confederation, and a Charter of Rights in Europe in order to induce revolt against the Nazis;
(b) an international Consultative Parliament should prepare the way for a new world organization;
(c) an allied Reconstruction Commission should be set up to plan the transition from war to peace.[35]

The Peace Aims Committee produced its report early in 1942. It was a lengthy document of some 25 000 words. At Easter, the Annual General Meeting of Federal Union approved it for publication under the title *Federation: Peace Aim – War Weapon*.[36] As regards world government, it was relatively modest. It quoted Field Marshal Smuts on the need for some form of world organisation more ambitious than the old League of Nations. 'We want a league which will be real, practical, effective as a system of world government'; but it recognised 'that no such government can be established within any foreseeable period after the war'. It saw the existing 'United Nations' – the name given to the wartime Alliance – as providing the germ of both the institutions it believed to be necessary: a 'Federation of Democracies' working within a 'World Confederation'. Explaining the difference between confederation and federation, the report recognised that 'to found a world government whilst the States which it is to govern retain their sovereignty is a contradiction in terms'; but it expressed the hope that the proposed 'World Confederation' would evolve in a federal direction.

The report's detailed proposals included a 'Confederate Council' on the lines of what became the UN Security Council, but with special powers giving it a near-monopoly of armed force and a responsibility for maintaining peace in the world, and an International Parliament not unlike the later UN Assembly, but with delegations elected by proportional representation. Within these global arrangements the report envisaged a core of democratic nations, roughly coterminous with what later became the Atlantic Alliance, which would themselves establish a Federation of Democracies 'open to accession by any member of the Confederation able to fulfil the conditions of membership'. The report deliberately chose 'a political rather than a geographical test for membership', and the idea of a European federation, 'including the United Kingdom and Ireland', was but one of a number of possibilities which would require revision of Federal Union's policy, 'if the situation were to develop along any of these lines'. The careful wording concealed but could not reconcile divergences of view about Europe that were to surface, with unfortunate consequences, in Britain's attitude to European unification after the war.

In some respects, however, the report was highly prescient – notably in its admission that the peace negotiations would result in a confederal system, with some spheres of influence being dominated by the Soviet Union. A number of those who were later to be associated with the post-war United Nations – including Gordon Evans, an initiator of the UN Development Decade – welcomed the Federal Union report as a real contribution to wartime thinking about post-war reconstruction.[37] It undoubtedly influenced the general climate of opinion within which the Allied governments took some of their key decisions. And yet, no less certainly, these fell far short of their more ambitious aims.

At the San Francisco Conference the victorious Allies drafted the Charter of the United Nations, signed on 26 June 1945. It provided for a Security Council, but without the powers sought by Federal Union's peace aims report, and a General Assembly, but without proportional representation. It was an improvement on the League of Nations: at the very least, the United States and the Soviet Union were members from the start. But it was very far from being even an embryonic 'government'. Moreover, the world itself was soon to assume a very different alignment. East and West were to diverge; former colonial systems were to be impugned and dissolved; the disparity in size between the United States and the countries of Western Europe was to hamper tranquil co-operation; the plight of what came to be known as 'the Third World' remained unsolved.

All these shifts and changes threw into relief the problems which faced the advocates of federal union. Looking back on Federal Union's peace aims report, Charles Kimber acknowledged that 'it was far too long to have the popular appeal which might have revived and united the movement'. He also recognised its more fundamental weakness. 'It showed,' he admitted, 'too many signs of trying to reconcile views which were widely separated.'[38]

It was not just a matter of economic and political debate between Left and Right. The clear-headed Professor Joad put his finger on the nub of what he called 'the controversy which has been bombinating up and down the movement for the last eighteen months'.[39] Four divergent aims, he said, needed to be considered: a union of West European countries, an Anglo-American union, Commonwealth union, and world federation. Federal Union must adopt a 'concrete objective' if it wished to become a political movement; otherwise it would have to remain 'primarily an educational and propagandist organization'.[40]

Federal Union's first reaction was to eschew the controversy that choice of a clear political objective would involve. An Extraordinary General Meeting held in London on 15/16 January 1944 to settle the matter could do no better than resolve that 'Federal Union should not at present advocate the setting up of any specific federation, but should encourage the establishment of any federations and international organizations which tend to lead to ultimate world federation'.[41]

Joad's challenge remained unanswered. With the Commonwealth so disparate, and America replacing Britain as a world power, Commonwealth union and Atlantic union looked less feasible. The real debate, it now seemed, was between advocates of world federation and those whose immediate objective was union in Europe. Neither, in the very long run, was incompatible with the other: but those campaigning for a stable and more peaceful international system had to choose their priorities. After Yalta and Potsdam, did it still make sense to press for world government? Or should the advocates of union set themselves a more immediate task?

4 Postwar Debate

Peace found Federal Union not only with new problems, but also with new premises and new staff. At the 1945 General Election, the political professionals returned to the fray. Some of them were members of Federal Union. R. W. G. Mackay, Henry Usborne and John Parker were elected for Labour; so was Wing-Commander Ernest Millington, a federalist and like Mackay a Common Wealth supporter. T. L. Horabin won his seat as a Liberal. Several other adherents of Federal Union were also elected; but any notion that the movement might itself have turned into a political party was now finally scotched.

At the beginning of 1946, Federal Union moved its headquarters, as planned, from Gower Street to No. 20 Buckingham Street, a rickety building which already housed a number of often eccentric voluntary organisations. It had suffered during the war: one visitor found herself standing on a projecting piece of masonry almost falling into the street below.[1] Another described with feeling the 'sombre semi-Dickensian atmosphere of hideous poverty and indomitable good cheer'.[2] The poverty was certainly real: that summer, a new financial crisis arose when the movement lost the £600 annually subscribed by one generous member.[3] With membership below 2000, the movement was in no position to compete with the big battalions.

The year 1946 saw some changes, too, in Federal Union's officers. E. E. V. de Peyer, an opera singer and member of a well-known musical family, became Treasurer. Another musical connection was in Scotland, where Sir Robert Grieg, a kinsman of the Norwegian composer, was a member of the movement's Edinburgh Council.[4] In London, the new National Council included Major Neville Coghill, future adaptor of *The Canterbury Tales*, and now just returning to civilian and academic life.[5] Yet there was continuity as well as change. Miss Josephy in particular remained as active as ever. As an anonymous federalist poetaster put it:

FU's directors come and go,
But Joad and Jo remain . . .
Josephy's passion sways the crowd
While Joad with logic wins –
So let F.U. with praises loud
Acclaim these Heavenly Twins.[6]

Finally, Federal Union had a new Secretary, J. Keith Killby. A member since 1940, he had learned as a prisoner of war in a group of mixed nationalities the possibilities of international action. 'We found we could co-operate in baffling the Germans', he wrote. A man of broad sympathies and much liked, he suited the movement well. He first proved his administrative abilities at the international conference staged in Luxembourg at the end of 1946.

Federal Union's European Committee, under Jo Josephy's chairmanship, had during the war proposed that an international conference of federalists be held after the war was over.[7] Already in mid-1945, FU's International Section established an outpost in Paris; and one of its members, Henri Koch, was a native and resident of the Grand Duchy of Luxembourg who had been active in Federal Union's European Committee when working in London for the Belgian government in exile during the war. In the summer of 1946, with encouragement from his wife Alison, herself a British federalist, he issued invitations to a meeting in Luxembourg. This finally developed into an international conference with some seventy delegates from fourteen countries, including strong Dutch, British, and French representation. There was also a significant group of world federalists from the United States.[8] The ensuing debates between world and regional federalists brought to a head – but not to a conclusion – the latent conflict of priorities within the movement which Joad had identified three years earlier.

A UNITED WORLD?

The nuclear bombs dropped on Hiroshima and Nagasaki in 1945 not only put an end to World War II: they also transformed the nature of war itself. No longer did it put at risk only the lives of hundreds, thousands and millions of people and the irreplaceable work of centuries. Henceforward, it threatened the human race. For most federalists, this made the rightness of their cause still more evident, and the urgency of action more intense than ever. For many, this meant primarily action on a world scale.

Federal Union had always sought world-wide contacts, even during the war. In the spring of 1941, R. W. G. Mackay had paid a visit to the United States, where he had conferred with Clarence Streit and attended a meeting of Federal Union Inc.[9] Later he visited Australia and New Zealand, and had helped to stimulate federalist movements there.[10] In May 1941, Federal Union's Board of Directors in London had decided to set up an International Section, divided into three sub-sections – American, Dominion, and European. Some confusion persisted about its title; and that of the American sub-section was amended to 'The Anglo-American Corresponding Society' – in order, as Professor George Catlin put it, 'to preserve the historical association and to follow the nomenclature of similar committees already formed by Mr. Streit'.[11]

In July 1942, Miss Josephy had reported that the federalists in the United States were divided into three groups: Federal Union Inc. (Streit's organisation), the World Federalists (who had split from Streit to pursue policies closer to those of Federal Union in Britain), and a more diffuse movement advocating world government. The Directors agreed to correspond with the first and second of these three bodies.[12] In the years that followed, Federal Union sought to co-operate not only with them, but also with groups in Switzerland; it also made contact with sympathisers in Nigeria and South Africa. But any serious attempt to create a world movement, it was agreed, would have to wait until after the war.[13]

World Federation had been among Federal Union's aims since these were formally adopted at the foundation meeting of the National Council in March 1940.[14] But this had been qualified by the adjective 'ultimate'; and in 1942 the big policy document, *Federation: Peace Aim – War Weapon*, had envisaged as the practicable aim for the post-war world a World Confederation, which it was hoped would evolve in a federal direction as states came to accept the requisite limitations on their sovereignty.[15]

In September 1944, the Annual General Meeting of Federal Union proposed European federation as the immediate objective, with world federation as a long-term goal.[16] But the terrifying prospects opened up by nuclear weapons made action on a world scale begin to seem more urgent.

One leading advocate of such action was the Hungarian-born journalist Emery Reves, who put the case against national sovereignty and for world federation with great clarity and force in his book *The Anatomy of Peace*.[17] Originally published in the United States just before the end of the war in the Far East, this pungently expressed a very simple, fundamental, message: the only condition that creates war is the unregulated relationship between sovereign states. 'Peace,' Reves wrote, 'will exist . . . only when absolute national sovereignty, which causes anarchy in international relations, gives way to universal legal order.' To a mass audience – the book sold half a million copies in over twenty languages and appeared as a Penguin paperback in January 1947 – Reves was repeating the argument of Lord Lothian and other founders of Federal Union. In the editions that appeared after Hiroshima, he appended a postscript entitled 'World Government *is* the First Step'.

Even so dedicated a European as Miss Josephy wrote that

> one thing which the unleashing of atomic energy must inevitably change is the policy of Federal Union. European Federation, though still an essential part of the whole, is no longer enough even as a first step. World Federation, far from being a utopian dream, becomes at one jump a practical necessity . . . What is more, the time is now or never . . . The first essential is for the Security Council to be composed of representatives of more or less equal units. Here is where European Federation still has a large part to play. Only through federal institutions will the peoples of Europe ever be in a position to supply a common representative to the Security Council.[18]

Before long, Miss Josephy was devoting her energies once more to the immediate concern of European union, with world federation as a longer-term aim. But many members of Federal Union continued to seek direct steps towards world government[19] while an active minority remained more interested in Atlantic unity. For the most part, relations between these different groups were mutually tolerant. Some people worked hard on more than one front. It was in line with this eclectic policy that Federal Union had invited both European and World Federalists to the Luxembourg Conference.

DEBATE IN THE GRAND DUCHY

Controversy broke out on the very first day. The ceremonies were properly decorous. The Mayor of Luxembourg greeted the conference members in English; Miss Josephy thanked him in French. Both languages were used for the meetings – although some Federal Union members were enthusiasts for Esperanto. But the chairman at the opening session, Lieut.-Col. Evelyn King, a Labour MP and a member of Federal Union's National Council, spoke and understood only English. So did most of the Americans; the valiant efforts of the volunteer interpreters were not enough to prevent objections from some French-speaking delegates, which exacerbated the more important substantive dispute between those like King, Henry Usborne, and the Americans, who wanted the meeting to concentrate on world organisation, and those who wanted to work for European federation. Some of the world federalists, particularly the Americans, felt there should be no place for this in the world organisation. According to Miss Josephy, there was 'never . . . any difference of opinion between the two groups on the necessity for World Federal Government'. But their desire to work separately became as clear at Luxembourg as it later did in Federal Union itself; and two commissions were set to work out proposals for a European bureau and a world organisation. The final compromise was that 'A World Organisation should be set up and within this organisation a section for European federation.' Their recommendations were accepted with a few alterations, and 'thus were born the Movement for World Federal Government and the European Union of Federalists'.[20] The Movement for World Federal Government held a Congress in Switzerland in the following August. Miss Josephy acted as the temporary liaison officer for the European Union of Federalists until it met in Paris in December 1946.

Federal Union had thus been a prime mover in creating the international federalist movements at both European and world level. Meanwhile, controversies notwithstanding, the British delegates had found the Luxembourg Conference a promising start. As Miss Josephy reported, the 'most important part of any international conference is never the formal discussions, not even, important as they may be, the decisions eventually taken, but personal contacts between people of different lands'. 'I now know in person,' she added, 'the people who up to now have been mere names on a piece of notepaper, and that, when it comes to community of effort, in working with people of other lands it makes all the difference when, with your mind's eye, you can see the faces behind the names.'[21] Likewise, Keith Killby, as organiser of the conference, became well-known to most of the representatives of the thirty-seven federalist organisations represented there.

In a letter to the participants afterwards, Killby declared the meeting 'an unqualified success'. An American world government journal remarked that it was 'valuable in lifting the involuntary "iron curtain" of isolation and ignorance, and in providing delegates with the cheering news that they were among many the world over devoted to the cause'.[22] At the same time, however, one British federalist argued that the national federalist organisations should merge into one. 'If a picked group of federalists,' he said, 'cannot even discuss a merger of their national societies, can they expect to be taken seriously when urging whole peoples to surrender their national sovereignty?'[23]

What was more, world federalists and European federalists soon found that they must agree to differ. Within less than a year of the Luxembourg meeting, the European federalists joined with representatives from a conference of continental federalists who had met at Hertenstein in September 1946 to establish, independently rather than within a world organisation, the European Union of Federalists and to organise its founding Congress at Montreux, at the end of August 1947. For world federalists, Luxembourg was likewise seminal. Their next step was the foundation of the Movement for World Federal Government (subsequently renamed the World Association of World Federalists,[24] or WAWF), also at their first Congress at Montreux, immediately before the 'Europeans'.

5 World Federalism?

Many of the slogans and rallying-cries that were current during and after World War II ring strangely half-a-century later. One such is the phrase 'world government'. In a world seen as divided between political super-powers, fragmented by sectarian and other wars, and irremediably complex, even the abstract idea of a global 'environment' presents forbidding problems. In the late 1940s, however, the situation looked simpler, and men and women perhaps had bolder minds. The victors in war were tired but self-confident. Their plans for peace had produced the United Nations, the International Monetary Fund, the World Bank, and other global institutions. Was it not possible to improve on this embryonic world system? Could the United Nations not be strengthened? Could the USA and the USSR, so lately comrades in arms, not be persuaded to settle their differences and establish a durable framework for peace?

Since then, such questions have met equivocal answers. Many who advocated more law and order in relations between states came to see their hopes embodied, however imperfectly, in the European Community rather than the United Nations. But hindsight is a hindrance to historical judgement. It behoves the historian to be fair to idealists as well as to stubborn facts.

EARLY ADVOCATES

The idea of world government gained some distinguished British supporters. Already before the end of the war Sir William Beveridge had enlarged upon his earlier support for European federation and advocated world federal government in a book called *The Price of Peace*. In the following year the publisher Victor Gollancz declared at a Federal Union meeting: 'I sincerely, almost fanatically, believe in World Federation.'[1] The Foreign Secretary, Ernest Bevin, spoke of the necessity for 'a new study for the purpose of creating a world assembly elected directly from the people of the world'.[2] And in 1946, as well as playing a leading part in Federal Union's delegation at the Luxembourg conference, Henry Usborne established the Parliamentary Group for World Government. Usborne was at first assisted in this by Norman Hart; and soon afterwards Patrick

Armstrong, one of the co-founders of Federal Union, became the Group's secretary (or in House of Commons terminology, Clerk), and in this capacity did much to ensure the Group's success, with a membership often exceeding a hundred MPs. The Group's parliamentary supporters came from all political parties, and many were later to be prominent. Some were committed federalists, like Gordon Lang, the Group's first Chairman, and later Martin Maddan who, when he joined the Group on his election to Parliament, was Chairman of Federal Union's National Council. Others, busy men, were content to be on the side of the angels without being fully convinced. Henry Usborne himself was a Labour MP; and the Labour leadership was often explicit in its support for world government. Thus, in 1946, Sir Stafford Cripps declared that: 'World federation has hitherto been looked upon as a very long-term objective, but the atomic bomb has telescoped history and made it impossible for us to wait long years of acute danger of war, because from that war civilisation and mankind cannot survive.'[3] In the following year Harold Laski, Chairman of the Labour Party, said:

> We cannot rest content until we have a genuine World Government expressing, through the direct choice of peoples, in a parliament responsible to them, the will of the common folk, instead of being dependent, like the United Nations, upon the sovereign wills of nation states which express, in all vital matters, the purposes of their ruling classes and subordinate to those purposes the interests of the common peoples.[4]

An inspiring orator, full of brilliant schemes, Henry Usborne seemed to take a pessimistic view of Federal Union and its prospects, but was often ready with financial and other help when it was needed. During his years as a Labour MP, however, he failed to win large-scale support, as distinct from general sympathy, although Clement Attlee spent many of his last years advocating world government – as did Hugh Gaitskell in one of his final public speeches.

In June 1947 when East–West tension in Europe was steadily growing, Usborne and other members of the Parliamentary Group issued a brochure, *The Plan in Outline for World Government by 1955*. He introduced it to Federal Union's AGM as 'a draft for discussion' and *Federal News* printed it in full.[5] It proposed that every million inhabitants of each country should be represented at a

'Peoples' World Constituent Assembly' to be held in Geneva in 1950. Where feasible, unofficial nation-wide ballots were to be held simultaneously in the summer of that year. A sub-committee of the Parliamentary Group set itself the task of interviewing would-be candidates. Among those chosen, the majority were Federal Union members, from Sir William Beveridge to members of the Parliamentary Group such as Usborne himself. The hope was to persuade a quarter of the British electorate to vote; the campaign, it was estimated, would need 500 000 voluntary workers and a million pounds of voluntary finance. The brochure was widely distributed: 100 copies of it were autographed by Ernest Bevin.[6] A number of the Plan's supporters were practising Christians: they included Donald Soper, Lionel Curtis, Christina Dowson, Anglican secretary on the Federal Union Churches Committee, John Hoyland, and another Quaker, Leslie Harris, a Midlands industrialist and long-standing member of Federal Union, who on receiving the brochure immediately contributed £1000.

Usborne's initiative led to a further new movement, the 'Crusade for World Government', to promote the idea of the 'Peoples' World Constituent Assembly' (or as it was often called, the 'Peoples' World Convention'). It was a valiant, tactlessly named attempt to produce a sharp change of direction in politics at a time when armed conflict, and possibly a third world war, seemed perilously imminent. The initial response was encouraging. The 'Crusade' set up a national organisation in London, and such Federal Union stalwarts as Leslie Harris took office. Gerry Kraus, a refugee, acted as Secretary and edited the magazine *Across Frontiers*. Lancelot Hogben, a distinguished academic much concerned for the social responsibility of science, who had been among the early members of Federal Union's Council, also played a leading part.

Usborne was invited by American world federalists, including Albert Einstein and Carl Van Doren, to a conference in Pennsylvania to discuss the project of electing delegates to the 'Peoples' World Convention', which was 'envisaged as a useful device of mass education'. Mrs Anita McCormick Blaine, 'interested and inspired' by the discussions, offered a million dollars to further the cause of world government; and this became the basis for a Foundation for World Government, which donated $50 000 to Usborne's crusade.[7]

When the 'Peoples' World Convention' was eventually held in Geneva in 1950, it soon revealed – even to that perennial optimist

Henry Usborne – just how misplaced his faith in it had been. As he later declared: 'After a week of arduous, nearly continuous sessions, the conference broke up in total confusion . . . The 500 enthusiasts, . . . most of them, it seemed to me, were either communists or fellow-travellers.'[8] Few, if any, of the detailed questions discussed had been discussed before, and the Assembly found it almost impossible to agree on the ideas to which it sought to convert the rest of the world. What was more, in a planet whose population was numbered in billions, any movement for change would have had to be far larger to effect any significant shift in political attitudes.

However, the 'Peoples' World Convention' had attracted some distinguished support. Einstein was one of a dozen world figures who, when endorsing it, had signed an appeal declaring: 'The human race as such will cease to exist unless a world government capable of enforcing world law is established by peaceful means.' When the leaders of the 'Crusade' fell out over the question of coercing the Soviet Union if it would not agree to the international control of atomic energy, Einstein supported Usborne, arguing that 'It is not feasible to abolish one single weapon as long as war itself is not abolished. This can only be done by establishing effective world government.'[9] At a less celebrated level, too, the 'Crusade' attracted many idealistic militants, especially youngsters. They included Tony Lynes, a budding accountant, who later went on to found the Child Poverty Action Group; Michael Howard, who was later prominent in the early years of the Campaign for Nuclear Disarmament; and Helier Robinson, who later went to work in, of all places, the Antarctic. Other sympathisers, such as Keith Killby and David Barton, were inclined to see Federal Union as a more practical and cautious approach to the ultimate goal of the 'Crusade'. After the Geneva Assembly, in any case, it gradually lost impetus; and by the early 1950s its initial adherents had dwindled to a stubborn but virtually ineffective few.

THE 1947 MONTREUX CONGRESS

Outside the 'Crusade', meanwhile, other federalists had been pursuing the paths they had mapped out in Luxembourg at the end of 1946. Federal Union continued to press for world government, while American federalists established a new umbrella movement, United

World Federalists. This, like other participants, had great hopes for the forthcoming world federalist Congress, scheduled for Montreux in Switzerland in the summer of 1947.

From 17 to 24 August Montreux played host to 300 delegates and 24 observers from 24 different countries.[10] The British were the most numerous, with 73 delegates, including seven MPs. Next came the French with 65, followed by 44 from the United States and 32 from the Netherlands. Among the British, one of the most prominent was the formidable Monica Wingate, Principal of Balls Park College, Hertfordshire. Although the Wingate family first became famous among the British public through the exploits of Miss Wingate's brother, Orde Wingate, the brilliant and eccentric general of the Chindits, it was already well known in Federal Union. Orde Wingate was a sympathiser, reputed to have lectured his men on the benefits of federation during a lull in the battle in Burma. His brother Granville, a barrister, served as Vice-Chairman of the National Council and for many years as a trustee of the Federal Trust, and later became a judge. Monica Wingate had joined Federal Union in 1939, and became chairman of the National Council in 1947. A woman of exceptional personality and strength of character, purposeful and highly businesslike in the chair, she also had gifts of tact and warmth which proved of immense benefit to the movement.

They were needed at Montreux. The working languages were French and English. As one participant wrote, 'Here were we, a polyglot collection, few of whom had met before at Luxembourg, mostly strong minded individualists, and all without exception highly suspicious of everyone else.'[11] Deeply imbued with some of the reflexes of national sovereignty which they wanted to abolish, they could not agree upon voting and representation, or upon procedure or anything else in open session. To Monica Wingate 'it resembled nothing so much as a dog fight . . . or a drunken man, because he always finds his way home in the end, and that was precisely what we finally succeeded in doing'.[12]

The Congress began with Henry Usborne as chairman; but it soon dissolved into furious arguments over the election of a steering committee. The delegations were at loggerheads over many issues, major and minor, such as the alternatives of a 'Peoples' World Convention' or the reform of the United Nations; but these discussions were bedevilled, in Monica Wingate's view, by feelings of guilt over the war years, particularly among the French.[13] While the leaders were trying to thrash out some sort of agreement, Monica

Wingate saved the day by proposing as chairman the leader of the French delegation, and appealing to everyone present to think not of their narrower loyalties, but of the world as a whole.

The French chairman, Jean Larmeroux, proved an excellent choice. An eminent political scientist who had been an adviser to Poincaré, he guided the Congress with tact and skill. With his help, it drafted statutes and a declaration, and elected a President and Council to run the movement, which came to be called the World Movement for World Federal Government. The declaration, carried unanimously, included a clear statement of Franco-German reconciliation. The Council, largely composed of Europeans, included three British MPs – Victor Collins, Rev. Gordon Lang and Henry Usborne – as well as the Abbé Pierre, later to become famous for his work on behalf of Parisian slum-dwellers. Counting the votes for its election had been in the capable hands of Mrs Edith Wills, Birmingham's first-ever woman Member of Parliament. Towards the end of the Congress, Sir John Boyd Orr, the craggy Scots scientist who was Director-General of the UN Food and Agricultural Organisation as well as a member of Federal Union, urged the delegates to adopt a functional approach to world government. As it turned out, most of the arguments had been about procedures and priorities rather than between Left and Right; and mutual understanding grew as the participants came to know each other better.

Not surprisingly some of the liveliest delegates at Montreux were the young. The United States had started a Student Federalist Movement, whose British contact was Norman Hart, a Federal Union activist and a pacifist member of the Independent Labour Party. After the Luxembourg conference of 1946, he had helped organise a student conference in Britain, and had persuaded a dozen British students to come to Montreux. Altogether, some 150 students from various countries were present there. Before the Congress was over, they set up the World Student Federalists, led among others by Hart and an American colleague, Charles Haywood.[14]

So Montreux belied its stormy beginnings. When the Congress ended, a world organisation of federalists had come into being, with a united, multinational structure, a newly established office in Geneva, and a firmly based youth section to look to the future. In Britain, Federal Union celebrated the occasion with an enlarged edition of *Federal News*, printed in colour and on glossier paper. As Monica Wingate declared, 'We spoke now at last as World Citizens.'[15]

'MY COUNTRY IS THE WORLD'

It was true – and it was untrue. Looking back with a generation's hindsight, one can wonder at such innocent optimism. Yet, at the time, things seemed possible and urgently necessary which now seem no less urgent yet far less likely.

One event in particular seized the public imagination. In May 1948, a former US Air Force officer, Garry Davis, sat down at the Palais de Chaillot in Paris, where the United Nations Organisation was in session, asserting his right to be a citizen of the world, and defying UN officials to evict him. His gesture brought him world-wide publicity: many were shocked to see that the universal organisation entrusted above all with responsibility for keeping peace in the world lacked the power to compel even one solitary objector to leave its premises in the heart of a member state. How much less possible then, asked Garry Davis, was it for the UN to ensure a peaceful world? When the French police took over and removed the offending world citizen, the lesson once again was clear; the sovereign state, upon whose membership the United Nations rested, retained the power to get things done. The only long-term consequences of Davis's action were his own book, *My Country is the World*,[16] and the International Registry of World Citizens, initiated and maintained in Paris.

In the summer of 1948, a few months after the Garry Davis episode, the world federalists held their second Congress, this time in Luxembourg. Emery Reves was one of the speakers. He, by then, had begun to see European federation as a possible step towards world federation, in line with Federal Union's own policy; and the final Declaration endorsed regional integration as 'an approach' to world federation. Following the failure of the 'Peoples' Constituent Assembly', the Congress also stressed the part that parliamentary committees could play in drawing up a world constitution. Sir John Boyd Orr was elected President of the Council; Monica Wingate became Vice-Chairman; and the Luxembourger and former member of Federal Union's European Committee, Henri Koch, took over as temporary Secretary-General.[17]

By the time of the following Congress, in Stockholm in the summer of 1949, the World Movement's efforts were already being overshadowed by the developing 'cold war'. As chairman of the Congress, Monica Wingate had an immediate political controversy on her hands: a Communist fellow-travelling or 'front' organisation wished to attend. What was more, the movement was short of money. When its Secretary-General resigned at the beginning of the Congress and Keith Killby stepped into the breach, he felt 'like a ball in the middle of a rugger scrum in which some twenty teams were taking part'.[18] Such Federal Union members as Ota Adler, Miss Josephy, Norman Hart and Henry Usborne also played leading roles in the Congress. Richard Reader Harris, MP, took the chair for the final plenary session, and Lord Boyd Orr[19] was re-elected President. With financial help from, among others, the Italian government, the World Movement managed to survive; but its hopes of achieving real political progress remained dim. Its next Congress, in 1951, was generally admitted to have been a failure. In the following year, the Parliamentary Group for World Government held a second international conference of parliamentarians in London. Those taking part included Lord Boyd Orr, the Liberal leader Clement Davies, Harold Wilson, Hilary Marquand, Konni Zilliacus and Julian Snow; on the Right, one of the most active Conservative organisers was Walter Elliott. This event helped to revive flagging spirits; and the conference made proposals for reforming the United Nations, which helped the world federalists to tackle more substantial matters than Crusades and Constituent Assemblies.

REFORM THE UNITED NATIONS?

An opportunity to give the United Nations Organisation more effective power now, in fact, seemed to be looming. Article 109 of the UN Charter stipulated that a conference to review it should be on the agenda of the General Assembly in 1955 (the text read 'at the tenth annual session'); and while some doubted whether the UN was capable of being turned into an effective world authority with power to keep the peace, others like Federal Union's Douglas Robinson thought Usborne's bull-headed approach 'incredibly naive'.[20] The idea of reforming the UN's Charter, which fitted well with the British preference for existing organisations, was also very popular with American federalists.

A distinguished American lawyer, Grenville Clark, had published a book on the theme of UN reform in 1950:[21] and the world parliamentarians produced their proposals in 1952. Federal Union, however, was among the first of the World Movement's member organisations to undertake serious work on the subject. Together with the Crusade for World Government, now seeking a more realistic goal than the Peoples' Constituent Assembly, Federal Union set up a study group and in 1953 produced its detailed proposals for reforming the UN Charter into a world federal constitution.[22] It then published a pamphlet about its plan by John Pinder, in time for the Joint Conference of the World Movement and the World Association of Parliamentarians for World Government, held in the Parliament buildings in Copenhagen in August that year. Two weeks later the pamphlet was reissued together with the Conference proposals, themselves based mainly on the work of Federal Union and of Americans inspired by Grenville Clark.[23]

The idea of revising the UN Charter to give the organisation federal powers, being both imaginative and practical, perfectly suited Beveridge. Now a member of the House of Lords, he had also become President of Federal Union; and in March 1954 he led a deputation from it to the Foreign Office, for an hour's discussion with Selwyn Lloyd, then Minister of State and subsequently Foreign Secretary. Among other things, Federal Union proposed to set up a small independent committee to collect ideas and make a report to the government. Beveridge told Selwyn Lloyd that he was considering an invitation to chair such a committee and that a 'prime consideration' would be to obtain official observers from the Foreign Office. *Federal News* reported that Lloyd said he would 'consider Lord Beveridge's request'. A member of the deputation recalls that Beveridge also asked for some office facilities. Selwyn Lloyd replied that previous experience (presumably with the Beveridge Report) suggested that if Beveridge secured such a foothold he would soon have the whole office working for him.[24] Beveridge got neither observers nor other help from the Foreign Office, so the idea of a Beveridge Report on reform of the United Nations quietly lapsed.

In September 1954, the World Movement followed its Copenhagen meeting with a 'working congress' in London hosted by Federal Union. This continued to concentrate on revisions of the UN Charter but this time, in response to the concerns of its host organisation, it set up a committee on regional integration. John Bowyer, just down from Cambridge and starting work at the Bar, was in charge of the arrangements, assisted by staff and volunteers from Federal Union. Per Haekkerup, later to become Foreign Minister of Denmark, was chairman of the Executive Committee; Lord Beveridge was elected Vice-President of the World Movement. At the opening press conference, his manner so impressed the *Guardian*'s reporter that he commented: 'If there was any journalist who felt at all sceptical about the virtues of federalism, he kept his feelings well hidden from Lord Beveridge.' Altogether, indeed, the London Congress earned several hundred column inches in the British press, and was also well covered on the air.[25]

In 1955, the World Movement held its Congress in Paris, again in association with the World Association of Parliamentarians. The French government invited the participants to the Quai d'Orsay for a meeting addressed by the Foreign Minister Antoine Pinay; and there were several official receptions. At one of them, Monica Wingate reported, 'I saw to my horror that the worst of all the current grass-eating sandal-wearers had Bertrand Russell in her grip. She had some obsession about Italian women.' Miss Wingate 'looked around wildly' for his wife to rescue him; but she was pinned in a corner by a British MP. So she bore down on the ill-assorted pair and took Russell away, saying: 'Lord Russell, you really shouldn't let yourself be monopolised by all the conference bores.' To which he replied, 'I always hope they will say something interesting,' but added sadly, 'But I could make nothing of that one; she kept speaking of Italian mothers until at last I said, "But, Madam, *I* am *not* an Italian mother!"' In the more suitable circumstances of the Congress itself, Russell warned his audience: 'You can preserve peace for some time by negotiation, but without world government there will come a time when negotiation breaks down.'[26]

The Paris Congress again tackled the revision of the UN Charter: and not long afterwards there seemed some hope that this might come about. Britain and six other countries put forward a Resolution in the UN General Assembly, calling for a Charter Review Conference to be held, at a time and place to be decided, in 1957. The Assembly approved the proposal. But the votes against it included those of the Soviet bloc; and against Soviet opposition these practical measures made little headway.[27]

A UN POLICE FORCE?

The Suez crisis of 1956 revealed once more the danger of governments' taking the law into their own hands. When British and French forces went in to 'separate the combatants', as the face-saving formula had it, Federal Union set up a study group under Lord Pakenham (later Lord Longford) to examine whether and how a UN police force might be formed to handle such situations. Shortly afterwards, Federal Union and the Parliamentary group called a conference in London under the title 'United Nations International Force – a Basis for Peace'.[28] One of the star speakers was General Sir John Glubb ('Glubb Pasha'). Following the conference, Lord Pakenham's study group got to work. Its members included Capt B. H. Liddell Hart, James Callaghan, MP, and Frank Beswick, MP from the Labour side as well as such Conservative MPs as James Pitman, John Tilney and Vice-Admiral John Hughes-Hallett. From Federal Union, John Bowyer, Keith Killby and John Pinder were among those most actively involved, together with Pat Armstrong from the Parliamentary Group. Hughes-Hallett, a formidable retired sailor, was responsible for many of the ideas and Pinder for much of the text of the final report.[29]

This discussed three possible types of Permanent UN Force: a 'Light Force', comprising 20000 men not able to undertake offensive action; a 'Medium Force' strong enough to undertake military actions so long as they were not directed against a Great Power; and a 'Heavy Force' which would 'enable the United Nations to be the effective policeman of the world'. The latter two options were not discussed in as much detail as the first, because the Medium Force would not be 'acceptable to members of the United Nations at present', while 'a Heavy Force is inevitably related to the acceptance of the principle of world disarmament'.

The Report saw the Force as primarily suited to 'interposition' – occupying territory between opposing national armies. It also suggested that some new states might wish for the presence of UN troops while establishing independence. The Report proposed that the Force should have its own ships and aircraft, with international immunity. A base in each of the northern and southern hemispheres should be owned or leased by the UN, to include airfields and other facilities, with terrain suitable for training, and a climate attractive enough to encourage membership of the Force as a career. It was also suggested that the UN should offer hospitality to units of the Force in other camps or bases, to give it experience under a variety of climates and conditions.

The Report favoured direct recruitment to the UN Force, with a maximum of 10 per cent of personnel coming from any one country. It recommended one operational language, and the enrolment of highly motivated candidates – although these, it stipulated, should be approved by their governments in order to avoid hostility on the grounds that undesirables were being admitted. However, it also suggested suspending the nationality of members of the Force during their period of service, replacing it perhaps with something comparable to an Order of Chivalry.[30]

Published on 29 May 1957, the Report won banner headlines in the Liberal *News Chronicle*: 'WORLD ARMY PLANNED – 100 MPs call for big UN Force', plus twenty-five inches of text. The *Guardian* featured it similarly, if less prominently, under the headline 'WORLD "POLICE FORCE" PLAN'. *The Times* and *The Daily Telegraph* summarised it in eight and ten inches respectively. The provincial press mentioned the Report and both ITV and the BBC outlined it. It was Federal Union's best publicity for years. Field Marshal Sir Claude Auchinleck called it 'a masterly paper, very clear and comprehensive': Sir Harold Nicolson said it was 'an excellent document'.[31] The Report went into three editions, the third of them four years later, when the UN was embroiled in the Congo. A terser, illustrated version, largely composed by Roderick MacFarquhar, was also produced under the title *PUNF for Peace*. This stressed the core of the federalist message:

> One would want to see the establishment of a force strong enough to be the effective policeman of the world. This could only come about with the acceptance of world disarmament. It would also mean that governments and their peoples would have to merge a part of their national sovereignty to a world government.[32]

On 10 June 1958, Duncan Sandys, then Secretary of State for Defence, suggested in a speech in the House of Commons the possibility of achieving comprehensive disarmament at a single step, after first establishing a world security authority, and an international police force with 'unquestioned military superiority'. Shortly afterwards, ten Conservative Members of Parliament produced a report for the Conservative Political Centre entitled *A World Security Authority?* Its proposals were remarkably similar to those of the Federal Union Report – but this was hardly surprising. Three of the ten, including Hughes-Hallett, had been members of Federal Union's Commission, and the draft had come from the same pen.[33]

UNANSWERED QUESTIONS

And yet, despite the lessons of Suez, the prospect of a world authority seemed as far away as ever, and the prevailing climate of opinion made support – and resources – hard to secure. In 1958, for economy's sake, Federal Union and the Crusade for World Government agreed to amalgamate their staff for a trial period of one year. At the following AGM, in April 1959, the arrangement was made permanent.[34]

Also in 1959, Federal Union agreed to co-operate with the Parliamentary Group in studying a proposed World Investment Convention. A Commission was formed under the chairmanship of the Rt Hon. Arthur Creech Jones, MP, a former Secretary of State for the Colonies who had been a member of the Federal Union Research Institute's Colonial Research Committee in 1940,[35] and including the Liberal leader Jo Grimond among its ten MPs. The joint Hon. Secretaries were Patrick Armstrong and John Pinder, and the Commission's advisers included Nicholas (later Lord) Kaldor and Harold Wilson. Among those who came to discuss the problems with the Commission were the Hon. K. A. Gbedemah, Ghana's Finance Minister, Lord McNair, former President of the International Court and later to be President of Federal Union, and Dr Paz Estenssoro, previously and subsequently President of Bolivia. The Commission's final report began with the premise that 'A framework of law is a basic condition of economic progress.' It accepted that the ideal solution, 'to establish a world federal government, which would create and enforce a world-wide system of law based on an agreed charter of economic rights' was not imminent, and it therefore proposed more modest measures. These – 'a World Investment Convention, backed by a Secretariat to administer it, and an Arbitration Tribunal to deal with disputes' – would provide a framework within which the necessary system of law could grow.[36]

Federal Union members, including John Roberts, also supported the Parliamentary Group in setting up its Education Advisory Committee. For over twenty years, it organised conferences, lectures, meetings, and competitions. Under Sir Edward Boyle and other chairmen, it did its best to encourage the development of non-chauvinist history teaching: in 1962 it published *History Syllabuses and a World Perspective*, which sold several thousand copies.

Meanwhile, world federalist ideas continued to be publicly voiced. In March 1960 Lord Hailsham, opening the defence debate for the government in the House of Lords, declared that a World Authority or total disarmament were the only rational objectives for the world, and that of these a World Authority was the more so.[37] Later, relieved of the responsibilities of government, Hailsham was to accept the presidency of the Parliamentary Group for World Government. Then in June 1960, after the breakdown of the Paris summit meeting between Eisenhower, Khrushchev, Macmillan and de Gaulle, Federal Union organised a large-scale conference in Central Hall, Westminster. Norman Hart took the chair and the speakers included Monica Wingate, James Pitman, Bertrand Russell, Canon John Collins, and Earl Attlee. When hecklers from the League of Empire Loyalists interrupted the meeting, Attlee told them that they were 180 years out of date – a reference to the role of empire loyalists in the American War of Independence.[38]

That same year, 1960, saw another crisis to which Federal Union felt bound to respond. This was the United Nations' embroilment in the Congo, which brought to the fore once again the question of an international peace-keeping force. In conjunction with Federal Union, the Wyndham Place Trust, recently established to work on the federal idea in a religious context, asked Lord Pakenham to play the same role as he had in 1956–7. This time, the resultant Commission included Group-Captain Leonard Cheshire, VC, Laurens van der Post, Dr David (later Lord) Pitt, Lord Beveridge, Douglas Sanders, various churchmen, and members of Federal Union. Monica Wingate served as chairman of the Drafting Committee and John Bowyer as Director of Drafting. Other outside advisers included Field Marshal Auchinleck, Professor Norman Bentwich, Commander Stephen King-Hall, Professor A. C. Mace and Dr Andrew Martin.

The section of the Commission's report which proposed a 'Light Standing Force' acknowledged its indebtedness to the previous Pakenham Report. Appropriately, it declared that 'The Force must be far more scrupulous than national armies have sometimes been about its weapons and its methods in using them.'[39]

The proposals of the two Pakenham reports clearly influenced official thinking. In 1963 Lord Home, then Foreign Secretary, speaking in the Lords about an Anglo-American Plan for disarmament linked with an international force, indicated that Pakenham's model was 'largely responsible for the proposals put forward'.[40]

Although the majority of the Wyndham Place Trust's Commission held that nuclear weapons should be available to the peace-keeping force pending future disarmament, a powerful minority disagreed.

Some felt that such weapons were incompatible with a 'policing' role; others held that they were inadmissible in any event.[41] This disagreement, of course, mirrored a much wider and deeper controversy. From the time when the Campaign for Nuclear Disarmament had been launched in the late 1950s, some members of Federal Union had been much attracted by it. Two of its leaders, Bertrand Russell and Canon Collins, had spoken on federalist platforms – although they too had their differences. 'It's all very well for Bertie Russell,' Canon Collins had confided to Monica Wingate, 'if *he* gets arrested he's at once put into the prison's sick bay, and every comfort and delicacy are brought to his bedside, because the one terror of the government is that he might die on their hands. But if I went to prison, I'd get no such favoured class of treatment because no publicity would follow *my* arrest.'[42]

Many Federal Union members were sceptical of CND's simplified, perhaps simplistic message; but others were eager to do more than merely criticise it from the sidelines. John Bowyer was one of these; and with the help of some like-minded colleagues he persuaded Federal Union to produce a leaflet entitled *Law not War*, to be distributed at the Aldermaston March of 1961. It began with an open letter to CND marchers, explaining that Federal Union activists were joining them because they sympathised with their aims, but adding that in the opinion of federalists 'the only effective ultimate solution lies through the building up of the United Nations and its eventual transformation into a World Government [with] . . . a UN Peace Force'.[43] However, these arguments cut no more ice with CND enthusiasts than Federal Union's similar efforts to persuade the United Nations Association to place more emphasis on security through institutions such as a permanent United Nations force.[44]

In 1961, Bertrand Russell asked the rhetorical question 'Has Man a Future?' The one hope for humanity, he proclaimed in his book of that title, was to be found in world government.[45] But the policies he now advocated – unilateral nuclear disarmament, with pacifist overtones and echoes of 1930s appeasement – alarmed many members of Federal Union. Some people – including the novelist Edward Blishen – found Russell's arguments compelling, but he quoted an equally challenging statement by Harold Macmillan, who as Minister of Defence in 1955 had declared:

> Genuine disarmament . . . must be comprehensive, and it must provide a proper system of control . . . The control must provide

> effective international, or, if we like, supranational, authority invested with real power. Hon. Members may say that this is elevating the United Nations, or whatever may be the authority, into something like world government. Be it so, it is none the worse for that. In the long run it is the only way out for mankind.[46]

Like Macmillan, the federalists believed that disarmament required effective control. Many thought that CND would fail – or, if it succeeded, merely lead to a repetition of the Allied weakness of the 1930s.

Not everyone in Federal Union agreed. After some discussion, a paper was written to relate the question of disarmament to Federal Union policy. Completed in 1962, this was delayed and modified, and not published until two years later, by which time CND itself had passed its first heyday. General and complete disarmament, the paper argued, would be feasible only if it was supervised and policed by a world government; as a minimum, such disarmament would take some fifteen years. Like *Law not War*, the paper had little impact, partly owing to lack of backing by Federal Union: it was not even reviewed in the Movement's own publication. However, when CND enjoyed its spectacular revival from 1980 onwards, the Association of World Federalists issued a revised version of the 1964 pamphlet to make the same basic point.[47]

PRACTICAL VERSUS POLITICAL?

Meanwhile, some sought to bypass political obstacles by concentrated action in the economic field. Already in 1947 Boyd Orr had initiated the debate about a 'functional approach' among world federalists at Montreux. It was an idea that had first surfaced in Federal Union four years before: to think 'not in political terms of rights and powers, but in practical terms of jobs to be done and the appropriate authorities for doing them'.[48] But unlike David Mitrany, who had originated the theory of 'functionalism' in order to avoid the political battles involved in establishing a federation,[49] Boyd Orr saw agencies such as the World Bank, the Food and Agriculture Organisation and the World Health Organisation as forerunners of the ministries of a federal world government. Such a government, he said, would be needed if the agencies were to be entirely successful.[50]

During the 1950s, impressed by the success of the European

Community's institutions, British federalists began to wonder whether this example of 'a federation in the making' might have a wider application. Federal Union set up an Economic Commission consisting of David Allen, David Barton, Norman Hart, Jim Hunt and the rapporteur John Pinder. They produced a policy statement on *World Prosperity*,[51] published in 1956 and discussed at a conference whose speakers included Lord Boyd Orr, Lord Birdwood and André Philip. Several came from Third World countries, as did Raghavan Iyer, a former President of the Oxford Union who later edited successive volumes of the works of Mahatma Gandhi, and who at that time was active in Federal Union. Observing that any eventual world federation was 'decades rather than years distant', *World Prosperity* saw economic integration as a step towards it, encouraging the consolidation of international relations and the establishment of pre-federal institutions to supervise aid, training and commodity stabilisation. When possible, the report added, such institutions should include democratic assemblies. The Parliamentary Group's 1959 proposal for *A World Investment Convention*, also drafted by John Pinder, took the same functional line.

Federal Union contributed a report on 'World Order and World Development'[52] to the 1960 Cologne Congress of the World Association of World Federalists, or WAWF, as the World Movement had been renamed in 1956. This was followed by a session on Economic Development at the next Congress, in 1961 in Vienna, where the participants included Earl Attlee and Bruno Kreisky, then Foreign Minister and later Chancellor of Austria. Reflecting on the failure to achieve even so sensible a goal as revision of the UN Charter, Attlee had said that the world must be 'full of madmen'. John Pinder, introducing the working paper on economic development, suggested that a programme of world economic development, to bring the Third World up to current European living standards within fifty years, could help to overcome both North–South and East–West divisions. If the programme was carried out by a pre-federal World Development Authority, it could even pave the way for UN Charter revision, disarmament, and a world police force.[53]

This version of the 'functional approach', however, did not attract much support. Economics was not the WAWF's strong suit, and most of its leaders were not then much impressed by the European Community. World federalists in Britain were more drawn towards another approach, once again involving the idea of a UN police force and an aspect of world citizenship.

During the summer of 1961, a keen student federalist, Peter Watts, acted as Executive Secretary of Federal Union, pending the appointment of Roy Shaw as Director. Watts started work on a project which had been suggested by the world federalists' youth section, and discussed that year at the Vienna Congress. The idea was to draw up a Register of people willing to serve in a permanent, individually recruited World Police Force. A Council was formed, consisting of Field Marshal Sir Claude Auchinleck, Rear-Admiral Sir Anthony Buzzard, the journalist James Cameron, Group-Captain Leonard Cheshire, VC, Captain B. H. Liddell Hart, Lord Longford, Sir James Pitman, MP, Dr Donald Soper, Henry Usborne, MP, Peter Ustinov and Monica Wingate. With the aid of the Hon. Treasurer, Michael Montague – an industrialist who later became Chairman of the English Tourist Board – money was raised and leaflets were prepared. Major-General Dimoline, Secretary of the British branch of the Inter-Parliamentary Union, agreed to chair the Council; it was also joined by the Bishop of Chichester. To sound out public opinion, it commissioned the Gallup Poll to conduct a survey in October 1962. This revealed that 73 per cent of those questioned believed that the United Nations should have a permanent Emergency Unit to deal with such conflicts as Suez and the Congo, and that 29 per cent would be willing to register as volunteers to serve in it. An only slightly smaller 25 per cent declared themselves ready to do so if their allegiance were directly to the United Nations, and not to national contingents in the force.[54]

In the same month, two days after President Kennedy's ultimatum to Khrushchev calling for Soviet missiles to be withdrawn from Cuba, the World Parliament Association convened a conference in Paris. The chief speaker was the Rt Hon. Hugh Gaitskell, Leader of the Opposition in the House of Commons, who had recently won his battle to prevent the Labour Party's espousing unilateral nuclear disarmament (and had yet more recently, to the consternation of the Federal Union's 'Europeans', led the Labour Party Conference into opposition to British entry into the European Community). Now he declared: 'Somehow we have got to get more and more people seriously considering the prospect of World Government, thinking about it as a real possibility, getting more and more accustomed to the idea.' He asked: 'Can we not now set about the task of creating a great and powerful movement for World Government to enlist the maximum volume of support behind it?' He continued: 'A Movement of this kind will only thrive if there are short-term objectives as well';

and he went on to list some that he recommended:

1. the establishment of the nucleus of a permanent international police force;

2. the creation of a World Development Organisation to ensure that this decade really is a decade of development with the necessary supervisory authority over the international economic agencies;

3. the setting up now by the United Nations of a Disarmament Agency not only to supervise the execution of a Disarmament Agreement but to help secure it;

4. reform of the United Nations financial arrangements so that member states are obliged to pay their allotted share of the UN operations whether or not they approve of particular projects;

5. fullest support for the diplomatic activity of the Secretary General and his staff – and firm opposition to anything like the Troika proposals (for splitting the post of Secretary-General into three);

6. reform of the Security Council and the Economic and Social Council so as to make them more representative – particularly of the large number of newer nations which have come into existence recently;

7. a greater effort to make the United Nations universal, including in particular the admission of the Peking Government of China;

8. the acceptance by member states of decisions of the Security Council and recommendations of the Assembly when carried by an overwhelming majority.[55]

It was no coincidence that Patrick Armstrong had helped to draw up these proposals. For world federalists, they made even more tragic Hugh Gaitskell's premature death in the following year.

When Federal Union held a press conference to launch its Volunteers' Register campaign, it was Harold Wilson who now sent a message on behalf of the Labour Party. He declared: 'By volunteering for a police force owing its allegiance to the world to which we all belong, they (young people) can bring appreciably nearer the time when some form of World Government in the peace-keeping sphere can be a reality. I am glad to follow Hugh Gaitskell in pledging the support of the Labour Party to this aim.'

Spirits were further raised in the summer of 1963 when federalist groups in Japan invited the world federalists to hold their Congress in Tokyo. This drew messages of support from both Harold Wilson and Harold Macmillan, and brought Eastern and Western sympathisers together as never before. As one British participant wrote, describing the preparation of the Congress resolutions:

> Six world federalists got together during the Tokyo Congress to produce a draft. Two Japanese, one Indian, one American, one Dutchman, and an Englishman. Beyond the fact that the Japanese were friends and that the two Europeans had worked together . . . for years, none of them had ever met or heard of each other before, although their aim in life was identical . . . From such unlikely origins came the documents which express world federalist thought and spur others to action.[56]

Federal Union's own action campaign for a volunteer peace-keeping force went reasonably well. Some 300000 leaflets were distributed, and many recruits came forward – a proof that there would be no reason to fear a shortage of volunteers if ever a truly international police force were to be established. But no government, and certainly not the British government, was willing to see the United Nations equipped with such a force, although the subsequent history of UN and other 'peace-keeping' efforts, all involving national contingents, was to show how necessary more radical action was.

For the British General Election of 1964, Federal Union issued three questions, suggesting that supporters should put them to their local parliamentary candidates:

> 1. Why has your party not yet come out unambiguously in favour of strengthening UN peace-keeping machinery by, for instance, following Scandinavia's lead in setting up volunteer standby units for UN use?
>
> 2. Do you agree that the British Government should take the

initiative in bringing about a World Government, possibly by starting a similar thing within the Commonwealth?

3. Do you agree that it will be impossible to achieve disarmament without a permanent and individually recruited UN Force as the nucleus of UN supervision and enforcement?

It was not the first time, or the last, that Federal Union used this technique. Then, as so often, the questions remained without satisfactory answers, but they were none the less pertinent for that. Given official indifference, it was perhaps understandable that some people, as Ota Adler remarked, regarded world federalists as 'dreamers, utopians, and a waste of time'.[57]

Were they? Politicians and thinkers of the calibre of Attlee, Beveridge, Boyd Orr, Gaitskell, Hailsham, Macmillan, Sandys, and Bertrand Russell had all publicly espoused or supported world federalist ideas. Leading figures from each of the political parties, including Ministers of Foreign Affairs and of Defence, had advocated institutions to control and enforce any future disarmament which in themselves would have amounted to a federal organisation for world security. The British Association for World Government (now known as the Association of World Federalists), set up in 1965 by world federalist members of Federal Union, had Lord Attlee as its first President, while its Vice-Chairmen included Lord Beswick and Peter Kirk, MP. What was more, Federal Union had done much to establish the world federalist movement; and while Henry Usborne's 'Peoples' Convention' had been a nine-day wonder, his Parliamentary Group for World Government and the ensuing World Parliamentary Association had proved far more enduring and influential.

AGREEING TO DIFFER

Yet, however eminent its sympathisers and however compelling its rationale, the long-term goal of 'world government' seemed to many members of Federal Union less immediate and practical than action on a smaller, more limited front, either in Europe or across the Atlantic. Ultimately, there was perhaps no contradiction. In 1951 an editorial in *Federal News* went further than that: 'Just as European federalists have rightly said that it will be impossible to build a World Federation without first federating Europe, is it not becoming clear that it may not be possible to federate Europe without doing so as part of a far wider scheme of federation?'[58] But although most people in Federal Union saw the federal principle as applicable both in Europe and in the wider world, the time-scales appeared more divergent than the editorialist implied, and the programme of activities in both European and world fields came to be undertaken in practice by different groups, not closely integrated as the *Federal News* editorial had implied they should be. Eventually, although members of Federal Union continued to hold to the idea of working together in a single organisation, they decided in 1956 to set up a Regional Commission and, later, a World Commission, while retaining their links in the monthly meetings of the Executive Committee, the quarterly National Council and the Annual General Meeting.

Those involved in the World Commission included Jim Hunt, who was for a time its Chairman, Pat Armstrong, John Bowyer, Frank Higgins, Roderick MacFarquhar, Lucy Webster, and John Roberts, editor and moving spirit of the *World Federalist*, the bulletin of the Association of World Federalists. The AWF has to this day continued to provide the British contribution to the World Association, for which Roberts was from 1970 to 1972 Chairman of the Executive Committee; and as Vice-Chairman of the Institute of Mundialist studies he has, like other British federalists, been an active supporter of its summer schools in South West France.

Already before the 1950s were out, however, Federal Union's dual structure was causing problems. At the National Council in September 1959 the Secretary had reported that 'the proliferation of sub-committees had left him nothing but administrative matters to report on'. By October of the following year Norman Hart introduced a memorandum to the National Council which proposed the division of Federal Union into a European and a World Section, with separate memberships but united in representation on the Council. The aim was to remove 'confusion in the minds of the public as to our aims' and 'to permit support from people only interested in a single aspect of our policy', and thus to increase the federalists' impact while not losing sight of 'the federalist theory on which we base our work'. When Roy Shaw, who already had much political experience in the Co-operative Party, became Director in 1961, he managed the complex Federal Union structure capably and sensitively. But the die was cast. The hiving-off of the European and world tendencies had become inevitable.

The 1963–4 Annual Report gives every sign of a flourishing movement. Ota Adler was chairman of the Council, Roy Jenkins and John Wakeham were not only officers of Federal Union but also members of the Executive Committee, along with leading members of a dynamic new generation. The President was Lord McNair, a President of the European Court of Human Rights and former President of the International Court of Justice. There had been a splendid 25th anniversary dinner in the Saddlers' Hall in the City of London. A lengthy policy statement expounded a reasonable relationship between European, Atlantic, and world approaches; British membership of the European Communities 'as soon as political circumstances permit'; the development of a European political and defence community leading towards a United States of Europe; the development, in an integrated Europe, of closer links with the United States and with Commonwealth countries; and 'concrete steps towards world federation' including general controlled disarmament, a permanent UN force, a greater role for the International Court, a 'great drive for world economic development', and strengthening the UN as a political force. But despite the coherence of this combined federalist programme, it was the individual parts of Federal Union, and the European part in particular, that were flourishing in action. This was to be the last annual report published by Federal Union as such. From now on the political action was to bifurcate into the European and world organisations established by the two wings of Federal Union.

Not until the 1980s, in fact, did the lines, which for a time had run parallel, once more begin to converge. Then, with Bruce Ritchie as Chairman and, as Secretary, Irene Watson, who originally joined Federal Union in 1939 after hearing Wickham Steed advocate European federation, the AWF began to move towards rapprochement with the European federalists. Meanwhile, the 'Europeans' themselves had been looking at the wider world. The European federalist movement in Italy increasingly saw European Union as a step towards a federal order for the world as a whole;[59] and in Britain, European federalists had never lost sight of the world context for the uniting of Europe. In 1987, at the World Association's Congress in Philadelphia, celebrating the bicentenary of the US Federal Constitution, Christopher Layton presented the conclusions of his report *One Europe: One World*.[60] Its purpose was to show how a federal Europe in the making could contribute to better order in the world. In many respects, this was a return to first principles. It was also the fruit of years of effort by Federal Union in the narrower field of Europe.

6 Groundwork in Europe

The idea of uniting Europe as a first step towards better order in the world had deep roots in Federal Union's short history. In 1939–40, the Federal Union Research Institute (FURI) had seen it as a way to prevent the war, then as a development of the alliance with France but open to accession by post-Nazi Germany, then as a peace aim offering the Germans an equal place in a post-war federal Europe.

WARTIME PROPOSALS

Some of those who contributed to the FURI studies had already been advocating European federation before Federal Union had been formed. One was Ivor Jennings, who had produced a paper 'The Idea of a United States of Europe' for the London Institute of World Affairs in 1938. Returning in October 1939 to the London School of Economics from a spell as Professor of Political Science at the University of British Columbia, he immersed himself in the work of the Federal Union Research Institute, attending almost every meeting of each committee. On the basis of these discussions, he drafted his constitution for a European federation, published in the spring of 1940 in his brief, clear, and cogent short book entitled *A Federation for Western Europe*.[1]

'Most "federalists",' he declared, 'start, like the present writer, from the assumption that "ultimately" complete international government will be necessary.' But 'Europe is the cauldron in which most wars are brewed':

> It is therefore a primary purpose of the Federation proposed in this book to prevent war in Western Europe. A federation which included Germany, France, and the United Kingdom would include the major participants in the three major wars of the past sixty years. It would, however, do far more. It would prevent war elsewhere in Europe ... No nation, not even an imperialist Russia, would dare to go to war if a great Western European power said nay and meant it.[2]

Lionel Robbins (later Lord Robbins) had shown equal energy in working for the Federal Union Research Institute and writing papers for the conferences it held in Sir William Beveridge's Master's Lodgings at University College, Oxford, in the winter of 1939–40. He too had already proposed a United States of Europe before the war. In 1937 he had expounded 'the necessity of replacing the independent sovereign states by larger federal unions';[3] and he ended his *The Economic Causes of War*, only days after the outbreak of World War II, with an eloquent appeal for a post-war European federation:

> We are fighting Germans. If European civilization is not to perish, we must destroy the tyranny which rules over them. No one with any sense of history and art will deny the existence of a real German problem in Europe . . . But for all that, Germans are Europeans. They are part of our civilization; and Europe can never be completely healthy till Germany is healthy too. Somehow or other we must create a framework in which the German *Geist* can give its best, not its worst, to Europe. A draconian peace will do nothing. The Nazis must be extirpated; but we have neither the strength nor the will to keep Germans in subjection for ever. What more appropriate outcome of our present agonies, therefore, what more fitting consecration of the blood which is being shed, than a peace in which this great people, purged of its devils, shall be coerced into free and equal citizenship of the United States of Europe?[4]

The author and journalist H. N. Brailsford also stressed the ideals of fraternity and of European civilisation, in a Federal Union pamphlet late in 1939:

> What shall we have gained if we can realise anything resembling this project of Federation? Firstly and chiefly we shall abolish internecine war in Europe, the homeland of our civilisation . . . In the positive sense we shall achieve vastly more: we shall rescue the priceless values of this civilisation itself . . . If we abandon the old concept of the Sovereign State, it will not be because we have changed our views about a legal theory. It will be because we have reached an ideal of human fraternity that embraces our neighbours, who in other languages think the same civilised thoughts. We can end war only by widening . . . Our Federation will . . . respect the rich variety of a Continent, that has preserved many stocks, many cultures, many tongues, through all the vicissitudes of its history.[5]

'To create such a federation,' Robbins had warned his readers, 'will not be easy.':

> We have a common culture. But we have no common language. We have a common history. But it is riven by fratricidal quarrels. No one who has realized the nature of the interests involved in the perpetuation of the present powers of the independent sovereign states can be blind to the strength of the opposition to any attempts to eliminate their disunity.[6]

It was partly for this reason that Harold Wilson, with what in retrospect seems startling prescience, suggested that 'a federal union should begin as unambitiously as possible in the economic sphere'.[7] Duncan Wilson, then at the Ministry of Economic Warfare and later Ambassador in Moscow, agreed: 'It may be doubted whether European nations have a sufficient sense of solidarity to desire any closer union. Economic motives, however, will probably drive them to it sooner or later.'[8]

In April 1940, a group of the Federal Union Research Institute's economists, who had been working on its plan for a European federation including Britain, France and a democratic post-war Germany, went to Paris to confer with their French counterparts. It was not Federal Union's first attempt at Continental contacts: in the previous year, Derek Rawnsley had visited Switzerland. But, as R. W. G. Mackay pointed out in his *Federal Europe*, published that month, 'The crux of any post-war settlement is security for France'[9] – which needed economic as well as political guarantees. Both sides at the Paris meeting were talented and distinguished. The French delegation included Jacques Rueff, Vice-Governor of the Banque de France, and Henri Bonnet, then Director of the Institut International de Coopération Intellectuelle of the League of Nations and after the War French Ambassador in Washington, plus half a dozen other weighty academics and industrialists.[10] The British delegation was led by Sir William Beveridge, whose *Peace By Federation?* was just about to be printed as the first of the *Federal Tracts*. Among its number were Ransome, Robbins, von Hayek and Barbara Wootton.[11] The journey out, she recalled, 'was rather rough, and I retain an endearing mental picture of Beveridge with a cloth cap drawn well over his forehead plunged into the depths of airsick gloom'.[12]

Within a few weeks, gloom was far more general. France was invaded, occupied, and divided. As the Nazi tide swept westwards, refugees and exiled governments settled in London, which in some respects became more 'European' in wartime than ever before or since. A number of civil servants from Allied governments in exile in London formed The New Europe Circle, mostly from the West but also including Czechs and Poles. It held large public luncheons, at one of which Paul van Zeeland made public the plan for a Benelux union after the war.[13] Federal Union members were in close touch with the New Europe Circle, and Federal Union itself invited a number of such continental Europeans to form a European Committee under the chairmanship of Miss F. L. Josephy. Soon, it numbered eighteen different nationalities, including Germans, and it held private meetings for research and discussion, as well as more public functions. In May 1941, its Anglo-American lunch with Vernon Bartlett, Vera Brittain, and Ritchie Calder attracted 260 people. In July 1941, 150 attended a Franco-British lunch with Maurice Desjeans and Francis Williams, including some twenty to thirty British guests but also Americans, French, Belgians, Norwegians, Yugoslavs, Russians, and Sudeten Germans. In September 1941, the committee staged a meeting in the Aeolian Hall which was so popular that 300 people had to be turned away. On this occasion, there were speakers or representatives from Britain, America, France, Germany, Italy, Belgium, Austria, Hungary, and Poland.[14] Federal Union's European committee also circulated a federalist questionnaire to all the political organisations run by Continental exiles in Britain, and elaborated in a further report, *How Europe should be Governed*, European aspects of the report on *Federation: Peace Aim – War Weapon*. Many of the Continentals who took part in these activities were to help establish federalist movements and to influence their countries' European policies when they returned home after the war.

ALTIERO SPINELLI

During the war, the Committee saw its main task as one of communicating with the European Resistance movements, many of whose leaders were thinking along similar lines. They knew, as Miss Josephy put it, that 'how you thought was much more important than the language you spoke'.[15] On four occasions between March and July of 1944, leaders of Resistance circuits from eight occupied countries (plus, after the first occasion, two members of the German underground movement) met secretly in Geneva, and issued a

Manifesto calling for a federal union among European peoples, whose member states would surrender sovereignty to it in defence, foreign policy and trade, and for a world organisation which would 'permit of development in a federal direction'. Among those in Britain who reacted enthusiastically were Lord Layton and the London-based Socialist Vanguard Group, comprising British and exile socialists who were in touch with Federal Union.[16] When Federal Union's members examined the Manifesto, they were especially pleased to find that it echoed some of the language they had used in documents of their own.[17]

This was no accident. The moving spirits of the Geneva meetings were Altiero Spinelli and Ernesto Rossi, who had drafted the document on which the Manifesto was based. Spinelli had been liberated in 1943 from Ventotene, an island off the coast between Rome and Naples, after sixteen years as a political prisoner under Mussolini's fascist regime. His fellow prisoner Ernesto Rossi was a friend of Luigi Einaudi, the great liberal economist and first President of the post-war Italian Republic. Spinelli described in his memoirs how he and Rossi, in Ventotene, came to receive the writings of the contemporary British federalists:

> Requested by Rossi, who as Professor of Economics was authorised to write to him, Einaudi sent him two or three books on English federalist literature which had flourished towards the end of the thirties as a result of Lord Lothian's influence. Apart from Lionel Robbins's book *The Economic Causes of War*, which I subsequently translated and which was published by Einaudi, I cannot recall the titles or authors of others. But their analysis of the political and economic perversion that nationalism leads to, and their reasoned presentation of the federal alternative, have remained to this day impressed on my memory like a revelation.
>
> Since I was looking for mental clarity and precision, I was not attracted by the foggy and contorted ideological federalism of a Proudhon or a Mazzini, but by the clean, precise thinking of these English federalists, in whose writings I found a pretty good key to understanding the chaos into which Europe was plunging and for devising alternatives.[18]

Einaudi had no doubt obtained these books from liberal economist friends like Lionel Robbins. Spinelli's translation of Robbins's *The Economic Causes of War* was but the first of a stream of British federalist works to be translated into Italian and other languages during the years that followed. They still profoundly influence Italian federalism today.[19] Until his death in 1986, Spinelli himself remained faithful to them throughout his long quest for federation, culminating in the Draft Treaty for European Union, of which he was the architect and which was passed by an overwhelming majority in the European Parliament in February 1984.

During the war Spinelli and Rossi studied the federal unionists' writings intensively. The results emerged in 1941 in the clandestinely published *Ventotene Manifesto*,[20] one of the basic documents of the European Federalist movement,[21] and the intellectual foundation-stone of the Italian federalist movement, the Movimento Federalista Europeo (MFE), launched in August 1943. It was soon after this that Spinelli and Rossi went to Geneva to 'organize a meeting of resistance leaders from as many countries as possible to work out a common programme'. The MFE's policy, derived from the Ventotene Manifesto, was itself the principal source for the document discussed at the Geneva meetings; and the final Declaration, drafted by Spinelli, which was issued by the national committees of the European resistance and liberation movements, 'preserved its basic ideas'.[22] Einaudi, who was then also in Geneva and in close touch with Rossi, provides further evidence of the continuing influence of the Federal Union thinking on these Italians. Writing in his diary on 17 May 1944, after a visit from Rossi when they discussed the meetings of the resistance groups, he declared that 'the best project' was that of Federal Union.[23] So it is hardly surprising that the British Federal Unionists found the Geneva Declaration 'spoke the same language' as Federal Union itself.

EUROPE AND THE WIDER WORLD

The emphasis that some other leading Federal Unionists placed on Europe did not pass unchallenged. Lionel Curtis, in particular, felt impelled on that account to sever his connection with Federal Union. Earlier, the FU Board's guidance for speakers had been careful to avoid offending opponents of regional federation, as witness its instruction, in January 1942, that 'speakers should make it clear that though they might be seeking one form of federation at the moment, any such federation must be built up within a larger framework which should include the whole world, and must be considered only as a first step towards a wider federation'.[24] Despite this caution, Lionel

Curtis believed that *Federal Union News* had 'identified the organization . . . with a scheme for European federation which would, in my view, destroy the British Commonwealth and ensure the control of Europe by Germany'.[25] Rather than risk losing any more disgruntled members, the general meeting in January 1944 simply avoided the issue.[26]

In September 1944, however, the members of the Board who were convinced of the need for a European federation grasped the nettle and decided to propose to the Annual General Meeting that, while 'the long-term aim of Federal Union remains the establishment of a World Federation . . . the immediate aim . . . shall be the promotion of a democratic Federation of Europe as part of the post-war settlement'.[27] There had been a conflict in the Board between this group, led by Joad, Josephy and Mackay, and others who preferred that Federal Union should be an educational movement. The latter included two of Federal Union's founders – Kimber and Ransome – together with Curry and Wootton, and all four resigned from the Board. A majority of two-thirds at the AGM supported the resolution, however; and two months later a campaign based on this policy was launched at a meeting of 1300 people at the Central Hall, Westminster, addressed by Lord Huntingdon and Commander Stephen King-Hall as well as Joad and Josephy.[28]

Thus Europe was again the priority for Federal Union, as it had been in the first half of 1940. Robbins had already given his reasons for this choice:

> Of course, it is quite Utopian to hope for the formation in our time of a federation of world dimensions. There is not sufficient feeling of a common citizenship. There is as yet no sufficiently generalized culture. In present conditions, even the electoral problems of such a body would present insurmountable difficulties . . . But it is not Utopian to hope for the construction of more limited federations . . . In particular it is not Utopian to hope for a structure of this kind in that part of the world now most menaced by the contradictions of its present political organization – among the warring sovereignties of Europe.[29]

R. W. G. Mackay had been still more categorical: 'An examination of the position of some of the Great Powers and of some of our national States in the different Continents will show at once how exceedingly unreal and impracticable is the suggestion of World Union.'[30]

Mackay's words, written in 1940, proved tragically prophetic. As World War II drew towards its close, the position of at least one of the 'Great Powers' – the Soviet Union – became still less propitious. From 1943 onwards, when the 'London' Poles found themselves facing the Communist-backed intransigence of their counterparts in Lublin, the shadow of the future 'Cold War' began to fall across Europe. The fear of what Jennings in 1940 had called 'an imperialist Russia' had always been real. 'Great Britain and France,' he had written then, 'could not allow the Soviet Union to swallow up the nations of Europe one by one, for we should then get rid of Hitler only to be compelled to face Stalin.'[31] As for including the Soviet Union within any future federation, Curry believed that 'her political and economic system differs in too many important respects'. 'It is essential,' he went on, 'that the constitution of the Federal Union should guarantee free speech and publication throughout the whole Union. It should also guarantee elementary civil liberties. So long as the Russian government is not prepared to concede these points it is difficult to see how Russia could be included.'[32] And Mackay pointed out that, as well as ideology, 'Numbers make the inclusion of Russia in any scheme of European Federation impracticable.' With, at that time, a population well over 150 million, the Soviet Union was simply too big not to dominate her neighbours.[33] Lionel Curtis was on one occasion heard to exclaim that world federal government would be impossible if it included 'a slave state like the Soviet Union'.[34]

It took time for full knowledge of the Soviet system under Stalin to filter into British public opinion after the euphoric sense of solidarity against Hitler engendered by World War II. Within Federal Union itself, illusions were slow to disappear; and the argument that a West European federation could antagonise the Soviet Union was for some a crucial objection.[35] The movement hesitated a long time before publishing Miss Josephy's pamphlet, *Europe – The Key to Peace*, even in the wake of the 1944 AGM's decision to give priority to European federation; and at least one member thereupon urged that it be balanced by another devoted to world federation.[36] But despite such doubts among some of the members, European federation remained a prime objective; and after the war Federal Union played a leading role in founding the European Union of Federalists.

THE EUROPEAN UNION OF FEDERALISTS

As the Allied armies liberated Europe, Federal Union learned of a series of federalist developments on the Continent. By January 1944, news of the foundation of the Italian MFE had filtered through.[37] In October, the Geneva Declaration of the Resistance Movements was reproduced in *Federal News*.[38] Then came a report of a Conference on European Federation that had been held in Paris in March 1945 to follow up the Geneva Declaration. The proceedings were opened by Albert Camus, then editor of the resistance newspaper *Combat*, and the second speech, according to Mary Saran, reporting in *Federal News*, came from the 'Italian representative'.[39] There are no prizes for guessing that this was Altiero Spinelli. With Ursula Hirschmann (also a founder-member of the MFE, who became Ursula Spinelli), he had undertaken a difficult and risky journey to take part in preparing the conference.[40] Together with French politicians, editors and resistance leaders, federalists from Italy, Switzerland, Austria, Germany, Spain, and Greece took part, as well as John Hynd, a Labour MP, who with his brother Harry Hynd, MP was to be involved for many years in Federal Union. Spinelli recalls that George Orwell, too, was present.[41] Later in 1947, when the post-war Labour Government was turning its back on European federalist ideas, Orwell wrote 'I cannot imagine [socialism] beginning except through the federation of the Western European States.'[42] At the end of the Paris conference, John Hynd and Spinelli were invited to join the French members of the Central Committee of the Comité International pour la Fédération Européenne (CIFE), whose aim then was to bring the democratic and socialist parties of different European countries together to promote federation.[43]

It was a time of optimism and opportunities, when even governments were prepared to consider fresh ideas. The post-war constitutions of both France and Italy envisaged the limitation of national sovereignty, and the Basic Law of the German Federal Republic looked ahead to a united Europe. But times were hard; and for about a year after the end of the war, progress in establishing the European federalist movement was agonisingly slow. Nor was Federal Union quick to carry out the proposal of its European Committee that it convene an international conference of federalists.[44] But contacts with the budding organisations on the Continent multiplied. Dutch, Belgian and German branches of Federal Union were formed.[45] The Dutch group, Federale Unie, set up in April 1945, was particularly significant. One of its founders was later to recall how, on 11 November 1944, he had started a conversation with a British soldier who took him to his quarters, showed him copies of *Federal News* and of Curry's *The Case for Federal Union*, and inspired him to become an active federalist.[46] Another member of this Dutch group was Hans Nord, who visited London to make contact with Federal Union as soon as possible after the liberation. As President of Federale Unie he played a big part in establishing the European Union of Federalists (EUF) and in determining its aims, which included world as well as European federation.[47]

The two European federalist organisations least scarred by war were Federal Union and the Swiss Europa Union Schweiz. Each of them, unaware of the other's plans, arranged an international federalist conference in the autumn of 1946. The Swiss convened a meeting on 15–22 September at Hertenstein near Lucerne,[48] which concluded with a demonstration on the Rütli plateau, commemorating the first Swiss federal oath there 655 years before. Seventy-eight people attended the conference – 41 Swiss, 13 Dutch and small groups from a dozen other countries, including one British participant, and two Belgian members of Union Fédérale, which 'regarded itself as a branch of the Federal Union'.[49] Alongside the contribution of the Swiss, the policy of the Dutch federalist movement 'formed the basis of the Hertenstein Programme',[50] which was influential in establishing the EUF. It remains to this day the basic statement of aims for the organisation's powerful German section, Europa Union Deutschland.

While Federal Union's influence on the Hertenstein conference was indirect, through Hans Nord and others who were in tune with its thinking, it was the principal organiser of the Luxembourg conference held a month later.[51] While the total number of participants there was similar, the spread was more even, with 19 Dutch, 18 British and 15 French as well as 23 from eleven other countries. From a European federalist viewpoint, however, too much time was taken up with the respective merits of world or European approaches, and whether these needed separate organisations.[52] The Luxembourg conference produced no document with the intellectual force of the Hertenstein Programme. But it agreed that an autonomous European Union of Federalists (EUF) be established, linked with the world-wide Movement for World Federal Government: and a Conseil Européen des Fédéralistes was formed to carry the project forward.[53] This led rapidly to a merger with the 'Aktion Europa-

Union: International Movement for the Unification of Europe and the World', which had been launched at Hertenstein. On 8–9 December 1946, Miss Josephy visited Basle to meet the leaders of Aktion Europa-Union; and it was agreed that she should invite all the individual organisations to a merger meeting in Paris on 15 December.[54] That meeting, chaired by André Voisin of 'La Fédération', decided to found the EUF, and to arrange a larger meeting in Amsterdam in April 1947 and a first congress of the EUF in Switzerland in August. Hendrik Brugmans was elected provisional chairman and Alexandre Marc secretary general, shortly to be joined by Henri Koch as Marc's deputy.[55]

At Amsterdam in April 1947, Federal Union's representatives played a leading part among the eighty delegates from eight countries.[56] Jo Josephy chaired the first day; and Henry Hopkinson, at that time Head of the Conservative Parliamentary Secretariat, later Minister of State for the Colonies and then Lord Colyton, presided and spoke at the banquet; while Evelyn King, MP addressed a public meeting. The other Labour MP, the Reverend Gordon Lang, made an important contribution to the Political Commission. Keith Killby worked out with André Voisin a structure for the EUF, based on federal principles. Ota Adler was elected to a three-man finance committee, and Hopkinson, Josephy and King were appointed to the General Committee which was to prepare the first EUF Congress in Montreux in August. Duncan Sandys came as an observer – a portent of dramatic events in the next three years.

The delegates from different countries, most of whom had never even met each other before, reached a remarkable measure of agreement in a short two days. In a special resolution on Germany, they insisted, as Federal Union had insisted in 1939–40, that post-Nazi Germany should be part of the European federation. When an Italian delegate suggested that Britain might remain outside, 'the British delegation had difficulty in stating their case as so many [of the others] wanted to say that there could never be a true European Federation without Britain'.[57] The future European federation, the resolution declared, was to play its part in the world organisations and, in line with FU thinking, help create a world federation. Despite the plain evidence by then that Eastern Europe had been appropriated for the Soviet bloc, federation was seen as 'essential to overcome bloc politics and thus to avoid a new conflict' which would result from 'the division of the world into spheres of influence'.[58] But the Soviet rejection of US Marshall Aid in June a few weeks later made reality brutally clear, and the other conclusions of the Amsterdam meeting provided a sound base from which to launch the EUF at its first Congress in Montreux towards the end of August 1947.

MONTREUX, AUGUST 1947

Federal Union was again strongly represented at Montreux, where 150 delegates met for three days.[59] Jo Josephy spoke, accompanied by W. B. Curry (who had left the Federal Union Council, but now returned briefly to the fold). Henry Hopkinson chaired the economic commission and made a 'brilliant and constructive' speech.[60] In the finance commission Ota Adler was active, and likewise in the legal commission Niall MacDermot, later Financial Secretary to the Treasury in the Labour government from 1964 to 1967, but then representing the New Europe Group as well as Federal Union. Gordon Lang, MP and Duncan Sandys spoke at a public meeting in the Palais des Sports. All of these except Curry and Sandys, who was again an observer, were elected to the Central Committee.

The opening speech was made by Denis de Rougemont, who in Paris in the 1930s had been one of a brilliant group of authors, including Alexandre Marc, who repudiated 'all forms of state-worship' and advocated 'a federalism built on family, professional and local communities' as the basis for a 'true European and federal new order'.[61] Not long before, de Rougement had 'urged the political union of Europe according to the federalist formula', with the strong support of Karl Jaspers; and Stephen Spender had then joined him in an effort to 'draw up a federal charter'.[62] Now, de Rougement stirred the Congress by showing how federalism could be seen as the antithesis of totalitarianism: as a community of free persons, organised in a variety of groups which together comprise the federation.[63] This theme, stemming from the Proudhonian tradition which was little known among the British, was incorporated in the general resolution of the Congress,[64] along with the concept, central to the Hamiltonian tradition so familiar to British federalists, of entrusting a part of sovereignty to a European federal authority based on representative government and the rule of law. Federal Unionists were also at home with the world framework within which the resolution was set: 'The aim of federalism is a World Government . . . Our motto is and remains: One Europe in One World.' Thanks to Federal Union's initiative in convening the Luxembourg conference of both European and world federalists the previous autumn, the founding Congress of the world federalist movement was held just before the EUF Congress, also in Montreux. Many Federal Unionists attended both. All the leading members of the EUF participated, and more than half of those elected to both the World Movement's Council and its Executive Committee were European federalists. For the time being, the British had succeeded in linking the two wings of the federalist movement. The economic commission of the EUF Congress, under Hopkinson's chairmanship, discussed proposals by Maurice Allais and Daniel Serruys. A former chairman of the Economic Council of the League of Nations and Secretary to the French Delegation led by Clemenceau at the Versailles Peace Conference after World War I, Serruys must have worked closely with Lord Lothian who was then (as Philip Kerr) playing a key role as Lloyd George's Private Secretary.

These proposals foreshadowed much that was later to be done in the European Community: a coal and steel pool, a customs union, a common agricultural policy, an atomic energy pool, and – still to this day awaiting realisation – an economic and monetary union. In view of the growing division between East and West, the general resolution recognised the need to 'start our efforts at unification in the West of Europe'.[65] This more realistic view of Soviet policy was reinforced by the presence, in a strong Italian delegation led by the writer and senator Ignazio Silone, of Altiero Spinelli, who insisted that it was now impossible in practical terms to fight for a federation embracing the whole of Europe.[66] But although the EUF was henceforth, like Federal Union in 1939–40, to focus on the West European group of democracies among which federalism was a more practical proposition, one British reaction to the Montreux Congress was that, whilst strong on federalist principles and theory, it was weak on proposals for political action.[67]

One person present who was not politically inactive, however, was Duncan Sandys. Another was the remarkable Joseph Retinger, a Polish exile who had been General Sikorski's closest adviser as well as a friend of Joseph Conrad, and who, like Sandys, was an observer at the Congress with an urge to do something about European unity. Retinger recalled 'talking with Sandys at Montreux the whole of one night' and deciding together to put all they had got into organising a large-scale Congress of Europe.[68] The nature of that Congress, of Sandys' relations with the federalists, and of Britain's relationship with the Continent for many years to come, was presaged by a clash, on a Swiss radio programme, between de Rougement, who urged political federation, and Sandys, who envisaged more modest intergovernmental co-operation.[69] The federalists had on their side an idea, 100 000 members, youthful enthusiasm and outstanding leaders from the Resistance movements;[70] Sandys had political nous, energy, and Churchill for a father-in-law. For a time, Sandys' assets were to prove the more effective.

CHURCHILL, SANDYS AND THE FEDERALISTS

'An iron curtain has descended across the continent': with characteristically dramatic words, Winston Churchill, in his Fulton speech of 3 March 1946, was the first Western statesman to articulate the uncomfortable fact that the West's Soviet comrade-in-arms had absorbed Eastern Europe into its totalitarian system. The editorialist of *Federal News* was not very pleased with the old warrior: to recognise an East–West split was a 'policy of despair', whereas there was a 'need for faith' in developing the United Nations to become a world federation.[71] *Federal News* had evidently fallen prey to wishful thinking of the type so common in the 1930s, and forgotten Lothian's critique of the League of Nations and Mackay's hard-headed realism about the Soviet Union. Nor, in his eagerness to take Churchill to task for anti-Soviet militarism, did the editorialist notice Churchill's further observation that 'the safety of the world requires a new unity in Europe'. But Churchill himself forced this idea on the world's attention in his speech at Zurich University on 19 September 1946.

After contrasting the miserable state of most of the Continent, still dazed and disrupted in the aftermath of war, with the freedom and well-being prevailing in Switzerland, he said that there was a 'sovereign remedy . . . We must build a kind of United States of Europe.' Then, although France was still weak and demoralised and Germany a pulverised pariah nation, he had the remarkable foresight to suggest that 'France and Germany must take the lead together'. The effect of the speech on Europeans was electric. A united Europe began to seem possible; and many, beyond the already convinced federalists like those who were at that very moment meeting, not far away in Hertenstein, decided to do something about it. Few noticed, in the general excitement, that Churchill's slogan of a 'United States of Europe' was ambiguous and that Britain was not fully part of the plan. This did not escape the attention of Jo Josephy, who immediately wrote to *The Times* to affirm that it would be 'a major calamity' not only for Europe but also for Britain, which would 'find herself precariously perched on the perimeter of a united Europe'.[72] Events have shown that Miss Josephy was right. But it was to be some time before British governments were to learn that lesson – if indeed they yet have.

Meanwhile, Sandys lost no time in organising a committee to promote the united Europe idea. By 16 January 1947, Churchill was chairing the first meeting of a 'provisional British Committee to further the cause of a United Europe', which unanimously approved a short declaration.[73] The twenty-one members of the Committee included four representatives of Federal Union: Jo Josephy, Evelyn King, MP, Gordon Lang, MP, and Commander Stephen King-Hall, the famous broadcaster and founder of the Hansard Society. Lionel Curtis was also a member, already mellower about Europe than he had been when he had broken with FU some three years before. Three years later he became a latter-day returning prodigal grandfather, as an International Patron of the Federal Pact promoted by the EUF.[74]

The Committee's declaration, drafted by Duncan Sandys, responded to Miss Josephy's criticism of Britain's role, if in a rather grudging way: 'Britain has special obligations and spiritual ties which link her with other nations of the British Commonwealth. Nevertheless, Britain is a part of Europe and must be prepared to make her full contribution to European unity.'[75] But on the political structure of the united Europe the declaration was lamentably vague. Citing as examples of nations which 'group themselves in larger units' the Pan-American Union, the British Commonwealth, and the USSR, it went on to declare 'It would be premature to define the precise constitutional relationship between the nations of a unified Europe. Unity can grow only from free consultation and practical experience of concerted action.' It was a calculated slap in the face for the federalists.

Why did FU representatives agree to serve on a committee and vote for a declaration which clearly implied that they were talking rubbish? Miss Josephy assured the National Council of Federal Union towards the end of January that co-operation with the Committee would 'bring it more on federal lines', and she wrote to Brugmans the next day that 'the presence of King and myself on the group has meant that the statement is . . . very much more federal' than it would otherwise have been.[76] Since it could hardly have been less federal as regards Europe's political structure, she must have been referring to other aspects of current federalist policy; and here indeed the FU representatives could claim some success. The statement referred to world government (as an 'ultimate ideal') and eschewed any *a priori* anti-Soviet stance ('United Europe would . . . seek the close friendship and cooperation of the Soviet Union and the United States').

These two points were important in Federal Union's own micro-politics. The Chairman of the Executive Committee, Jack Fidler, was stressing that world government was FU's policy, whereas he thought it debatable whether a United States of Europe would be divisive or make for peace;[77] and many federalists still hoped for a Soviet blessing on European unification.[78] But arguments about the external posture of a future united Europe were academic if the form of the institutions which would determine that posture were neglected. In this respect, British federalists acquiesced in a policy that later caused untold strife between British and Continentals in the European Movement. What was more, adopted by British decision-makers for more than a decade, the policy shunted Britain into a siding where it remained for a quarter of a century.

POST-WAR PROBLEMS FOR FEDERALISTS

British federalists faced real difficulties, given the post-war mood of key civil servants and politicians: 'We'd just won a war. We were still the centre of an Empire . . . We thought of ourselves still as one of the great world powers.'[79] Not only had the nation-state become once again a source of satisfaction to those who were responsible for making British policy; they were also 'highly sceptical about Europe. Europe was a collection of aliens and foreigners . . . who were erratic. They were unreliable. Some of them had let us down. Some of them had fought against us. All of them were seen, in 1948, to be liable to communist intervention . . . not the sort of area that we . . . wanted to tie ourselves down to.'[80] The wartime experience of being saved by America also told against close ties with Europe, with the fear that 'if you moved towards the surrender of sovereignty towards Europe, the Americans would go away'.[81] Yet the federalists were not without resources in their relationship with Sandys. King and Lang, the FU representatives, were the only two Labour MPs on the United Europe committee, since the Labour Party Executive Committee had put it out of bounds to party members, ostensibly because this might 'embarrass' the government's relations with the Soviet Union,[82] in reality because they probably felt that Churchill and Sandys were playing the European card to win party advantage. This Labour representation was therefore of some significance. Lang, indeed, was a joint Honorary Secretary with Sandys. Sandys also needed to build Continental support for his campaign; and the federalists could deliver one of the few multinational European groupings – hence Sandys' presence at the EUF meetings at Amsterdam and Montreux. At the inaugural meeting of Sandys' United Europe Movement in the Royal Albert Hall on 14 May 1947, the federalists brought a 28-strong French delegation, led by André Voisin, together with Henri Barré as the only non-British speaker. Above all the federalists' view that institutions were required was to prove more prescient than Sandys' belief that a 'loose association of states similar to the British Commonwealth'[83] was all that could be achieved. It might surely have been possible to persuade such an astute man, by reference to the potential of federalist feeling already awakened on the Continent, that he was backing the wrong horse – or at least that it was worth while to keep his options open.

Unfortunately, there had been a diaspora of those who had led the British federalists when they rode so high in 1939–40. Lothian was dead. His close friend Lionel Curtis had left FU in protest against its European stance. Beveridge had transferred his affections to world federalism and Robbins to Atlantic Union.[84] Barbara Wootton had resigned, together with Curry, Kimber and Ransome. Rawnsley had been killed during the war. Jennings was Vice-Chancellor of Ceylon's University. Mackay's commitment was undimmed, but he had transferred his field of action to the House of Commons – where he was later to secure the backing of nearly one-third of the Members for the calling of a constituent assembly to launch a European federation. Most of those who could have inspired the British federalists or given them political or intellectual standing were no longer active in Federal Union's own policy-making. Those that remained were no match for so able a politician as Sandys.

Nor were the Continentals who joined the British federalists to form the EUF much more effective at that time. EUF had not been created until nearly two years after the end of the war. Disruption and hunger had made things difficult, and travel remained a problem. Retinger later described how shortage of foreign currencies was a serious obstacle for many who wished to reach The Hague for the

Congress of Europe as late as 1948.[85] Ota Adler recalled, in the absence of scheduled air services, co-piloting a light aircraft with Naomi Allen, a Federal Unionist who had flown Spitfires as an Air Transport Auxiliary during the war, to attend the Luxembourg Conference in October 1946. Their wartime flight map did not show Luxembourg airport and, running short of fuel in their search for it, they landed at Trier, then occupied by highly suspicious French, who nevertheless finally gave them a map reference for the airport and let them go. They arrived for the meeting, but late.[86]

Physical and technical obstacles would, however, surely have been overcome, if federalists had had the will to overcome them. Spinelli had reached Geneva and Paris through regions disrupted by war; Nord had visited London quite soon after the liberation. But the spirit seems not to have been willing until well into 1946, after what a historian called 'a year of resignation in the face of what seemed like a diktat by the two world powers acting in concert'.[87] The US Administration certainly did not at that time dissent from the Soviet view that any autonomous regional organisation should be discouraged. There was no external federator, friendly or otherwise; and some key figures were elsewhere. From the end of 1945 until the middle of 1947, Spinelli undertook, first party political (in the secretariat of the Partito d'Azione), then administrative work;[88] he returned to the federalist movement not long before the EUF's Montreux Congress. In September 1945 Jo Josephy gave up the chairmanship of Federal Union's Executive Committee in favour of a world federalist who was equivocal about Europe: she left on a lecture tour of the British forces in Asia which lasted until May 1946. When the Swiss and the British did convene international meetings in the autumn of 1946, it was some time before their feet touched the ground of practical politics. Finally, the federalists were too slow to recognise that they would have to work for a united Western Europe without the blessing of the Soviet Union. Instead of exploiting the coincidence that Churchill made his Zurich speech during the course of the Hertenstein Conference, its participants defeated by a large majority a proposal to send him a telegram of congratulations – not because of his vagueness about the political structure of the United States of Europe but because the federalists hoped that a European federation would secure Soviet support if it stood neutral between the Soviet Union and the United States. By August 1947 in Montreux this vain hope had been shed, but the federalists had lost further precious months.

Finally, at Montreux, Spinelli was to express the widely held view that everything depended on 'a British initiative' similar to 'the appeal it addressed to France in the chaos of her defeat in 1940'.[89] Until Jean Monnet launched the Schuman Plan in 1950, continental federalists continued to assume that, if not a British lead, at least British participation was essential to any attempt at unification. This enabled the British government to feel confident of imposing its own outdated pattern on the process. The federalists would have been more effective if they had made it plain sooner that there were limits to the extent to which Britain should be able to block progress in a federal direction.

As had been seen at Montreux, the EUF was then stronger on federalist theory than on political action. It was not until its next Congress, in November 1949 in Rome, that the federalists began to concentrate on action relating to current political problems and thus to exert more influence.[90] Meanwhile, as the establishment of the United Europe Movement was followed by Sandys' plan for the Congress of Europe at The Hague, which he and Retinger had discussed through the night at Montreux, the fledgling federalist movement began to fear that the Congress 'could crush us'[91] under the weight of its prestige; and crushed the federalists were – more or less – for the period surrounding the Congress. Just as Sandys had persuaded Federal Union representatives to serve on the United Europe Committee, with a policy hard for them to accept, so he secured the agreement of the EUF representatives to a 'Joint International Committee of the Movements for European Unity', which he established in the autumn of 1947 to prepare for the Hague Congress next May with a majority of 'unionists'[92] who envisaged, as he did, a loose association of European states. The federalists put up a good fight; but the unionist tendency dominated, and its British protagonists were able to believe for another couple of years that they could prevent supranational developments in the direction the federalists desired. If the federalists had organised themselves more rapidly, the future balance of forces might have been reflected more accurately at The Hague, and the British might have been able to avoid the misjudgements that led their European policy so grievously astray.

THE CONGRESS OF EUROPE

The Congress of Europe, held from 7–10 May 1948 in The Hague, took place against a background of rapid change in Europe and the world. In 1947, the United States had come to the rescue of bankrupt Europe with Marshall Aid – a condition of which was that the European recipients should form a joint organisation to administer it. This became the Organisation for European Economic Co-operation, a purely intergovernmental body with no political, still less federal, overtones. American efforts to persuade the Europeans to form a customs union ran into the sand of opposition and indifference. Marshall Aid had been offered to Eastern as well as Western Europe; but after initial signs of interest, notably from Czechoslovakia, the Soviet Union had vetoed such a move. It was but one more in a series of such vetoes which had already paralysed the United Nations. One by one, the countries of Eastern Europe were succumbing to Communist dictatorship and Stalinist empire-building: Czechoslovakia, in 1948, was the last to go. The two halves of Germany, meanwhile, were developing separately: soon, the Soviet Union was to impose its blockade on Berlin, to be answered by the Western airlift and ultimately the formation of NATO, the North Atlantic Treaty Organisation. Europe and the world were dividing; Western Europe was forming a new, more intimate relationship with the United States.

Churchill's immense prestige as President of The Hague Congress, together with Sandys' organising ability, ensured that it would be a great and glittering occasion.[93] The eight hundred people who attended came from every part of the Continent, and included eminent individuals from many spheres of public life, but especially from politics: there were several score of former and future Ministers, Prime Ministers and Foreign Ministers among them, including Paul Reynaud, Konrad Adenauer, Alcide De Gasperi, Paul-Henri Spaak and François Mitterrand. Reynaud, who on the eve of his replacement by Pétain in June 1940 had been so eager to accept Churchill's offer of union with France, led the federalists' call for a directly elected constituent assembly,[94] while Mackay, who headed the Federal Union delegation, was also in the forefront of that battle.[95] The most the federalists could achieve, however, was to ensure that formulations such as 'the pooling and transfer of sovereign rights', and 'union or federation', appeared in the final resolutions.[96] The principal outcome of the Congress stemmed from its proposals to establish the Council of Europe and the European Movement. It was thanks to the efforts of the federalists that the Council of Europe was set up: it was thanks to the efforts of the British government that it was virtually bereft of power. It comprised a Committee of Ministers and a Consultative Assembly: but the latter was composed of national delegations, not directly elected, and at first did not even have the right to draw up its own agenda. The European Movement, meanwhile, had Sandys as Chairman of its International Executive Committee and Retinger as Honorary Secretary General.

If the federalists saw Sandys as a formidable block on the road they wanted Europe to follow, Sandys could point to the prevailing mood in early post-war Britain – the same mood as made life hard for the British federalists. Federalists might with some justice have replied that the British mood would change if people such as he were to devote some of the energy which they were applying to rebuff the federal idea, to trying to persuade their compatriots that there might be something in it. As far as the Labour leadership was concerned, this was becoming an increasingly uphill task.

IN LABOUR

Not all the omens in the Labour Party were unpropitious. In February 1947, seventy-two Labour MPs, including R. H. S. Crossman, Michael Foot, Ian Mikardo and George Wigg, had signed a motion calling for an affirmation of 'Britain's readiness to federate with any other nations willing to do so'.[97] In September, Mackay sent a copy of his book *Federal Europe* to all Labour MPs. Building on their reactions, he formed a Labour backbench Europe Group in December, with himself as Chairman and John Hynd as Vice-Chairman. By April 1948 there were not far short of a hundred Labour signatories for an all-party motion, promoted by Mackay and the Conservative MP, Robert Boothby, which called for a long-term policy to create a European federation, based on common citizenship, representative institutions and human rights, with powers including foreign affairs, defence, currency and trade, and to be designed by a constituent assembly which the West European governments should convoke as soon as possible.[98] At the 1948 Party Conference, Fenner Brockway proposed a resolution seeking 'co-operation with European Socialist Parties . . . to achieve the United

States of Europe . . . in complete military independence from the USA and the USSR'. This third force version of a European federation was accepted by the Conference; but Hugh Dalton, on behalf of the National Executive Committee, expressed a preference 'for the practical British functional approach rather than for any theoretical federalism'.[99]

Dalton's robust reaction reflected well enough the negative view that the Labour government then took of any plans for European integration. In the autumn of 1947 the Foreign Secretary, Ernest Bevin, had been moving towards a more European policy and by February 1948 he strongly supported the idea of a West European customs union, although this was opposed by the main economic Departments.[100] In January he said in the House of Commons 'I believe the time is ripe for a consolidation of Western Europe . . . we are now thinking of Western Europe as a unit', and this was followed in March by the Brussels Treaty for mutual security, signed by the Benelux countries, Britain and France. Paul-Henri Spaak for one, doubtless interpreting the speech over-enthusiastically, was enormously encouraged by Bevin's attitude at that time, only to be bitterly disappointed later at what seemed to him a volte-face, commenting that Bevin was 'already a sick man'.[101]

Those who remembered Bevin's enthusiastic support for the federal idea in 1939 must also have felt disappointed at his apparently intractable post-war opposition, at least to its European version. Christopher Mayhew, who worked closely with Bevin as Parliamentary Under-Secretary to the Foreign Office, recalled 'mentioning the word federation to him once and he bit my head off'.[102] Bevin, no less than many other British people, was affected by the disillusion with Europe and confidence in America engendered by wartime experience. He told Henry Usborne, MP in 1947 that, in order to prevent the Soviet Union from occupying any more of Europe, Britain must remain a sovereign state, backed by the US, because a federal Parliament in Strasbourg, faced by Russian troops, would vote to capitulate. 'Hitler could never take over this island . . . but the Russians might take it over by a vote in a European Federal Parliament without our being able to fire a single shot.'[103] Roger Makins (now Lord Sherfield), who returned in 1947 from the Embassy in Washington to assume responsibility in this field at the Foreign Office, was reported to have strongly influenced Bevin, and certainly not towards British participation in European integration projects. But it is also likely that Churchill's display of European fireworks put Bevin off.[104] He appears to have resented the lack of consultation when Churchill made major pronouncements on European policy; and he doubtless felt, with others responsible for Labour Party policy, that Churchill was playing party politics.[105] Hence the attempt to ban Labour Party members from the United Europe Committee. Hence also an instruction to discourage them from attending The Hague Congress, and a reprimand from the whips for some twenty-seven Labour MPs, including John and Harry Hynd and Gordon Lang as well as Mackay, who defied the ruling and went.

There is no known cure for the caprice and amour-propre of leading politicians. But a stronger federalist presence both in the Labour Party, where the hard core around Mackay was small, and among other influential people and the general public, where Federal Union no longer counted for much, might have countered Churchill's centrifugal effect. As it was, the agitation and pressure that followed from The Hague Congress could elicit no more from Bevin than 'we've got to give them something and I think we'll give them this talking shop in Strasbourg, the Council of Europe'.[106]

THE COUNCIL OF EUROPE AND R. W. G. MACKAY

Sandys and Retinger lobbied to such effect that, within a year of The Hague Congress, a Treaty was signed to establish the Council of Europe, and the first session of its Parliamentary Assembly was convened in Strasbourg in August 1949. But the negotiations leading to the Treaty had cast doubt on the Council of Europe's future. The British government had insisted on concentrating all power in a Committee of Ministers voting by unanimity – against those Continental governments which wanted an Assembly of representatives from the member states' parliaments. Bevin conceded this only on condition that its role be purely consultative.[107] Contention and frustration were the result.

The Assembly's first session seemed promising. Paul-Henri Spaak, up to then Prime Minister and Foreign Minister of Belgium, was unanimously elected President, with Churchill and Paul Reynaud among his sponsors. Edouard Herriot, Harold Macmillan, Guy Mollet and André Philip were also on hand.

So was Mackay; and he at once set about using the Assembly to promote the federal idea. He had done his utmost on that score in the more sceptical House of Commons. The motion by the all-party

European group which he and Robert Boothby led had secured nearly 200 signatures by April 1948 – just before The Hague Congress; it had considerable impact on continental politicians, notably in France, where a similar resolution received 169 signatures in the Assemblée Nationale.[108]

Mackay 'set up office in the Pension Elisa and from there organised the federalist Representatives from all the other member countries'. Jo Josephy was to recall the day when 'he and Senator de Felice, an ardent French federalist, sat down (with me as interpreter) to work out what the aim of the Council of Europe would be. The phrase, "the aim of the Council of Europe is to create a European Political Authority, with limited functions but real powers", was born at that meeting, and Kim [Mackay] spent the years of his membership of the Assembly in trying to get it carried into effect.'[109] Miss Josephy was being modestly forgetful: the phrase 'limited functions but real powers', which was to become the slogan of the federalist campaign in the Consultative Assembly, had already been foreshadowed in July 1943 by Federal Union's European Committee, of which she was the chairman. This had declared: 'The European Council, if it is to be successful, must be a legislature whose decisions have constitutional authority . . . a European government with definite but limited power.'[110]

The phrase once coined, Mackay lost no time in promoting it. On 4 September 1949, less than a month after the Assembly held its inaugural session, it unanimously resolved that the aim of the Council of Europe was 'the establishment of a European authority, endowed with limited functions but with real powers' – a good working description of the federal principle. Paul Reynaud was among its leading champions; Robert Boothby was a strong supporter. More remarkable, perhaps, was the lack of opposition, or even abstention, by either the Labour Party representatives or the leading Conservatives present. The Committee of Ministers, however, rapidly rejected this and most of the Assembly's other resolutions, provoking Reynaud to exclaim: 'on ne pouvait ignorer avec plus d'insolence les voeux de l'Assemblée'.[111] Apart from the European Court and Convention on Human Rights, adopted in 1950, the bulk of the Assembly's output was ignored or vetoed by the Ministers, and above all by the British, whose attitude was quaintly but vividly depicted by Bevin when he was heard to say of the Council of Europe: 'If you open that Pandora's box, you never know what Trojan horse will jump out.'[112]

However, despite such obstruction, Mackay and his friends were able to develop a strong federalist group in the Assembly. Nor was it a stage army of ineffectual idealists. As later events showed, it represented powerful political forces in France, Italy, Federal Germany and Benelux.

Already in March 1948, under pressure from Spinelli, the Movimento Federalista Europeo (MFE) had begun to campaign in Italy for the idea of a European constituent assembly, which Mackay was promoting in the House of Commons and which Reynaud later championed at the Congress in The Hague. In 1949 the MFE called for the Council of Europe's Consultative Assembly to become a constituent assembly with the task of drafting a Federal Pact – a constitution for the United States of Europe. Spinelli sent a memorandum to all its Italian members, seeking their support for this and for a supranational federalist group to be formed within the Assembly. Almost all of them agreed; and they kept their word.[113]

Meanwhile, the broader European Union of Federalists (EUF) had become more politically active since its Rome Congress in November 1948, where the novelist Ignazio Silone had retired as chairman of the Central Committee in favour of Henri Frenay, former leader of the French resistance circuit *Combat* (whose newspaper Camus had edited), and then Minister for War Prisoners in General de Gaulle's first government after the Liberation. In May 1949 the EUF Committee also called for a constituent assembly to be formed, and asked the members of the future Council of Europe Assembly to support the idea of a Federal Pact. Frenay, Spinelli and Usellini, the EUF's Secretary-General, formed close links with members of the Assembly; and the federalists set up a 'Council of the Peoples of Europe' – representatives of European social and political forces – to sit in Strasbourg and monitor what the Assembly did.

By January 1950, the balance of power within the European Movement as a whole had swung far enough in the federalists' direction to ensure that it adopted the principle of a Federal Pact. In France, the federalists obtained the signatures of thousands of mayors to a petition in favour of the Pact; in Germany there were successful local referenda and the project was approved by the Bundestag; in Italy the MFE collected half a million signatures for the Pact, including those of Prime Minister De Gasperi and Foreign Minister Carlo Sforza, as well as securing its approval by the Parliament. E. G. ('Tommy') Thompson, a young British federalist then working for the European Youth Campaign in Paris, helped to organise a demonstration of young Europeans who symbolically (and peacefully) burned the wooden barriers of a frontier post separating France and Germany near Strasbourg. Many cheered; many more silently applauded.[114] To add technical substance to the political campaign, the EUF convened a commission, chaired by Germaine Peyroles, Vice-President both of the EUF and of the French Assemblée Nationale, to draw up a draft treaty as a basis for the Federal Pact. An international conference at Lugano approved it in April 1951.

BRITISH RELUCTANCE

Support for a federal Europe, spearheaded in the Council of Europe's Assembly by Mackay, was most marked in the six countries that were soon to establish the European Coal and Steel Community (ECSC), and later the EEC and Euratom: France, Germany, Italy, Belgium, The Netherlands, and Luxembourg. But Mackay became increasingly isolated among his British colleagues in the Assembly and in his own political base at home. In 1950, the Labour Party's National Executive Committee produced a pamphlet entitled *European Unity*, which attacked the idea of supranational or federal European authorities as alien to 'British democratic socialism'; and the Party engineered Mackay's removal from the Assembly's Political Commission.[115] He battled on until he left the House of Commons in 1951 and returned to business. Even then he continued to write about Europe and the federal idea. A review of his posthumous book, *Towards a United States of Europe*, treated him more kindly than the Labour Party had done. The reviewer wrote in *World Affairs*:

> He can be criticised in detail but he chose the important subjects and he reached the right conclusions. He is probably the only British political figure of his generation of whom this can be said, which seems the best epitaph that a politician and statesman can earn. He earned it largely because he was so conscious of the unfolding of history; and when history has unfolded, it will surely recognise him as one of its prophets.[116]

Kim Mackay made three decisive contributions to British federalism: first, in wartime, when he rescued Federal Union from its financial crisis in 1940; then, when he showed that so many backbenchers in the House of Commons, given a lead, were ready to support the

European federal idea; finally, when he showed how constructive and effective a British parliamentary representative could be in the early days of the Council of Europe.

In the first two sessions of the Council of Europe's Assembly, in 1949 and 1950, Spaak felt that 'the Conservatives had seemed more European-minded than their Labour opponents'.[117] From the standpoint of Sandys and Retinger, who were working hard for the European Movement both inside and outside the Assembly in Strasbourg, the contrast between Tories and Labour looked sharper: 'The Conservative delegates, led by Churchill, played a leading part and their speeches . . . were enthusiastically received by their continental colleagues.'[118] In August 1950, Churchill initiated a resolution in the Assembly which called for the immediate establishment of a united European armed force, under the authority of a European Minister of Defence and subject to European democratic control.[119] The resolution was passed with 89 votes for, 5 against, and 29 abstentions, including those of the Labour Party representatives. Churchill referred in his speech to the European Army 'in which we would all play an honourable and active part'.

In the Assembly's third session, however, when the Conservatives had been returned to office, they played a different tune. Sir David Maxwell Fyfe, now Home Secretary, delivered to the Assembly what Spaak thought 'a disappointing speech'. After calling a federalist approach 'illusory', and explaining that Britain wanted good relations with the European Coal and Steel Community from the outside, he nevertheless said that while he could not promise full participation in the European army project – which was then being negotiated by the six members of the ECSC – there was 'no refusal' on Britain's part. If this was disappointing, it was pure gold compared with what was to come a few hours later that same day. Anthony Eden, now Foreign Secretary, was adamant that Britain would not take part in a European army on any terms. Churchill, when taxed later with his government's failure to live up to the words he had used in opposition, said 'I really meant it for them and not for us'; and he was later heard to say that a European army would be a 'sludgy amalgam'.[120] Whatever role he had originally seen for Britain in Europe, he was not willing to fight, as a very elderly Prime Minister, for any real alternative to the policy of the Labour government which he had criticised in opposition, but which now seemed to suit Eden and the Foreign Office of the time so very well.

Britain's performance bitterly disillusioned Paul-Henri Spaak.

Maxwell Fyfe and Eden had spoken on 28 November 1951. On 10 December, the federalist representatives led by de Felice, Paul Reynaud, and Pierre-Henri Teitgen, and organised by Frenay and Spinelli, proposed in the Assembly the establishment of a federal political authority by the six member countries of the ECSC. They lost the vote by only 41 votes to 47.[121] On the same day, no fewer than four Foreign Ministers – Konrad Adenauer, Alcide De Gasperi, Robert Schuman and Paul van Zeeland – came to address the Assembly and seek support for the European army. The British were bent on staying aloof; and many other delegates either followed them or had doubts about the project if Britain refused to join. Spaak decided to resign from the Assembly's Presidency. From 1942 to 1951, he explained, he had

> persistently advocated Britain's participation in the building of Europe and even urged that she should be Europe's leader. However, after Churchill's return to power I came to realize that we must do without Britain's support if we were to make any headway . . . to rely on Britain, whether Conservative or Labour, means, in the present situation, to give up the very idea of building Europe.[122]

As the Assembly broke up at the end of the session, Lord Layton said to Jo Josephy: 'It's the end.' She replied 'No, it's a beginning.'[123] Both were right. It was the end of a period when Britain was generally seen as a necessary partner, if not leader, in the unity of Europe and could, merely by refusing to participate, prevent more federalist-minded countries from building anything more solid than a loose intergovernmental association. It was the beginning of a period when the Six of the ECSC were prepared to move further towards federalism, without Britain if necessary.

Spaak realised what this meant. So did Sandys, who in 1950 resigned from chairmanship of the Executive Committee of the International European Movement. Spaak became his successor. The tables had been turned. Apart from the small minority of federalists, the British had failed to appreciate how far other Europeans were ready to follow the logic of the federalist argument, rather than be bound by conventional notions of what can and what cannot be done. Looking back, Hendrik Brugmans declared: 'If Duncan Sandys had devoted his tireless energy, personal charm and incomparable sense of tactics to defending the federal standpoint . . . instead of attacking it, then at least as many British as French MPs would have signed the [federal] pact, and we should have had a European federation in 1950.'[124] Brugmans was over-optimistic. Duncan Sandys was not the only British advocate of European 'union' who shrank from more radical measures; and very many of his fellow citizens were opposed or indifferent to any such union at all. The task of turning round the entrenched opinions and assumptions of the Ministers and civil servants who were then responsible for Britain's European policy, or the lack of it, was more than any one man could achieve. It involved a long, slow process of information and education. This was a process in which Federal Union had a significant part to play.

7 New Thinking: The Federal Trust Begins

For a few months in 1939 and 1940, a very distinguished group of British federalists and sympathisers had come together in the Federal Union Research Institute. They had included Sir William Beveridge, Ivor Jennings, Lionel Robbins, and Barbara Wootton; and their work had done much to give federal thinking force and conviction – notably in the design for a post-war federation of Europe. But after the fall of France in 1940, most of them had dispersed to other more pressing tasks. The Institute's intense activity had begun to peter out. True, in the following year a distinguished group of scholars, including Gilbert Murray and Salvador de Madariaga, took part in a study of the educational functions of a federation;[1] and in 1943 a collection of papers written for the Research Institute was published as *Studies in Federal Planning*.[2] By that time, however, the Institute had effectively died a natural death.

After the war, as events in Strasbourg and elsewhere amply showed, the need for something like the Federal Union Research Institute was as great as ever. There was a deep gulf between federalists and British public opinion; there was much ill-informed discussion of matters which needed thought and debate.

To Douglas Sanders, in particular, it had already seemed that Federal Union ought to engage in educational work. Political action and propaganda had their part to play; but deeper and (in the best sense) more academic study, reflection, and research were essential too.

A Quaker banker who had set up a Federal Union branch in Bristol in 1939, Sanders hit upon the notion of forming an educational charitable trust. Discussing this idea one evening with a group of members, he was offered some money by Ota Adler to help prime the pump. In July 1944, he wrote to the Executive Committee of Federal Union to propose various future trustees. Negotiations with the Inland Revenue, to ensure the benefits of charitable status, took several months. Federal Union's Executive Committee agreed to the project, and in 1945 the Federal Trust for Education and Research (originally called the Federal Educational and Research Trust and now usually known as the Federal Trust) was established. Sanders, still over four decades later a member of the Trust's Council, was the first Chairman. The other founding Trustees were Ronald Gillett, another Quaker banker who was subsequently chairman of a City discount house, and Patrick Ransome, as a founder of Federal Union and the secretary of the Research Institute, of which the Federal Trust was to be the successor. Lord Beveridge, who had been Chairman of the Institute, Granville Wingate, and Sir Adrian Boult were soon to join them as Trustees. Debarred from political action by its status as an educational charity, the Trust was also free from political pressures and conflicts. It grew slowly, but worked hard. Its first activities were among young people.[3] In 1949, with a shoestring income from personal covenants, it launched a series of essay competitions, on subjects such as the suitability of federal government either for the nations of the United Kingdom, or for a combination of states in Europe, or in the world. The themes of a poster competition included a Parliament of Man, a United States of Europe and a Law above Nations; the judges included the cartoonists David Low and Feliks Topoloski; and the best posters were displayed in Charing Cross underground station.

Judges for the essay competitions included Lionel Curtis, James Meade (still in 1990 one of the Trust's Patrons), Herbert Agar, Hendrik Brugmans (Rector of the College of Europe in Bruges), Trygve Lie (former Secretary-General of the United Nations), Sir Sarvepalli Rhadakrishnan, who was then Vice-President of India, and the Rt Hon. Kenneth Younger, later Director of Chatham House. The Trust also attracted support from the world of the arts. At the end of its first decade in 1955, at the opening of his play *Romanoff and Juliet*, Peter Ustinov spoke of the need for international federations; and in the same year Sir Adrian Boult advocated the federal idea in the programme of an Albert Hall concert at which he and Vaughan Williams gave their services as conductors and Clifford Curzon did the same as the soloist in Beethoven's Emperor Concerto. Other artists who helped the Trust were Claire Bloom, Dennis Matthews, Donald Swann, Phyllis Sellick and Cyril Smith.

'Building a World Community', the title of a conference in Manchester for older secondary school children, was a typical theme for the Trust's activities in those years. Other conferences, on 'Britain, Europe and the Commonwealth' and on 'Unity in Africa and Unity in Europe', reflected the mounting concern about Britain's self-exclusion from the new Community in Europe that had been launched with the Schuman Plan. Much of the Trust's activity in the following years was concerned with the European Community, although it never forgot wider interests.

One channel for them was the Wyndham Place Trust, set up in 1962 to pursue the federal idea in a religious context. Once again, Douglas Sanders, this time with Monica Wingate, was one of the moving spirits and the first Chairman. Martin Maddan introduced Jim Prior, MP (subsequently a Cabinet Minister) to the Trust, of which he became Treasurer for a time;[4] and the Archbishop of Canterbury, the Chief Rabbi, the Earl of Longford and the Bishop of Masasi were among the Patrons. Its first major project was its commission on the problems of creating an international police force.[5]

EUROPE, FACTS, EDUCATING INDUSTRY

From the early 1950s the Federal Trust had been producing publications on Europe. Jointly with Basil Blackwell of Oxford, it published two books by R. W. G. Mackay, *The Economic Aspects of European Federation* and *Whither Britain?*.[6] From 1952 onwards, the Trust also issued a regular bulletin entitled *Facts*, giving information about a wide range of international organisations, notably the new European institutions. Its editors included Norman Hart, Colin Jones, then at the Economist Intelligence Unit and later with the *Financial Times*, and Stuart Whyte, who was to become a senior official in Western European Union.

John Bowyer had become the Secretary of the Trust in 1954. His energetic initiatives had included the Albert Hall concert, the poster competition, and activities relating to world economic development, including conferences and a review of development plans by John Roberts. In 1957, with the signing of the Rome Treaties, the Trust's European activities began to gather pace. The British were still largely ignorant of the historic steps being taken to establish the European Community, and Bowyer identified the need for business to be better informed. He therefore applied the Federal Trust's growing organisational skills to a series of two-day conferences on the Community and Britain's relationship with it, directed primarily towards company executives.

The conferences began in a modest way, with a score of participants in a hired room and with lectures on 'The New European Market' by the federalists and their friends, who had what at that time was unusual European expertise. Their knowledge was evidently of use; the numbers participating grew, and the Trust became able to draw on a wider range of expert speakers, including people from the EC Commission and the member countries. After the half dozen such conferences in 1958 and again in 1959, they were held at the rate of about one a month during the negotiations on the terms of British accession in 1961–3. The subjects soon covered such specialised fields as agriculture, finance and investment, transport, labour law and tax; the speakers came to include figures like Raymond Barre, Valéry Giscard d'Estaing, Edward Heath, George Brown, and Robert Triffin. The numbers attending rose to over one hundred, sometimes more than two hundred; Douglas Sanders recalls entering one such meeting which was so crowded that he found the Governor of the Bank of England sitting on a stool in the corner.[7] Participants were charged a fee, so that well-attended conferences brought in income for the Trust, and the series as a whole was self-financing. Those who came were quite senior people. Decision-makers in a number of companies became much better informed, and the Trust won a reputation as a sensible and significant organisation.

After General de Gaulle's veto on British entry to the Community in January 1963, the Federal Trust did its best to maintain interest in the Community on the part of companies in a Britain that was now marooned outside. It ran conferences on subjects such as 'Establishment Inside the Common Market', or 'The Common Market Today and Tomorrow' (at which one of the speakers was Fernand Braun, then a young Commission official but later the Director-General in charge of the programme to complete the internal market by the end of 1992). There were orientation courses on France, Germany, and Eastern Europe, and fact-finding missions to Brussels, Frankfurt, Paris and Geneva.

The standard was maintained by a series of able Directors of Conferences in the mid-1960s, including Gerry Reynolds, MP, Roy Hattersley, MP, and Dennis Thompson, all capably assisted by Eileen Usher who was Executive Secretary from 1961 (when she moved to the Trust from the Economist Intelligence Unit) to 1968. By 1966, when the Labour government was preparing the ground for a second application to join the European Community, and public interest in it was reviving, the Trust was again able to organise a dozen conferences in a year. But business was now better informed, and in any case the scope of the Trust had always been wider than business education; so its focus shifted towards the Community's economic, institutional and political development, and those attending its conferences began to include a wider range of policy-makers and other Community-watchers.

'THE FUTURE OF EUROPE'

In July 1965, the academic journal *Journal of Common Market Studies* published a special issue under the title 'The Future of Britain's Relations with Europe'. In it, ten people associated with the Federal Trust – all members of the 'Criterion' or 'Eurodiners' group convened by Roy Pryce – wrote about the prospects for Britain as a member of the European Community.[8] Coming just after General de Gaulle had begun a partial boycott of the Community institutions, the essays and the seminar at which they were publicised, held in the house of Georges Berthoin, the EEC representative in London, caused some stir in the press.[9] Seven of the ten had become Trustees in the preceding years and one, François Duchêne, was to become a Trustee subsequently. Of the seven, David Howell remained until 1980, when he became a Minister in the Conservative government; Dennis Thompson has continued to be active in the Trust although living in Brussels and Geneva; and John Bowyer, Christopher Layton, Richard Mayne, John Pinder and Roy Pryce still remain members of the Council. They, in fact, have formed part of the core of the Trust's leadership for a quarter of a century.

Their writings, here and elsewhere, focused not only on the prospect of British membership, but also on the development of the Community in a federal direction. David Barton, also by then a Trustee and later to be the Trust's Chairman for many years as well as President of a European accountancy association (UEC), had in the late 1950s ranged more widely when he initiated a series of pamphlets on 'Britain in the Second Half of the Twentieth Century': two on the European Community, one on Atlantic Union, one on Britain and the Commonwealth, and one, by Lady Barbara Ward Jackson, later also to be a Trustee, on the general issues the series raised.[10] Roy Pryce had focused on institutional developments in his *The Political Future of the European Community*, published for the Federal Trust in 1963.[11] And all ten contributors to the 1965 symposium in the *Journal of Common Market Studies* combined their specifically British concerns with further thinking about how the Community should develop.

A first step was a weekend conference at Ditchley Park in February 1966, where the Federal Trust group discussed 'The Future of Europe' with a lively and constructive gathering of Europeans and Americans. This was followed by a dozen similar meetings with groups of Europeans, most of them organised with great flair by Diarmid McLaughlin, who became Director of the Trust in 1967. The results were remarkable friendships and understandings between a very wide range of British and Continental politicians, civil servants, academics, and others. These contacts and the thinking they generated certainly helped pave the way for eventual British membership.

Another outcome of this series of weekend meetings was the forging of links that were to lead to the formal establishment of TEPSA (the Trans-European Policy Studies Association), initiated by the Trust with some of those who had taken a leading part in the meetings, including the Belgian Jacques Vandamme, who was to be TEPSA's President, Altiero Spinelli and his Istituto Affari Internazionali, Robert Toulemon who returned to Paris after serving as a Director-General at the Commission, and Katharina Focke, whose institute (now known as the Institut für Europäische Politik) continued to be the German partner after she had become a Minister in the Brandt and Schmidt governments. It would have been anomalous to think about integrating Europe without a network of like-minded bodies to integrate the thinking in the various countries; and the informal network that the Trust created in the 1960s provided the basis for the formal creation of TEPSA in the 1970s.

A NEW PHASE

Christopher Layton had written, in his introduction to the special issue of the *Journal of Common Market Studies* in July 1965, that the 'crucial years' for Britain's chance to enter the Community would be after 1967, and certainly not long after 1970. While waiting for that opportunity, it was important to maintain British interest; and the Federal Trust's weekend meetings endeavoured to do so. The Trust also continued to run conferences for business. Two particularly significant meetings, in February 1966 and May 1967, and both entitled 'Britain and the European Community', counted among the speakers a future British Prime Minister (Heath), a future French President and a former French Prime Minister (Valéry Giscard d'Estaing and René Mayer), and no fewer than six past, present or future Foreign or Finance Ministers (George Brown, Joseph Luns, Reginald Maudling, Jean Rey, Baron Snoy, and Michael Stewart), as well as friends of the Trust such as Lord Gladwyn, Christopher Layton and Pierre Uri.

By 1970 the question of British membership had, as Layton foresaw, become practical again. In May, while the Labour government was preparing its negotiating position, the Trust conferred at Wiston House, Sussex, about 'Key Problems of Enlargement' with friends from Community countries, including Michel Albert, Etienne Hirsch, the former President of the Commission of Euratom who was one of Monnet's right-hand men and also President of the French Mouvement Fédéraliste Européen, and Altiero Spinelli. In October, when Heath's new Conservative government was well into the negotiations, the Trust held another big conference for business on 'Industry and the EC'; and as the negotiations reached a climax, it organised business seminars almost weekly from March to May 1971. The high point of that period was, however, a conference in May at Wiston House, on the economic effects of British membership; it was another example of policy studies timed and carried out so as to maximise their relevance to political action.

What enabled the Trust to contribute in this way to the crucial debates about entry was the breadth of its contacts and friendships in the academic world; it knew where current research on such crucial issues as trade, the EC's budget, and agricultural policy was far enough advanced to be presented to a wider audience. The relationships with official and business economists and economic journalists which the Trust had built up over the years of conferences, seminars, and weekend meetings also helped it to assemble at short notice most of the key people who were advising or writing about the economic aspects of entry. The findings of the Wiston House conference, most of which have stood the test of time, helped to put the economic debate into proportion well before the House of Commons voted on the principle of entry in October 1971. The conference papers, indeed, were published in August as a book edited by John Pinder, who also contributed an introduction synthesising the results. The Trust also published a 50-page summary by Stuart Holland, then a lecturer at Sussex University and not yet drawn into political opposition to the Community.[12]

While the Wiston House conference drew on the substantial stock of goodwill among the economists that the Trust had accumulated in previous years, it also reinforced that goodwill and helped to launch the Trust on the next stage of its development. Its priority now was to study ways in which the Community's policies and institutions might be improved – policy studies, as in the title of TEPSA. Richard Mayne, who was the Trust's Director from 1971 until he became head of the Commission's UK offices when Britain joined the Community in 1973, steered the Trust through this period of transition. But the need to provide information was still very real – especially so long as British membership remained the subject of political dispute. During the referendum in the mid-1970s and when the Labour Party adopted its policy of withdrawal in the early 1980s, the Trust had again to provide expert and unbiased research findings as it had done during the long-drawn-out approach to British entry, from the late 1950s to the early 1970s.

With the Labour Party in opposition when entry was decided, there was an evident danger that Labour would become hostile to the Community, even though those who had been responsible for the previous Labour government's negotiating position affirmed that the final terms of entry corresponded to their own negotiating brief.[13]

Ever since launching its first conferences for business, the Trust had been concerned to inform trade unionists as well. In March 1973, following a number of meetings designed for trade unionists, it held a weekend conference on 'Trade Unions and the European Community'; and during the period 1974–84, when the Labour Party's opposition to the Community rose to its highest point, the Trust arranged over fifty seminars for trade unionists. Organised by Jim Skinner and Penny David, who had been for six years Executive Secretary of the Trust, the seminars were held in co-operation with a diversity of Unions, including the Transport and General, the General and Municipal, the electricians, local government officers, and teachers, and in a diversity of places up and down the country, from Portsmouth to Glasgow, from Newcastle to Norwich, from Derby to Durham, from Cardiff to Carlisle. The participants, often numbering over a hundred, heard experts from Britain and the Commission explain the nuts and bolts of Community policies, and the ensuing discussions showed how much the participants valued the chance to get behind the alarmist headlines and into factual data.

The Trust's main contribution to the continued debate about British membership, however, lay in its economic studies. These were masterminded by Geoffrey Denton, who was the Trust's Director from 1976 to 1983, after a couple of years as Research Director. As Reader in Economics at Reading University and head of

Economics at the College of Europe in Bruges, he had acquired wide knowledge of the economics of the Community, which he applied to good effect in assessing the costs and benefits for Britain.

With three other economists he produced a report on *The Economics of Renegotiation* in time for the referendum on renegotiated terms in 1975.[14] On the vexed question of the Community budget, the Trust held seminars almost every year, the most notable in October 1977 examining the Commission's recently published report of its study group on 'The Role of Public Finance in European Integration'. At this, the speakers included the study group's Chairman, Sir Donald MacDougall, and Michael Emerson, the Commission official who had written much of the report.[15] The Trust was thus well placed to consider the future of the EC budget, on which it produced a book-length report, *The British Problem and the Future of the EEC Budget* in 1982, and one the following year on *The Economy and EEC Membership*, both by Geoffrey Denton.[16] Soon, however, the spectre of British withdrawal was finally laid to rest, and the Trust could focus its studies on themes that would help people to think about the future of the Community in which the British were now firmly anchored and about the wider world of which it is an important part.

8 The Birth of the European Community

The European Community, to which the Federal Trust had devoted – and still devotes – so much close attention, did not arise from a federalist blueprint. The 'rising tide of opinion'[1] to which Federal Union and its sister organisations had contributed had certainly encouraged serious thinking about political institutions for Europe, even as early as 1948. But the Community's true founder was Jean Monnet, and there was no need for his opinions to rise with any tide. He had long been firm in his view that states, if they were to live together in the modern interdependent world, must merge some national sovereignty in common institutions. This conviction lay behind the plan for Anglo-French union that Monnet had put to Churchill in June 1940; and it lay behind the sustained effort that he undertook, after World War II, from his vantage point at the head of the French planning commissariat, to establish the European Community.

Monnet's first approach had been to Britain, in the hope that the idea he had mooted in 1940 could now be applied through joint economic planning, in effect merging the British and French economies. He invited Sir Edwin Plowden, then Chairman of Britain's Economic Planning Board, and two colleagues to spend four days discussing the idea with him in April 1949.[2] Sir Roger Makins's observation that 'Sir Edwin Plowden's solid realism and good sense should be helpful in expounding the United Kingdom view'[3] had a discouragingly sceptical chill to it. Monnet found Plowden 'full of goodwill', but the reactions that followed Plowden's return to London showed that there was no breaking through the mental block which prevented British policy-makers from sharing Monnet's enterprising, imaginative thoughts.[4] So Monnet turned to Germany.

Not only Monnet, but a number of others in Paris saw that keeping Germany permanently down was not a viable policy, and that the alternative was 'to incorporate a revived German economy in a safe European framework'.[5] Such had been the gist of the proposals made by Daniel Serruys at the Montreux Congress of the European Union of Federalists (EUF) in 1948; and such was the rationale of the Declaration which Robert Schuman, the French Foreign Minister, launched, at Monnet's instigation, on 9 May 1950, proposing that France, Germany, and other European countries willing to take part establish a High Authority over the coal and steel industries as 'the first concrete foundation of a European federation which is indispensable to peace'. The word 'federation' was not just decorative rhetoric. During the negotiations among the French, German, Italian, Belgian, Dutch and Luxembourg delegations which Monnet chaired in his uniquely collegial manner, some markedly federal features were incorporated in the treaty: an executive High Authority independent of the member governments; a parliamentary Assembly with power over the Community's budget, its members eventually to be directly elected at a date to be agreed by the member states; and a Court of Justice to have the final word on matters of Community law. The Council of Ministers, representing the member states, was brought in as their link with its High Authority. Apart from an increase in the power of the Council at the expense of the Commission (as the executive later came to be called), the institutions of the Community today are remarkably similar to those which Monnet and his colleagues designed in 1950.

In his inaugural speech as the first President of the High Authority, Monnet underlined the federal character of 'the first European Community which merges a part of the national sovereignties and submits them to the common interest'. He pointed out that the Assembly, the Court and the High Authority were all independent of the member states; that the acts of the High Authority could be challenged before the Court of Justice, not before national tribunals; that the executive obtained its financial resources 'not by contributions from States, but from levies imposed directly on production', and that it was 'responsible, not to the States, but to a European Assembly'.[6] The writings emanating from Federal Union and the Federal Union Research Institute had made very similar points about the nature of federal institutions; and the resemblance was more than coincidental. For Altiero Spinelli, with his commitment to the ideas in Federal Union's literature, helped Monnet in drafting that particular speech;[7] and the Federal Union ideas chimed with the inherent logic in the new Community's embryonic institutions. If societies based on parliamentary democracy and the rule of law were to transfer sovereignty to a supranational authority, that authority should be democratically controlled and subject to a court of appeal. Monnet was no federalist theoretician: but he had a logical mind; and the widespread acceptance of federalist thinking in the six ECSC countries in the early 1950s ensured that, there at least, such logic was widely accepted by both politicians and public.

BRITAIN'S RESPONSE

The British Labour government's hostile reaction to the Schuman Plan is well enough known. Herbert Morrison's comment, on being informed of it as Acting Prime Minister in Attlee's absence owing to illness, may serve as an epitome: 'It's no good. The Durham Miners won't wear it.'[8] Yet to single out the Durham miners as the symbol for Morrison's parochialism was hardly fair; their leader, Sam Watson, was a great internationalist and later became a pillar of the organisations that Federal Union sponsored to promote British membership of the Community. But Morrison gauged accurately the stance that the Cabinet was to adopt.

The possibility that Britain might now have taken a different and more promising course is less well recognised. That politicians were ready to follow a lead towards a federal Europe had been shown by the hundred or so Labour MPs who signed R. W. G. Mackay's uncompromisingly federalist motion in April 1948, joined by a similar number of Conservatives led by Robert Boothby. If two backbenchers could muster such support, the government would surely have had little trouble in securing a majority for what was no more than a small first step in a federal direction – a direction which Attlee accepted as legitimate when he responded to the Mackay–Boothby motion with the assurance that he believed a European federation must eventually be established.[9] Nor, to judge from the adoption by the 1948 Party Conference of Fenner Brockway's resolution in favour of a United States of Europe, would there have been difficulty with the Labour Party as a whole. The Chancellor of the Exchequer, Stafford Cripps, did not appear to think that the Schuman Plan or the prospect of federalism in the longer term were politically off limits for Britain. When Monnet came to see him on 15 May 1950 about the project, Cripps said 'that in his personal opinion the United Kingdom should accept to negotiate at once on the basis proposed by the French, subject to the clarification of certain points', which seems to have been more forthcoming than the Dutch position at the time. Cripps added that 'he realised that the proposal might lead to political federalism but thought that this would not come until later'.[10]

Cripps's openness towards a supranational proposal and federal perspective did not appeal to the civil servants most closely involved. Sir Edwin Plowden, who was present at this conversation, 'impressed on M. Monnet that these were the Chancellor's personal views which he had not discussed with his colleagues'.[11] Makins, then at the Foreign Office, later recalled the advice he gave at the time not to 'join a Federal Europe' – which was his way of describing Monnet's proposals – and went on to suggest that, had he and his civil service colleagues given the contrary advice, 'we would no doubt have been applauded by present-day historians. But in fact, of course, we would have been thrown out, because there was not the faintest chance of the Attlee government accepting the principle of a Federal Europe. Attlee, Bevin, they would not have agreed to it.'[12] The relationship of civil servants with ministers is subtle, and it is hard to know how much Attlee and Bevin were influenced by those who served them. But at least it seems clear that their principal advisers were doing nothing to encourage Attlee and Bevin to consider the federal prospect that Attlee had accepted in principle in response to the Mackay–Boothby motion, or to take up again the train of thought that both of them had earlier found valid, when Attlee had coined the slogan 'Europe must federate or perish', Bevin had helped with the founding of Federal Union, and both had supported the proposal for Anglo-French Union as members of the Cabinet in 1940.

Cripps and his welcome for Monnet; Mackay and his federalist motion in the Commons, accepted by Attlee as a long-term goal; Brockway's 'United States of Europe' resolution at the Party Conference: these indicate at least the possibility that Attlee and Bevin, had they so wished, could have swung the Labour government round to accepting the Schuman Plan. But instead of trying to persuade them in this direction, most of their civil service advisers set out to scotch any idea of British membership. They also tended to denigrate the federal idea and to tar Monnet and the Schuman Plan with this opprobrious brush.[13] It may well be that the persistent unpopularity of the word 'federal' in post-war British politics, in sharp contrast to its widespread acceptance earlier, dates from this official opposition to British participation in the Schuman Plan and in other European initiatives of that period.[14] The taboo on the use of the word by British politicians, except as a term of invective, still limits the capacity of the British to discuss the future of Europe with their Community partners, most of whom see federalism at least as in the spectrum of legitimate approaches.

Churchill, with his Zurich speech and The Hague Congress, had led the Conservative opposition in a more European direction than the Labour government, and had criticised its refusal to take part in the negotiations on the Schuman Plan. But when the Conservatives took office in 1951, Churchill gave Eden as Foreign Secretary his head. Eden was by then an irreconcilable anti-federalist, and the new government soon adopted the practice of giving the ECSC 'the blanket description "federal", irrespective of its actual characteristics',[15] as a justification for continuing the policy of non-participation, which they had attacked when in opposition.

Britain's anti-federalist stance, with its suspicion of Monnet and the Community development, thus became the policy of the two dominant parties – largely, perhaps because of the choices made in 1949–50 by a few key people, reinforced, from 1951 onwards, by Eden's influence as Foreign Secretary and then Prime Minister. A small number of MPs in the two parties, notably Edward Heath and Roy Jenkins, felt this policy to be misguided. The Liberals strongly agreed with them. Their 1948 Assembly, in line with the all-party motion sponsored by Mackay and Boothby in the House of Commons in April of that year, had resolved that 'the long-term policy should be to create a democratic federation in Europe . . . [with] defined powers with respect to external affairs, defence, currency, customs . . . production, trade, power and transport . . . [through] a constituent assembly'. The hand of Jo Josephy, long an active Liberal as well as federalist, can surely be detected here. In 1950, the Liberal Assembly welcomed the Schuman Plan and deplored the government's refusal to join the negotiations. In 1954 it called for British membership of the ECSC and of a European Defence Community; and in 1956, during the negotiations to establish the European Economic Community and Euratom, it advocated British participation in European economic integration.[16] The Federation of British Industries, too, had supported the idea of European economic integration.[17] But with the two big parties and the civil service set in an anti-federalist mould, Liberals and open-minded industrialists cut little ice; and Federal Union became a voice crying in the wilderness. Miss Josephy, as the British speaker at a crowded meeting in the Rathaus in Aachen at the time of the EUF Congress there in 1952, startled the more stolid among the local audience by describing the British federalists as 'die einzigen Engländer die nicht verrückt sind'. Adenauer, who spoke after her, assured her soothingly that not all the British non-federalists were mad: one should have understanding for the British government's policy.[18] But if Miss Josephy's rhetoric, like her hair, had ginger in it, she was fundamentally right. British policy was profoundly regrettable and was later profoundly regretted. And before establishment opinion turned, there were further sorry episodes, including the failure of the European Defence Community, which could have succeeded had Churchill delivered on his promise of British support.

THE EUROPEAN DEFENCE DEBACLE

Winston Churchill's proposal of a European Army, made on 11 August 1950, had followed the outbreak of the Korean war in June. With American forces committed in Korea, the US began to press hard for a substantial German contribution to the defence of Western Europe. This confronted France with a dilemma similar to that which she had faced by proposing the ECSC. Western Europe's main ally, on which its economy and security depended, was making a reasonable demand for a revival of German power; yet German power itself was still seen as a potential threat.

Monnet was among those who saw that the way out of this dilemma could be a European Defence Community (EDC), harnessing German power to European institutions, after the pattern of the ECSC. He had considerable influence with René Pleven, who had worked for him at the Anglo-French Coordinating Committee in London during the war, helping among other things to draft the declaration on Anglo-French union which Churchill transmitted to Reynaud on 16 June 1940. Between late August and October 1950, Monnet persuaded Pleven, who was now French Prime Minister, to endorse the idea of the EDC, and on 24 October Pleven announced to the Assemblée Nationale the French government's proposal for a European Army, under a European Minister of Defence responsible to a Council of Ministers and a European Parliament.[19]

Federalists saw this proposal as opening the way to a European federation. Federal Union welcomed it,[20] as did other member organisations of the European Union of Federalists. Monnet, in his *Memoirs*, put his finger on it: 'the army, its weapons, and basic production, would all have to be placed simultaneously under joint sovereignty'; a joint European army 'touched on the core of national sovereignty' and 'the federation of Europe would have to become an immediate objective'.[21] Yet the representatives of the six Community member governments, in the negotiations that followed Pleven's proposal, proved reluctant to grasp this nettle. It was Spinelli who impressed its importance on De Gasperi,[22] and his efforts resulted in article 38 of the draft treaty, providing for the EDC's assembly, on its establishment, to draft a European Constitution.

The federalists were understandably unhappy about a treaty that would involve commitment to a European army while leaving the arrangements for its democratic control until later.[23] They persuaded the European Movement to form a constitutional committee, with Paul-Henri Spaak as its president and Fernand Dehousse, Vice-Chairman of the European Union of Federalists, as its secretary. This successfully pressed for the task of constitution-drafting to be given to the Common Assembly of the ECSC.[24] The ECSC Council of Ministers, at its inaugural meeting on 10 September 1952, agreed to entrust the Common Assembly (slightly enlarged and called for this purpose the 'Ad Hoc Assembly') with the drafting. Spaak was elected its President and Dehousse a member of its constitutional commission. In March 1953, Spaak duly presented the draft of a quasi-federal European Political Community (EPC) to Georges Bidault, who by then was the French Foreign Minister and currently chairman of the Council of Foreign Ministers of the Six.

During the following year the EDC Treaty, which had been signed by all six governments, was ratified by the Federal Republic of Germany and the Benelux countries, while the Italians were waiting only on the French. With French ratification, the EDC would be assured; and there can be little doubt that, with French concurrence, the EPC would also have been agreed. But Bidault lacked Schuman's commitment; the French political climate was deteriorating; and in August 1954 Pierre Mendès-France, by then Prime Minister and far from favourable to the project, presented it to the Assemblée Nationale, which voted to put it on the shelf, where it has remained ever since. The prospect of a giant step towards federation in Europe receded indefinitely.

Much blame for the failure of the EDC, and hence of the EPC, has been directed at the British. It has been reasonably argued that, even if they could not then bring themselves to accept membership, the degree of commitment to Continental defence that Britain made immediately after the EDC debacle, in Western European Union (WEU), would, if given earlier, have been enough to encourage the French to go ahead.[25] Yet apart from Federal Union and the Liberal Party,[26] there was virtually no British support for EDC membership;

and there was precious little concern to encourage the Continentals to proceed on their own.

Blame has also, again fairly, been directed at French politicians. It has been suggested that, if the project had been presented to the Assemblée Nationale in 1952 or even in 1953, it would have been ratified. Opinion polls were favourable and the political complexion was not unlike that which had enabled the Assembly to approve the project in principle in February 1952.[27] Yet the matter was delayed until too late.

The federalists, too, must take a share of the blame. Many were initially lukewarm towards EDC; and the EUF failed to launch its campaign for a constituent assembly until 1952,[28] despite the fact that Spinelli had been pushing the Italian government in this direction from the start. Even Monnet blamed himself, in private, for having left the EDC largely to others and concentrated on launching the ECSC. By the time that the ECSC institutions were inaugurated in the summer of 1952, he 'was concerned exclusively with laying solid foundations for this first enterprise, which would make possible all the rest'. Although he too 'believed that we must build a federal Europe', he was not prepared to give his attention to the Ad Hoc Assembly or to the promotion of the EDC.[29]

For want of timely enough pressure and strong enough support, the EDC project failed. Monnet reacted to the ensuing crisis in European politics by resigning from the presidency of the ECSC High Authority and establishing his Action Committee for the United States of Europe to press for further steps in building up the Community. Its members were the majority of democratic political parties and trade unions in all the Community countries. For a time, the federalist movement found itself torn between those who supported Monnet's gradualist approach and those, led by Spinelli, who advocated more radical action.

FEDERALIST DIVISIONS

To the British government of the time, the establishment of Western European Union – which provided a loose European framework for German rearmament within NATO after the collapse of EDC – was a triumph of British diplomacy. Federalists saw it as a figleaf for a traditional type of alliance, with German power controlled by American power. It was certainly not the key to a new, more democratic and federal relationship between states which the EDC and EPC had offered. Suddenly, the prospect of long strides towards federation appeared to have been set back by years, if not decades.

Federalists reacted in two distinct fashions. One group, led by Spinelli, with strong support in Italy and a measure of support in France, stressed the need to oppose governments which had shown their inability to act in the interests of their peoples. This group promoted the idea of a constituent assembly – which could be the Assembly of the ECSC if this were directly elected (as the ECSC Treaty had stipulated).[30] Inspired by Spinelli, these federalists launched a Congress of the European People, to organise 'primary elections' in major cities, appointing delegates to press for a European federation through the adoption of a constitution which the Congress would draft. Such elections were held a number of times from 1957 onwards, culminating in nearly half a million votes registered in Rome in 1961.[31] But the project got no further than that, and Spinelli abandoned it, to pursue his remarkable quest for federation by other means. Eventually, in 1979, the direct elections to the European Parliament (as the Assembly of the ECSC had by then become) enabled him to relaunch the idea of a constituent assembly, by promoting the Parliament's own Draft Treaty establishing the European Union.

The other group of federalists, including Europa Union in Germany, La Fédération led by Voisin in France, the Dutch federalist movement and the majority of Federal Union, attached more importance to the ECSC as 'the first concrete foundation of a European federation' and supported moves to build up the European Community through what has been called 'a series of federal pacts of limited scope'.[32] In June 1955, less than a year after the failure of the EDC, the foreign ministers of the six member countries met in Messina to launch the process that ended with the establishment of the European Community and Euratom on 1 January 1958. In January 1956, Federal Union held a meeting in London to hear representatives of the two schools of thought. Hans Nord argued that the federalists should concentrate on persuading the governments to set up the EEC and Euratom. Professor Mouskhely advocated the constituent assembly. The Federal Unionists concluded that the approaches were compatible and should be combined.[33]

In this the Federal Unionists saw eye to eye with a third group in the EUF, led by Henri Frenay, of those who wanted to accommodate both the constituent and the Community approaches. This group made some headway in 1955 and early in 1956. The argument came to a head at the EUF's Sixth Congress in Luxembourg in March 1956. Under the EUF's constitution, the Federal Union delegation, comprising Ota Adler, Jo Josephy, John Pinder and Tommy Thompson, had voting strength proportionate to Britain's population, rather than to the size of Federal Union's membership; and this was enough to tip the scale. The British first agreed to back Frenay in the middle ground. But feelings ran high, and when it came to the point, Miss Josephy could not refrain from following her old friend Spinelli. The other three then switched to the Community approach. Frenay lost. Before long the EUF had split into two: a Mouvement Fédéraliste Européen (MFE) with the Spinellist policy of the Congress of the European People and the constituent assembly; and a Centre d'Action Européenne Fédéraliste (AEF), based mainly on Dutch, French and German groups.[34] At first, Federal Union contributed to both organisations, but put its main effort into the work of the AEF, which focused on the development of the Community and, in the case of Federal Union in particular, on its enlargement to include Britain. It was nearly two decades before the AEF and the MFE were to reunite in a single organisation, called this time the Union of European Federalists (UEF), with Etienne Hirsch as President, and with a rule-book drawn up by a committee chaired by Tommy Thompson.

'Co-operation,' Monnet used to say, 'does not come naturally to people'; and federalists are no exception to this human rule. Seeking unity in Europe and the world, they have often been prey to disputes among themselves. Shortly before the quarrel in the EUF over European tactics, there had been a divergence within Federal Union over strategy. This time, the disagreement was not between European and world federalists, but over the possible emphasis to be given to Atlantic union as a complement to both.

9 Atlantic Union?

One of the reasons that British officials later gave for looking askance at the beginnings of unity in Western Europe was their fear that it might damage transatlantic relations.[1] If genuine, the fear was misplaced. Support for European integration – including Britain – was a relatively constant feature of US policy throughout the post-war period, from before the Marshall Plan, with its project for a European customs union, to the late 1980s. What the British remembered, of course, was American isolationism; and some suspected that if Europe were truly united, the United States might be tempted once more to withdraw. They devoted much effort, therefore, to warding off so ominous a possibility; and if this led men like Sir Roger Makins to exaggerate the prospects for 'an Atlantic Community', and downgrade those of unity in Europe, the mistake was understandable at the time. Others, after all, were then still speaking confidently of a 'special relationship' between Britain and America, although it looked far more hollow in Washington than it was thought to be in London.

Some British federalists, too, looked westwards. Clarence Streit's *Union Now*[2] had had a great impact when it was published in the spring of 1939. Federalists like Lionel Curtis and Lord Lothian, who saw Britain and the United States as the kernel of a future world federation, were immediately receptive to the idea of a federation of the democracies, of which the US, Britain and France were then the most important; and many of Federal Union's first members were first inspired by Streit's vision. When the project for a European federation founded by Britain and France, on which Federal Union had come to concentrate in the first half of 1940, was undercut by the fall of France, divergences arose between those who stuck to the idea of a federation of Western Europe and those who supported the idea of an Anglo-American federation. As a compromise, Charles Kimber in 1941 suggested a democratic federation of Britain, the Commonwealth Dominions, the countries of Europe and the United States, or any combination of them;[3] and this concept of a federation of the democracies emerged again in 1942 in Federal Union's policy statement, *Federation: Peace Aim – War Weapon*.[4]

The divergences were to reappear after the war. Alongside the resurgence of European federalists and the emergence of the world federalist movement, support began to grow in Parliament and elsewhere for closer unity of those Atlantic states that were members of the North Atlantic Treaty signed in 1949. In Federal Union, a National Council resolution was passed in January 1950 welcoming efforts being made by the Atlantic Union Committee (of the United States) to form an Atlantic federation but with the proviso that a European Federation should have priority; and Ota Adler explained this policy to the First Annual Congress of the Atlantic Union Committee, held in Memphis, Tennessee, in 1951.[5]

When Clarence Streit joined two British speakers, Joad and Mackay, in presenting the three approaches – European, Atlantic and world – at a meeting organised by Federal Union in 1951, he spoke of an Atlantic Union to embrace all countries guaranteeing civil liberties, including Australia and New Zealand; and the editor of *Federal News* argued that the three approaches were not only compatible but interdependent.[6] After the European Coal and Steel Community had been established in 1952 with the British government still set on remaining outside, Federal Union's internal politics were complicated by a resurgence of efforts in a more Streitian direction.

The occasion was Keith Killby's leaving the secretaryship of Federal Union to work in his family business. He was succeeded by Douglas Robinson, then in his early twenties, with immense energy, charm and flair for public relations. There was an impetus towards high-profile activities such as the initiation of special supplements in daily newspapers and of statements signed by notables, in the various fields of FU policy.

First attracted to Federal Union by reading Streit at the age of sixteen, Robinson had long been keen on Atlantic co-operation although he later said that: 'Atlantic Union always worried me'. After Britain's failure to take part in the European Coal and Steel Community, talk of 'interdependence' was in the air; and, rather than trying to increase membership for what he saw as idealistic and for the moment distant goals, he preferred to 'influence people who influence others' in a more immediate and practical direction.[7]

Already, earlier in 1952, David Barton had proposed a resolution to the National Council on the comparative economic weakness of Western Europe and the need for any proposed federation to be part of a larger entity including the United States and the Commonwealth.[8] At a later meeting, Douglas Robinson and Ota Adler welcomed the formation of the Friends of Atlantic Union and proposed co-operation with the new body within the limits and principles for which Federal Union stood.[9] Taking this a step further, Barton and Robinson pressed for an unofficial Atlantic–Commonwealth Congress from which would develop a possible Consultative Assembly. This may well have been the original concept for the later Atlantic Congress and for the NATO Parliamentarians Conference, in both of which Robinson was to take an active part. Ted Leather, MP, continued the debate with a pamphlet on *The Commonwealth, Federation and Atlantic Union*.[10] Federal Union kept its options open by publishing this as well as pamphlets on Europe and on UN Charter reform.

SUPPORT WIDENS

Unlike the Council of Europe, what came to be known as the NATO Parliamentarians Conference, later to become the North Atlantic Assembly, was neither the product of a great continental movement for federal unity, nor the result of an intergovernmental agreement. Its origins were far more modest.[11]

The proposal for an Atlantic Assembly was first presented to the House of Commons in July 1953 by Geoffrey de Freitas, MP, a former Under-Secretary for Air in the Attlee Government. He suggested that 'The Council of Europe is dying' (it was then but four years old) and urged that its Assembly and Committee of Ministers be transformed into 'An Atlantic Council, with a Committee of Ministers and a Consultative Assembly'.[12] He labelled Strasbourg 'parochial' and called for the inclusion of American and Canadian representatives in the new Assembly. He also felt that the question of federalism would never arise; the North Americans would never countenance the idea in an Atlantic context. The proposal was also backed by Denis Healey, MP, a relative newcomer to the House of Commons, who declared 'very reluctantly, and against much personal experience at Strasbourg . . . that there is a very strong case for the establishment of some sort of Parliamentary Assembly for the principal countries of NATO'.[13]

But the most powerful early support for the idea came from a group of American Atlantic Unity activists who had established contact with middle and high level State Department officials, Senators, Congressmen and like-minded citizens of the European NATO allies. Livingston Hartley, a later Director of the US federalist Atlantic Union Committee, had published an article in the

November 1951 issue of Clarence Streit's federalist journal *Freedom and Union*, on the possibility of encouraging national legislatures to initiate a movement for an Atlantic Assembly.[14] At an Atlantic Conference in Oxford in September 1953, sponsored by a group called the British Society for International Understanding, Walden Moore, Executive Director of the Atlantic Union Committee, heard Douglas Robinson propose a resolution for 'a conference of individuals and organisations comparable to The Hague Congress as a first step'.[15] Although the resolution was defeated, Hartley and Moore made contact with Federal Union to seek support for an Atlantic Assembly. In fact, Moore had already written in 1952 to the Conservative MP John Tilney, a Vice-President of Federal Union, to suggest 'an exchange of views between our people and our friends in Britain, France and Canada prior to the meeting of Congress in January'.[16] Robinson took up Moore's suggestion and found himself playing a leading role in finding British signatories of a 'Declaration of Atlantic Unity' (DAU), of which David Barton and Martin Maddan, MP became United Kingdom sponsors and of which Walden Moore had previously become the first Director. A tall American with the rather shambling gait of a professor, Moore combined the characteristic persistence of his fellow-countrymen with an encyclopaedic knowledge of the personalities and problems of the Atlantic Alliance and an ability to persuade without giving offence. His 'walligrams', letters copied to international signers and sponsors on the flimsiest of paper, were to become his hallmark. He was the pivot around whom the signers and sponsors of the DAU revolved.

The Declaration secured 270 signatures of influential citizens from all the non-Communist political parties in thirteen NATO countries. They included two Vice-Presidents of Federal Union – Rt Hon. Clement Davies, leader of the Liberal Party, and John Tilney, MP.

Robinson's efforts in obtaining signatories for the Declaration were reported to the National Council. One of the proposals for an advisory Atlantic Assembly was deemed more acceptable to Federal Union critics by his success in incorporating the words 'observers could be invited from associated states of the North Atlantic Treaty countries'[17] – a reference in British eyes to the Commonwealth and a reminder of the Kimber compromise of 1941.

That the activities of Douglas Robinson as Secretary of Federal Union were raising eyebrows, especially left-wing ones, among members of the National Council was shown by reactions to a resolution expressing interest in an International Atlantic Union Movement and asking the Executive Committee to negotiate with other organisations to form an International Committee. Although the resolution was passed, there were four dissentients.[18] To add insult to injury, a dinner was held early in 1954 in the House of Commons at which Sir Hartley Shawcross, a former Labour Attorney General, spoke on 'the concept and development of an Atlantic Community'.

The attitude of Federal Union to the 'Atlantic Unity' idea remained ambivalent; but the seeds of conflicting views were germinating below the surface. The issues came to a head in 1955, after six leading members of Federal Union, including Keith Killby, John Bowyer and Norman Hart, wrote to *Federal News* expressing their 'deep concern' at 'seeking to build links between European and American parliamentarians on a largely military foundation'.[19] There were fears that any move towards an Atlantic Community might intensify the Cold War and be seen in the Third World as a rich white man's club. The more Atlantic-minded members saw at least short-term advantages in the existing current of opinion towards greater interdependence in the Western world, while British entry into the European Community and revision of the UN Charter seemed remote prospects. The compromise worked out in Federal Union's National Council stressed the importance of political and economic unity among the nations of the Commonwealth and North Atlantic area irrespective of race, colour and creed, and recommended an Atlantic–Commonwealth Assembly and more effective aid to less developed countries through international bodies; but it nevertheless allowed the advocates of greater Atlantic unity to press for a possible common market in the North Atlantic Treaty area.[20] Douglas Robinson felt free to proceed with his work on the Declaration of Atlantic Unity. Among other proposals, this was seeking to use Article II of the North Atlantic Treaty to promote at least a North Atlantic free trade area, as well as an Atlantic Assembly to which observers from Commonwealth countries could be invited. Later, it suggested a stronger and better-funded International Development Association.

In December 1955 Douglas Robinson resigned as Secretary of Federal Union to take up an appointment as executive secretary of the embryo NATO Parliamentarians Conference. Martin Maddan, MP and David Barton continued their work in the Atlantic field within the ambit of the September resolution and under the watchful eye of the National Council. Meanwhile the DAU had moved into action to some effect, both to emphasise the importance of Article II of the North Atlantic Treaty and to promote a North Atlantic Assembly. The National Council of Federal Union in March 1957 noted the British Foreign Secretary's recent reference to the need for an Atlantic Assembly representing the peoples of North America and Western Europe but regretted, not surprisingly, that no mention was made for representation from the expanding Commonwealth.[21]

THE DECLARATION OF ATLANTIC UNITY

The aim of the Declaration was to form a network of correspondents which, when appropriate, would react to Atlantic developments by making representations in print and by deputation to the political leaders of the Alliance.

The Declaration was released to the press on 4 October 1954. Its British signatories – thirty-four well-known figures from all walks of life – included the Rt Hon. Clement Davies, Sir Oliver (later Lord) Franks, Jo (later Lord) Grimond, Sir Will Lawther, Barbara Ward (Lady Jackson). Among other signatories from the NATO area were Averell Harriman, Christian Herter, Hubert Humphrey, General Marshall, Adlai Stevenson, Harry Truman, John Diefenbaker, Roy (later Lord) Thomson, Raymond Aron, Michel Debré, Valéry Giscard d'Estaing, Prince Bernhard of the Netherlands, Hans Nord, and Paul van Zeeland.[22] Moore already had a fairly clear picture of Atlanticist activity in Britain through Douglas Robinson, who wrote to him on 31 October 1952: 'Whenever European Federation had been mentioned, or, on occasion Atlantic Union, they (the leaders of the three main parties) have almost without fail mentioned that Britain is the centre of the three inter-linking circles, namely Europe, Britain and the Commonwealth, and the US.'[23]

ARTICLE II OF THE NORTH ATLANTIC TREATY

In September 1956, Theodore Achilles, soon to be United States Ambassador to Peru, wrote an article about the beginnings of the North Atlantic Treaty, in whose drafting he had been closely involved.[24] He maintained that its real father was Ernest Bevin, the British Foreign Secretary, and went on to say that in December 1947, the Council of Foreign Ministers – the so-called 'Big Four' who were trying to draft peace treaties – broke down for the final time. The night after the last unsuccessful meeting, Mr Bevin and General Marshall, then the US Secretary of State, had dinner together. Mr Bevin said that he had reluctantly reached the conclusion that, for the foreseeable future, there was no hope of the Soviet Union's dealing with the West on any normal terms; and that, to safeguard Western Europe and western civilisation, it would be necessary to establish 'some form of union, formal or informal in character, in Western Europe backed by the US and the Dominions'. He continued that what was necessary was 'such a mobilisation of moral and material force as would inspire confidence and energy within and respect elsewhere'. General Marshall agreed with him. At that time he was trying to get the Marshall Plan through Congress. He told Mr Bevin: 'I would like you to apply this same principle of self-help and mutual aid in Western Europe. See what you can do toward establishing a collective defence organisation in Western Europe.' Thus was NATO duly born. The heart of the Treaty was Article V; it contained the obligation for each signatory to undertake to recognise that an attack on any one of them was an attack on all. Article VI defined the area within which an armed attack would bring Article V into effect.

Much neglected was Article II; and it was on this that the DAU focused its attention. The Article stated that

> The parties will contribute towards further development of peaceful and friendly international relations by strengthening their free institutions, by bringing about a better understanding of the principles upon which these institutions were founded and by promoting conditions of stability and well-being. They will seek to eliminate conflict in their international economic policies and will encourage collaboration between any or all of them.

The Article was the only section of the North Atlantic Treaty which dealt with non-military aspects of NATO. In the early 1950s, despite an occasional half-hearted assertion to the contrary, Article II remained virtually ineffective. The North Atlantic Council was so lukewarm about the economic aspects that *The Economist* wrote: 'There is clear danger lest NATO . . . become a technocracy of military men and diplomats remote from public opinion',[25] – clearly endorsing the view expressed by Federal Union in its Atlantic–Commonwealth resolution of September 1955. A technocracy, in fact, was precisely what NATO had become. Articles about it appeared from time to time in the press, but the average citizen, at least in Britain, would have been hard pressed to describe what NATO was. A letter from David Barton to *The Economist* stated quite frankly that most people could not answer the question 'What is NATO?'; and the Chairman of the newly organised British Atlantic Committee was forced to admit in his reply that the necessary public information was indeed lacking.[26] This indifference hardly helped the Atlanticists and was perhaps as great an obstacle to their progress as any opposition in the North Atlantic Council or elsewhere.[27]

As to the North Atlantic Council, David Barton recalled a visit to France as a guest in the country house of General Pierre Billotte, the French sponsor of the Declaration. In May 1940, while commanding a unit of tanks, Billotte had met twenty German panzers head on, destroying twelve and scattering the rest. Later captured, he escaped from a German prison camp to the Soviet Union and eventually led his brigade into Paris, the first of the liberating forces to reach it, an hour and a half before General Leclerc, winning the bet he had made with him three months earlier.[28]

Barton rehearsed with Billotte in the early hours the arguments to be put on behalf of the DAU in favour of implementing Article II. The next day, at the Palais de Chaillot, they met the Committee of Three (the 'Three Wise Men') appointed by the Council to hear various proposals, namely Lester Pearson of Canada, Halvard Lange of Norway and Gaetano Martino of Italy. The memorandum they presented began: 'The measures brought to your attention are practical ones, resting on living realities and would seem able to be accomplished in a reasonable time since the Atlantic governments already have the authority to undertake them from the North Atlantic Treaty.' The memorandum went on to expand on the development of Article II and how best it could be done.[29]

The recommendations of the 'Three Wise Men' were approved on 13 December 1956 by the North Atlantic Ministerial Council, which called them 'A major forward step in the development of NATO in the non-military field.' The sponsors of the DAU were less optimistic; their statement included the words 'We concur in this view *provided the report is implemented by our governments*.'[30]

CONFERENCE OF NATO PARLIAMENTARIANS

Meanwhile, Douglas Robinson had begun without much success to press for the formation of a British NATO Parliamentary Association similar to that which the Canadians were forming under the guidance of Senator Wishart Robertson, Speaker of the Canadian Senate. At the same time, Herbert Hoover Jnr, acting US Secretary of State, indicated that the State Department had given its blessing to a congressional NATO Association, an unofficial Parliamentary Conference in Paris and an Atlantic Assembly.[31] Robinson persisted; but, even with the help of Clement Davies, there was no possibility of a NATO Parliamentary Group in the UK.[32] The Speaker of the House of Commons did however select ten delegates to attend the conference in Paris, including Walter Elliot, MP, a former Cabinet Minister. Invitations had gone out from other NATO countries to attend the proposed conference, including one to Vice-President Richard Nixon, and one to Speaker Sam Rayburn.[33] On 18 July 1955, Walter Elliot was elected to the Conference steering committee; and on the following day some 200 delegates from fourteen NATO countries met at the Palais de Chaillot. Elliot was to play a significant part in the Conference. Apart from discussing its own future, those attending heard in closed session addresses and briefings by Lord Ismay, Secretary General of NATO, and by military leaders of the Alliance. There followed three days of open plenary debate on the current situation in NATO and Western Europe, in which the British delegation played a prominent role. Elliot was appointed Treasurer, Robertson of Canada the President, and Colonel Fens of the Netherlands the Parliamentary Secretary.

The NATO Parliamentarians Conference continued to meet annually, and was eventually transformed into a North Atlantic Assembly, more on the lines originally conceived by the Declaration of Atlantic Unity than as first proposed by Geoffrey de Freitas. Meanwhile the DAU debated how best to follow up the report of the 'Three Wise Men' and made various proposals. It concluded: 'We agree with the Committee of Three that the moves towards Atlantic co-operation and European unity should be parallel and complementary not competitive or conflicting. At the same time, we suggest that the present dangers should make Atlantic Unity the highest priority with all governments.'[34]

Meanwhile, in 1957, preparations began for an Atlantic Congress to be held in London in July 1959. This was to some degree inspired by Douglas Robinson, who was to play a major part in its organisation. It was opened by Her Majesty the Queen in Westminster Hall to a trumpet fanfare specially composed for the occasion by William

Walton; then the 650 participants from the various countries dispersed to various committees to draft resolutions for the final plenary session.

Federal Union's National Council welcomed this development, and presented its view to the committee concerned with economic and technical assistance to the under-developed areas.[35]

THE GENESIS OF OECD

In December 1956, during the run-up for the Atlantic Congress, David Barton wrote to Walden Moore in New York: 'Now that the preparations for an Atlantic Congress are getting into their stride, I am wondering what proposals you have in mind for the signers of the Declaration of Atlantic Unity (DAU) to put forward.' The letter continued 'I have in mind that the Declaration should present fairly radical proposals in two fields, first political and second economic.' He added: 'in the economic field, as you know, there has been much talk and no action. My suggestion is that we should propose an Atlantic Economic Council rather on the lines of the Council for the Organisation of European Economic Co-operation (OEEC) served by top level government officials.'[36]

The fact was that times had changed since OEEC had been founded. It had done its initial job; Western Europe was no longer poor and no longer divided by quota restrictions on trade. The Six had begun tariff-cutting on their way to economic unity; the British proposal of a West European Free Trade Area had failed, and Britain had formed the smaller, seven-member EFTA. Europe, as the saying went, was at sixes and sevens. Britain was championing 'bridge building' between the two in the framework of OEEC: but the Six were suspicious of any move that might weaken their growing unity. If 'economic co-operation' were still needed, as it obviously was, it should surely embrace the whole Atlantic Area, not just Western Europe. Europe, too, should play its part in Western aid to the less developed world. Such was the logic of the Atlantic Economic Council proposal.

The proposal to be submitted to the Atlantic Congress was well received by Walden Moore and his colleagues, as well as by the Canadian sponsor.[37] It was also agreed to press for an Atlantic Development Fund to aid less developed countries. Maddan and Barton then set about producing a draft of the proposals from which emerged a combined UK/US draft to go before the Atlantic Congress covering political, economic and cultural proposals, the latter in the shape of an Atlantic Institute.[38]

The proposals, political as well as economic, were duly debated at the Atlantic Congress. They were opposed by certain British elements as being too radical, by Clarence Streit's followers as not radical enough. They emerged, however, more or less unscathed.

The DAU programme that was finally approved, and adopted with the concurrence of the sponsors in other NATO countries, contained a number of precepts: '2. Promote the creation of an Atlantic Economic Community by transforming OEEC into an Organisation for Atlantic Economic Co-operation (OAEC) in which the US and Canada would be full members. . . . 3. Support the establishment of an International Development Association with more adequate capitalisation than has been proposed.'[39]

In December 1959, while the UK sponsors were writing to Selwyn Lloyd, the Foreign Secretary, proposing an OAEC as well as increasing funding for the International Development Association,[40] the Americans were informally briefing their Secretary of State, Christian Herter, prior to his departure to the North Atlantic Ministerial Council Meeting on 16 December.[41] Both approaches were encouraging.

Events now moved forward at a higher level. Douglas Dillon, the American Under-Secretary of State for Economic Affairs, had visited London, Paris, and Brussels on the 7 December to discuss trade relations; and when the Dillon Committee of thirteen governments met in Paris in January 1960 to discuss the problems of European and world trade, it was perhaps not surprising that it was confronted with the basic differences between the Six and the Seven. To try to resolve them, a Frenchman, an American, an Englishman and a Greek formed the Group of Four and produced an agreed report. The word 'Atlantic' was to be dropped; the new body was to be called the Organisation for Economic Co-operation and Development. Both the neutral Swedes and the Austrians felt that the word 'Atlantic' would associate it too closely with NATO.[42] The American representative on the Group acknowledged the work done by the DAU. Economic policies were to be co-ordinated to obtain rapid economic growth and the need for greater co-ordination of aid to the developing countries was widely accepted. Following what came to be known as the Dillon Round, the agreement of the governments concerned having been obtained, the OECD was officially born on 14 December

1960, with twenty member states. Four other countries – Japan, Finland, Australia and New Zealand – joined later.

While Federal Union was not directly involved in these developments, the Chairman of the National Council, David Barton, welcomed the strengthened economic relationship between the USA and Europe.[43] At about the same time, in January 1960, he submitted a draft paper to the Regional Commission of Federal Union, drawing attention to the lack of opportunities for pressure-group activity now that the UK had become a member of the then 'apparently irrelevant' European Free Trade Area and that altering the structure of the United Nations looked unlikely. He went on to describe the work done by Douglas Robinson and others in collecting signatures for the DAU, the creation of the NATO Parliamentarians Conference and the calling of the Atlantic Congress with the subsequent importance of the Dillon proposals.[44]

This paper, intended to be controversial, was critical of the Regional Commission and of the World Commission for being too restrictive in their outlook. It pointed to the federal element in the Atlantic developments, and suggested that regional federations might well be a prerequisite of a world federal government. Failure to adapt to the changes in world affairs, it maintained, could bring an end to Federal Union in its present form; and there were other organisations ready to fill the gap and make the running in the European, Atlantic and world fields.

WHICH COMMUNITY?

The Atlantic Congress was the highlight of the Atlantic movement. Not only were the wounds opened between the United Kingdom and America by the Suez operation forgotten, but there seemed to be movement towards Churchill's vision of unity among the English-speaking peoples.

But other events were beginning to shape things to come. In 1961, Harold Macmillan offered to join the European Community. Meanwhile the formidable figure of General de Gaulle stood in the way of any closer relationship between France and the United States.

Nevertheless, encouraged by their success at the Atlantic Congress, the supporters of the DAU pressed on. One of their recommendations was to convene eminent citizens from the NATO countries into a kind of Royal Commission, the proposed Atlantic

Convention. This received the support of the NATO Parliamentarians Conference in Paris from 21 to 26 November 1960, significant among other things for the presence of Lyndon Johnson as the leader of the US delegation. As Walden Moore reported later: 'I chatted with him about five minutes during which he gave me the "Johnson Treatment" and made me feel very good indeed. However he did, I think, impress the delegations from other countries and made an excellent speech.'[45] As Representative Wayne Hays, a co-chairman of the US Committee for the Atlantic Congress, declared in a congressional debate:

> I see extensive advantage to be gained from the convention . . . If an unwieldy gathering of 650 leading citizens, meeting for only 5 days, can prove as valuable as the Atlantic Congress proved, a smaller meeting of less than 100 highly qualified citizens meeting for as long as necessary to examine exhaustively the problems of co-operation and unity, can produce much more valuable results.[46]

The Atlantic Convention duly met in Paris on 8 January 1961, and from it emerged what was known as the Declaration of Paris. It called upon the governments 'to draw up plans within two years for the creation of an Atlantic Assembly suitably organised to meet the political, military and economic challenges of this era'. To that end, it recommended the appointment 'within the earliest practicable period' of a Special Government Commission on Atlantic Unity, to 'propose such reforms and simplifications of existing institutions, and such new institutions as may be required'.[47]

Meanwhile, the DAU in a second Declaration of Atlantic Unity followed the resolutions passed at the Atlantic Congress with a call to governments to initiate certain radical proposals, political, economic and cultural, including an Atlantic High Council with weighted majority voting and an Atlantic High Court of Justice – in other words, an embryo Community not dissimilar to the European Community which Britain was now seeking to join. Adopted by the sponsors in April 1962, the Declaration was endorsed by the NATO Parliamentarians Conference on 12 November and presented to the North Atlantic Council on 15 November.[48]

The difference between the European and the Atlantic viewpoints in Federal Union could no longer be ignored. While David Barton was reporting to Walden Moore on the British move towards a European future and explaining the word 'Community' in a European context, the latter was in correspondence with Jean Monnet in

Paris. In 1960 Monnet had expressed interest in and support for the DAU and, indeed, had seen a similarity between the Declaration and his own Action Committee for the United States of Europe. But he had declined to sign its programme for that year, no doubt on the grounds that his prior commitment was to Europe. In a later exchange of correspondence in 1963, Monnet, while favouring the Atlantic concept, clearly meant Atlantic partnership rather than a more full-blooded Community such as the American sponsors of the DAU were seeking.[49] In an article in *The Observer*, Nora Beloff referred to the partnership concept as 'Operation Dumb-bell'. The entry of Britain into the EC would help to make it an equal partner with the US.[50] David Barton, however, in an article in *World Affairs*, had tried to give a more precise meaning to the expression 'Atlantic Community': he preferred it to 'Atlantic Partnership' on the grounds that the latter lacked supranational overtones. Essentially, he saw it 'as linking militarily, politically and economically large trading blocks or regional groupings' which would serve as an example for other regions and could ultimately lead to a World Community.[51] Most of Federal Union's 'Europeans' shared Monnet's view of the relationship, while accepting that a federal Europe should seek the type of relationship that Barton envisaged with the US and with such other regions as might be ready for it.

But by 1964 the DAU was in decline. Barton recalled a proposal in that year for setting up an Atlantic Council in the UK similar to the powerful US body, with an Executive Committee including a number of Federal Union Council members; he also attended a dinner in Paris later in the year where fellow-guests included General Billotte, Geoffrey de Freitas, Ambassador Dowling (Director-General of the Atlantic Institute), Walden Moore and Paul van Zeeland. In the following year Professor George Catlin put forward the idea of an Atlantic Community Association under the Presidency of Lord Attlee.[52] Nothing came from any of these initiatives.

At a meeting in New York on 15 July 1964, the veteran Clarence Streit repeated a speech that Lionel Curtis had made at a meeting of Federal Union in London on 1 July 1939.[53] It was a powerful plea, an attack on nationalism which ended with the famous lines of Arthur Hugh Clough:

> And not by eastern windows only,
> When daylight comes, comes in the light,
> In front the sun climbs slow, how slowly,
> *But westward look, the land is bright!*

Churchill had quoted these same words to Roosevelt during the dark days of the World War II. But times had changed. The supporters of an 'Atlantic Community' had shot their bolt. Little could be done against de Gaulle's nationalist opposition; and after his departure, it was Jean Monnet's idea of building up the European Community as a partner of the United States that made the running. The Atlanticists broadened their concept to include Japan as well as North America, Western Europe and Australasia. Federal Union Inc., founded in Washington by Clarence Streit soon after the birth of Federal Union in London, was in the 1980s renamed the Association to Unite the Democracies; and its new Director, Ira Straus, cultivated links with the European federalists to promote the idea of a union of democracies. European federalists, for their part, began to consider how a federal Europe might help to build a wider union of democracies, as a step on the long road to world federation.[54] But meanwhile, in the mid-1960s, the outlook for the Atlanticists had darkened. For Britain's patient pro-Europeans, however, the sun was just beginning to rise.

10 Europe Relaunched

Less than a year after the French Assemblée Nationale abandoned the European Defence Community, the six member governments of the ECSC agreed to start the negotiations which produced the European Economic Community and Euratom. The Messina declaration, which announced this decision to 'relaunch Europe' at a foreign ministers' meeting on 1–2 June 1955, contained an invitation to Britain to participate. But the British government merely sent a civil servant to the discussions with an ambiguous brief and, after a few weeks, withdrew him again.

Russell Bretherton, the civil servant in question, later summed up the reason for this nonchalant behaviour: the Foreigh Office thought 'that nothing would happen'.[1] Lord Butler, who was then Chancellor of the Exchequer, admitted that this showed 'a definite lack of foresight on the part of myself, and a much bigger lack of foresight on the part of the Treasury and a very big lack of foresight on the part of the Foreign Office'.[2] The collapse of EDC had clearly given the British some grounds to doubt the ability of the Six to carry forward the Community idea. But Miriam Camps, one of the shrewdest observers of Europe during this period, identified an underlying reason for this crippling failure to judge the potential of the Community:

> There had never been much real understanding in the United Kingdom of the depth of the drive towards real unity, as distinct from inter-governmental cooperation, on the Continent. Except for a handful of people, no-one really accepted or believed in the feasibility or in the desirability of the 'Monnet approach' to a United Europe.[3]

A NEW GENERATION

A fair number of this handful of people were to be found in Federal Union. This generation of federalists had absorbed the thinking of the earlier federal unionists and possessed the skills required to adapt it to current political circumstances. Most of them later became prominent in their various walks of life, but at the same time they remained a coherent group. The Chairmen of the National Council included David Barton and Norman Hart, of the Executive Committee John Pinder and Donald (now Lord Justice) Farquharson. Ota Adler chaired the Regional Commission, where the most active members included these officers as well as E. G. (Tommy) Thompson, John Leech, Roy Pryce, and Dennis Thompson, later to be a legal Director in the EC Commission. Harry Cowie edited *World Affairs*. Pat Armstrong chaired the World Commission, whose activists included John Bowyer, John Roberts and Lucy Webster. Soon after Douglas Robinson left, the Hon. Findlay Rea was appointed as Federal Union's Secretary. From a distinguished Liberal family, he had been a Labour Councillor in Chelsea. He combined an ebullient commitment to the federalist cause with a sharp and sometimes stinging wit, and a tendency to rid the office of many documents which would have facilitated the writing of books such as this.

Other members of the staff of Federal Union and related organisations included Robert Jarrett, Jim Hunt, Tony Morris, and Val Schur. Later entrants or occasional participants included Derek (later Lord) Ezra, Maurice Foley (later Minister of State at the Foreign Office, then a Deputy Director General in the EC Commission), Colin Jones (later of the *Financial Times*), Niall MacDermot (later Financial Secretary to the Treasury), John Wakeham (later Conservative Chief Whip, Leader of the House and a Cabinet Minister), Sir Anthony Meyer (later a Conservative MP), David Webster (later a senior executive in the BBC), Lucy Webster (later a pillar of the World Association of World Federalists) and Shirley Williams (later a Labour Cabinet Minister, then President of the Social Democratic Party). R. W. G. Mackay was a corresponding member and François Duchêne, Richard Mayne and Noël Salter gave sympathetic help from key positions on the Continent.

Most of this group were by then in their thirties and, in the late 1950s and early 1960s, they led Federal Union's new surge of activity. They were well described by another occasional participant, Uwe Kitzinger, after their efforts had been crowned with the success of British entry in 1973:

> Some of them served in the war, some had been conscientious objectors, some had been too young to be either and perhaps for that reason felt all the more keenly a personal responsibility to contribute to making any recurrence of war in the future impossi-

> ble. It was this generation that had been catapulted into political adulthood by Hiroshima . . . and who felt a corresponding commitment to peace aims and the construction of a new system of international order. Many of them were federalists in the late 1940s, and some of these regarded European federalism as a first step, both pilot project and pace-maker, for a new world system.
>
> They came from a wide variety of backgrounds: one the son of a peer, another who left school at fourteen, one the son of a small tailor, another the son of a bank clerk, several with family origins on the Continent, some candidates or local councillors of the Labour, some of the Liberal and some of the Conservative Party, some full-time trade unionists, some lawyers, some in public relations, one who worked for the British Council of Churches, another for *The Economist*, several at universities or various research institutions. . . .

But, Kitzinger insisted, one should not make out a conspiratorial theory of history about them, nor should one overrate their achievements, for

> their influence . . . would have remained minor had not national fortunes and demands, and therefore national policies, evolved in directions they had more or less anticipated and advocated. Nor was there ever any clear leadership. What mattered was that most of them, while pursuing their own chosen careers in different fields in which they could remain useful to the cause, had remained in close touch with several others of the larger inter-connected 'mafia', that their political thinking had remained along broadly parallel lines, and that underlying often sharp tactical disagreements there were common reflexes as to aims and strategy – very much indeed as had been the case with the older 'Establishment generation' against whose national patriotism and mismanagement of international affairs they were . . . in clear revolt.[4]

Ota Adler was to recall that what in 1956 would have seemed to most of their compatriots quixotic devotion to an idealistic cause was in the event to turn to advantage in the federalists' careers. 'We had a core of serious-minded practical men and many British civil servants – as former members of Federal Union – owe their present position to their membership, since they had the foresight to predict and aid the shift of British policy in relation to Europe.'[5]

The turn in the federalists' fortunes was certainly associated with a change in British perceptions about Britain's place in the world. The British had emerged from the war with the illusion that their country was one of the world's Big Three powers, in a different league from the neighbours in Western Europe. The need for a profound reappraisal of the role of the nation-state, which had been perceived by the federal unionists of 1939–40 and had, following the failures of the 1930s, convinced so many of their countrymen, had been eclipsed by Britain's wartime success. It took the first post-war decade for the reality to sink in.

AFTER MESSINA: EUROPE AND BRITAIN

Two days after the Messina conference in June 1955, the Annual General Meeting of Federal Union urged full British participation in the Common Market, as a step to a European federation. Not long afterwards, *Federal News* welcomed the establishment of Jean Monnet's Action Committee for the United States of Europe, and Federal Union organised a special conference to discuss the next moves in the campaign for European unity.[6] One was to establish a group containing the hard core of its supporters of the Monnet approach of Community-building. This held its first meeting in March 1956, only a week after the Congress of the European Union of Federalists which confirmed the split between the partisans of that approach and the more radical Spinellists.[7]

The name given to this group, the Regional Commission, reflected the divergence between regional and world federalists within Federal Union. It included some champions of Atlantic as well as of European federation; and some members of the Regional Commission were active in promoting the Atlantic Congress which was held in London in 1959. But the group as a whole worked mainly for Britain's participation in the building of a Community Europe; and it had a significant influence on the events which finally led to British membership of the EC in 1973.

Although Jo Josephy, still a member of Federal Union's Council, continued to support Spinelli's line, at that time one of disillusionment with the Community, there was never any doubt in the Regional Commission about the validity of the Community approach. Members of the Commission helped to draft a policy statement which saw the EC as a step towards a United States of Europe, in which an elected parliament and a federal government would incorporate economic powers such as those being vested in the European Community, and security powers which could be developed through Western European Union. It was in this general framework of ideas that Federal Union urged full British participation in the Community.[8]

The Regional Commission lost no time in planning how to change British opinion and policy. Industrial support was identified as vital; concern about the Commonwealth seemed the main hindrance. Studies, conferences and publications on these two themes now began to loom large in Federal Union's work. It initiated a series of pamphlets of which the first, by Sir Cecil Weir, was on the ECSC, to which he had been Britain's first diplomatic representative.[9] It launched a survey of the attitudes of members of Commonwealth parliaments;[10] a conference of economists; and a major research project on the effects of removing trade barriers within Europe. But first, it seemed important to demonstrate public support for Britain to join the Six in establishing the European Economic Community.

Federal Union accordingly drafted a statement calling for British participation, and persuaded some fifty prominent industrialists, trade unionists and economists to sign it. When it was published on 9 October 1956, its signatories included Sir Oliver (later Lord) Franks, Lord Layton, Professor James Meade, Lord Salter, S. G. Warburg, and Sam (later Lord) Watson. Martin Maddan, MP, then Deputy chairman of Federal Union's Council, helped initiate a similar Conservative resolution in the House of Commons, signed by eighty-nine Conservatives including Sir Keith Joseph and Geoffrey Rippon; and John Hynd played a similar role on the Labour side, where the eighty-two signatories included Richard Crossman and Roy Jenkins.[11]

Almost simultaneously, it began to become clear that the government, no longer able to ignore the progress of the Six towards establishing the Common Market,[12] had decided to change its policy towards Europe. Its aim at this stage was not to join the nascent Community, but to try to establish a European free trade area around it.[13] When the details were published, the government's proposal turned out to be narrowly focused on industrial free trade. It made virtually no concession to the concern of the Six for agriculture, for a common trade policy, for economic and social harmonisation or for Community-type institutions.[14]

In Britain, the Free Trade Area plan looked like a cautious step towards European involvement; but across the Channel it had a mixed reception. Some welcomed it as a move towards freer trade. But partisans of European unity feared that it might dissolve the Community, as the saying went, 'like a lump of sugar in a British cup of tea'.

Despite these fears, Federal Union's Regional Commission decided that, if the Community was a step towards federation, the free trade area could be seen as a step towards British membership of the Community. It would be worthwhile to persuade the public in general, and industry in particular, of the general benefits of European free trade, trusting that the movement of opinion, once started, would lead on to support for the Community, itself the best basis for a later campaign for federation. Too explicitly radical a stance, moreover, might, it was thought, jeopardise the recent shift towards Europe.[15] However, Federal Union's Executive Committee feared that so much discretion would endanger the federalists' identity and it decided that some openly federalist activities should be undertaken alongside the work of the Regional Commission.[16] The federalist line was explicit enough in the policy statement that soon followed.[17] But the Regional Commission continued to concentrate on the immediate objectives and, although all the hard core and most of the other members were federalists, they kept fairly quiet for the time being about the ultimate objective of federation.

BRITAIN AND EUROPE: A MASSIVE STUDY

'When it was announced at the end of 1956 that Britain was considering entering a European Free Trade Area, a small group of people concerned with European affairs met in London to consider what this proposal would really mean.'[18] So ran the first sentence of the Economist Intelligence Unit's book on the effects of free trade within Europe. In clear, it meant that the idea of the study had been conceived by members of Federal Union's Regional Commission, among whom Ota Adler, its chairman, and Tommy Thompson were particularly conscious of industrial concerns, while John Pinder and Caspar Brook, both at the Economist Intelligence Unit (EIU), were in charge of international research and of publications respectively. The cost of a detailed sector-by-sector study of the effects of European free trade on British industry was estimated at £7000.

The American Committee on United Europe, led by Paul Hoffman, who had played a leading part in the Marshall Plan, looked like a potential source of funds. The American Committee had financed the European Youth Campaign, for which Tommy Thompson had worked in Paris and whose Director in London was now Maurice Foley; and within a couple of months the Committee had agreed to help finance both the study and the Regional Commission's survey of Commonwealth parliamentary attitudes, provided that at least half the money was found elsewhere.[19] Sixteen British sponsors were rapidly assembled, mostly company chairmen, trade-union leaders or former ministers, mostly knights and lords, and largely from among the signatories of the recent statement urging British participation in the Community. They formed a committee with Martin Maddan, MP as Hon. Treasurer and Tommy Thompson, who did most of the work on behalf of the Regional Commission, as Hon. Secretary. The sponsors' signatures, covering much of the reverse side of a letter of appeal to companies and trade unions, looked sufficiently impressive to pull in some £14000 from about a hundred contributors: twice the sum originally envisaged, with the American Committee's contribution now no more than a quarter of the larger total the study received.

This massive piece of research, led at the EIU by Ann Monroe with a team of contributors who covered a score of industries and a dozen countries, was completed within six months and published early in December 1957, less than two months after the free trade area negotiations formally opened in the Organisation for European Economic Co-operation, and just before the EEC and Euratom treaties came into force. The research provided convincing evidence of the opportunities for competitive British firms in a tariff-free West European market, and hence of the potential dynamic effects on the British economy. Caspar Brook, with the expansive spirit that was later to achieve a mass circulation for the Consumer Association's *Which?*, sent out 40000 selling letters and over six hundred review copies; he organised simultaneous press conferences in London and New York, and persuaded *The Observer* to serialise the gist of the book week by week over a period of three months. Eight thousand copies were sold within six weeks of publication,[20] reflecting intense interest on the part of British industry.

The EIU took care to be guided by the facts: there was no suggestion from any quarter that its results were biased. But for the first time since 1940, Federal Union could congratulate itself on having achieved a mass impact – although with the limited objective of arousing interest in a form of economic integration.

There was also an unexpected financial bonus. After the cost of the research had been met, almost all the donors agreed to leave the balance of their contributions with the sponsoring Committee for use in further work on a single European market. This money could not be used for Federal Union itself. But the Committee was composed mainly of people who favoured British membership of the European Community; and its officers and committee included a number of members of Federal Union's Regional Commission. There was now the financial basis for a stronger organisation to work on the initial steps of free trade area or of Community membership, even if it had to leave open the question of the Community's ultimate political destination.

Thus began a period in which British federalists established organisations in which they could work for limited objectives with others who did not necessarily or explicitly share their federal goal. The federal idea was to remain the province of Federal Union and, when Federal Union went into hibernation, of the Federal Trust. Faced with the danger of permanent British isolation from the Community, and hence from any movement at all towards federation, members of the Regional Commission had little doubt where they should channel their energies.

FROM REGIONAL COMMISSION TO 'BRITAIN IN EUROPE'

With the residue of funds from the appeal for the *Britain and Europe* study, the Federal Union Regional Commission was able to ensure the establishment of a Britain in Europe Committee, soon to become the Britain in Europe organisation. Its chairman was Sir David Kelly, former British Ambassador to Argentina, Turkey, and the USSR. Its Executive was chaired by Lawrence Robson, chairman of Associated British Engineering Ltd, and a Federal Union member of several years' standing. The Vice-Chairman was Ernest Jones, President of the National Union of Mineworkers. Again Martin Maddan was Hon. Treasurer and E. G. Thompson Hon. Secretary. The Committee, over fifty strong, included Lord Cornwallis, chairman of Albert Reed & Co., and the chairmen of such firms as Glaxo, Rowntree, General Motors, and Metal Box. From the financial and nationalised sectors of British industry, it had the backing of the chairmen of several banks, of Lord Salter, and of Lord Douglas, chairman of

British European Airways. On the trade-union side, the committee included Frank Cousins of the Transport and General Workers Union; Tom Williamson, General Secretary of the General and Municipal Workers; Tom Yates, General Secretary of the National Union of Seamen; and Douglas Houghton, General Secretary of the Inland Revenue Staff Federation.[21] Federalists could play the Establishment game too. Britain in Europe also leaned towards the Establishment with the appointment of Eric Lingeman, a former ambassador, as Director-General of its tiny staff, although Jim Hunt, a member of the Regional Commission and of the Executive Committee of Federal Union, complemented Lingeman as Executive Secretary.

The aim of Britain in Europe was to interest industry in European free trade and integration. It co-sponsored some of the series of conferences which John Bowyer had initiated in 1957 on behalf of the Federal Trust, at which members of the Regional Commission, better informed than most of their compariots about the progress of integration on the Continent, were frequent speakers. It launched a Newsletter. It continued to commission research: suspecting that fear for Commonwealth links would undermine the policy of developing ties with continental Europe, it commissioned from the Economist Intelligence Unit a short report on the Commonwealth and Europe, which was published in September 1958; and it set about raising £11000 for a major EIU study of that complex subject. Sensitive to the possibility of Labour opposition to European integration, Britain in Europe also formed a trade-union affairs group, whose most active members included Colin Beever, Maurice Foley and Norman Hart from the Regional Commission, together with Shirley Williams, then Secretary of the Fabian Society.[22]

In parallel with the creation of Britain in Europe came the establishment of Europe House, likewise with pressure and support from the Regional Commission, after Walter Lessing had explained the idea to the Commission in March 1957. By November, Norman Hart was able to report, thanks to the goodwill of Sir Edward Hulton, Chairman of *Picture Post*, that Europe House had obtained for £1 a year a lease for premises at Hulton House in Fleet Street.[23] The speakers at the inaugural meeting on 4 March 1958 were the Rt Hon. Reginald Maudling, the Minister responsible for the Free Trade Area negotiations, Walter Hallstein, President of the EEC Commission, and K. G. Kiesinger, subsequently Chancellor of the German Federal Republic. John Leech, as its first Honorary Secretary, followed this with an impressive series of Europe House lectures during the next few years.

With so much being done by Britain in Europe and Europe House, Federal Union's Regional Commission focused on engendering ideas and seeking to co-ordinate the other bodies' activities. In September 1958, however, it published not only the short EIU report commissioned by Britain in Europe but also the Survey of Commonwealth parliamentarians: this showed predominant goodwill towards Britain's approach to Europe. Separately, Federal Union published its own detailed proposals, drafted by John Pinder, for association of the Commonwealth with an integrated Western Europe.[24] A further paper came from a study group on the scope for supranational development in a Free Trade Area;[25] and this commitment to the idea of supranational institutions, so rare in Britain at that time, was of a piece with the Regional Commission's links on the Continent, where such ideas were a matter of course.

Already in March 1957, Federal Union had attended a conference organised by the Centre d'Action Européenne Fédéraliste (AEF) in Paris, with a British delegation including Lord Salter, Sir Edward Hulton, and four Conservative and five Labour MPs. The French participants included two former Prime Ministers. René Mayer and Antoine Pinay, as well as many notables from France and other Community countries.[26] There was still much Continental support for the change in British policy towards Europe, but there was also a growing feeling that the free trade area proposals were too Anglocentric and neglectful of Continental ideas and interests. The British needed much more exposure to Continental thinking, and the British federalists' efforts to expose them went in the right direction. A similar but grander conference was held in Wiesbaden in January 1959. But General de Gaulle, sensing that support for the British proposals was insufficiently strong on the Continent and particularly in France, and having no desire to share European leadership with Britain, brought the Free Trade Area negotiations to an abrupt close in November 1958.

The federal unionists might well have brooded over their failure to do more to alert the British to the weakness of the free trade proposals. Had they swum too much with the tide instead of battling against it? But rather than spend time on regrets, they now began trying to persuade their compatriots that the practical successor to the Free Trade Area project should be a British application for full membership of the Community.

TOWARDS EC MEMBERSHIP

During 1958, with Britain in Europe working on the Free Trade Area project, Federal Union began to be convinced that its own role should be to press the need for Britain to go further and actually join the Community, and press the Community to establish stronger, more democratic institutions.[27] Christopher Layton, then on the staff of *The Economist* after a spell at The Economist Intelligence Unit, was close to John Pinder and other federalists in the EIU and had written in *World Affairs* about the blindness of Britain's negative policy towards European integration.[28] In the month after de Gaulle cut off the Free Trade Area negotiations, *The Economist* published an article in which Layton advocated British membership of the Community.[29] There could have been no better forum from which to establish that this was a respectable and responsible idea.

It certainly encouraged the distinguished delegation that Federal Union took to the AEF's Wiesbaden conference in 1959. Since the spring of 1958, Tommy Thompson and André Voisin had taken the initiative in designing the programme and inviting speakers; and the result was an impressive gathering of five hundred strong, including Robert Schuman, Walter Hallstein and Heinrich von Brentano, later German foreign minister. Nor did the Federal Union delegation fall below this standard. Led by the Rt Hon. Earl Attlee, it included eleven MPs, among them Roy Jenkins, Niall MacDermot, Martin Maddan and Geoffrey Rippon, as well as a dozen members of the Regional Commission.[30]

While Attlee gave lustre to the Federal Union delegation, he astounded the Continentals by speaking for no more than five minutes; and what he had to say about Europe was friendly but equivocal. He was clear that we must be 'prepared to depart from old conceptions and absolute national sovereignty and to accept the will of others'; and he was 'a profound believer in world federalism'. But, although we British 'are of Europe', some (including, it could be surmised, Attlee himself), 'would say we are like a semi-detached home, partly in Europe and partly outside'.[31]

More important for the future was the presence of Roy Jenkins in the delegation. During the next five years he was a strong supporter of Federal Union, becoming a member of the Executive Committee and Vice-Chairman of the Council before entering the Labour government in 1964. In the spring of 1959 he added distinction to the Federal Union group in two further international meetings: one on

'The New Europe and the Commonwealth', organised by the Regional Commission for the AEF in London; the other a demonstration of European solidarity organised by the AEF in Berlin.[32] By June 1960, opening a Federal Union study conference on 'A New European Policy for Britain', he was categorical that 'there is no alternative for this country except complete membership of the European Economic Community'; and he presciently predicted that 'there will not, at first, be immediate acceptance' of Britain's offer to join, 'but in the long run it will come'.[33]

After the breakdown of the Free Trade Area negotiations, the conventional reaction to de Gaulle's rebuff was to turn elsewhere: to a European Free Trade Association of countries on the periphery of the Community; to the Commonwealth; or to suggestions for a North Atlantic free trade area. Even the UK Council of the European Movement, led by the Establishment-oriented Sir Edward Beddington-Behrens, tended to look in these directions.[34] Federal Union's Regional Commission had, on the contrary, concluded that the next step must be a campaign to persuade British opinion to favour membership of the Community.[35] But to find people with the weight to turn round Establishment thinking was no easy task. The Rt Hon. Peter Thorneycroft, former Chancellor of the Exchequer, agreed in June that he would support a Common Market campaign,[36] but he was one of very few at that time. The search for others continued; but the Regional Commission was also preoccupied by a sharp deterioration in the finances of Britain in Europe and Europe House. As became usual after a setback in Britain's relations with the Community – and also, later, after successful achievement of an objective – company donations were no longer so readily forthcoming.

But although finances were low, activities continued at high speed. Reginald Maudling spoke to 160 people at a Europe House dinner in January 1959; and by mid-1960, John Leech was organising Europe House lectures at a rate of three per month.[37] Britain in Europe continued to publish its newsletter, and its trade-union group had launched a European Labour Bulletin. It also continued to organise two-day conferences for business jointly with the Federal Trust, and directed its research towards the issue of Europe and the Commonwealth.

Already in 1957, the Regional Commission and its offshoot, Britain in Europe, had initiated studies of the problems that British participation in a European Free Trade Area could pose for the Commonwealth. British federalists were therefore well placed to propose solutions to these problems at the same time as they proposed membership of the Community. On 2 April 1959, Federal Union published a report by a Working Group on *Britain in the Common Market: the implications for Commonwealth trade*, which made a detailed analysis of the difficulties, country by country and product by product, and showed how they could be tackled.[38] But although, during the 1961–3 negotiations for British entry, solutions were found along such lines, British fears for the Commonwealth still seemed likely to present a major political obstacle to Community membership. Weightier evidence would be required.

Early in 1959, therefore, Britain in Europe agreed with the Economist Intelligence Unit on the terms of reference for the £11 000 study of Commonwealth problems.[39] At the EIU, Ann Monroe was again responsible for the very intensive and complicated research, whose results were published as a 600-page book, *The Commonwealth and Europe*,[40] just before the Commonwealth Prime Ministers' Conference in September 1960. Edward Heath, soon to lead the negotiations for entry, was one of the many politicians, industrialists and British and Commonwealth officials who attended the press conference, at which Reginald Maudling, then President of the Board of Trade, called the book 'a monumental piece of analysis and research', 'showing tremendous thoroughness and competence and integrity', and demonstrating also that, despite their extent and complexity, the technical and trade problems could be satisfactorily solved.[41]

While the British government was evidently satisfied that the Commonwealth's economic problems were soluble, the forthcoming negotiations were dogged by doubts among politicians and the public.[42] At the level of populist politics, the EIU's research and Britain in Europe's rationality were no match for the Anti-Common Market League.[43] The federalists' achievement was, rather, to assemble an impressive enough array of facts, arguments, and Establishment figures in favour of entry to encourage the Prime Minister, Harold Macmillan, to take the plunge into negotiations in 1961, and to help swing enlightened opinion and business interests into line with his policy.

Through the spring and summer of 1959 Federal Union's Regional Commission made preparations for the Common Market Campaign, including a press statement, drafted with Roy Jenkins's help. Detailed planning was done by a dedicated preparatory sub-committee – so dedicated that, at its meeting in the evening of 9 August, the minutes record that Messrs Hart, Hunt, Leech, McLaughlin, Pinder, Rea and E. G. Thompson, who had been present since 7.00 pm, were joined at 10.30 pm by Douglas Robinson, who had come with some suggestions that doubtless kept them at it for another hour or two.[44] The problem was still to find a sufficiently weighty figure to lead the Campaign. The initial press statement had been successful, a number of people had agreed to join the Campaign Committee, and Federal Union had appointed Bob Jarrett, later an official at the EC Commission, as secretary of the Committee and of the Regional Commission.[45] But it was not until the end of the year that the ideally weighty figure emerged.

Lord Gladwyn had just retired after six years as British Ambassador to France. He had shared in the making of Britain's mistaken European policy in the late 1940s and the second half of the 1950s; and Federal Unionists had cause to remember his reception at the British Embassy in Paris in March 1957, when he had chaffed MPs in the Federal Union delegation for their allegedly excessive federalist zeal.[46] But the breakdown of the Free Trade Area project had convinced Gladwyn that Britain should join the Community; and, once freed of official constraints, this cause had no more trenchant advocate.

In mid-1960 financial stringency had forced a merger between Britain in Europe and Europe House. But the Europe House lectures were still run by John Leech with a committee comprising mainly members of Federal Union and its Regional Commission.[47] They invited Lord Gladwyn to make a speech on 7 December 1960, at which he envisaged a European Community including Britain, and called on the government to take a lead in this direction.[48] Four weeks later, Gladwyn became the President of Britain in Europe. Hitherto, this had kept a low profile about joining the Community; but Gladwyn, in his inaugural address, came out for a policy of pressing the government to seek British membership.[49]

On the same day, Lord Jellicoe chaired a meeting at which Roy Jenkins, MP, Peter Kirk, MP, and some industrialists met members of Federal Union's preparatory committee for the Common Market Campaign to make plans for launching a declaration signed by people prominent in public life.[50] But Jellicoe soon had to withdraw on his appointment as Government Whip in the Lords; and Federal Union's preparatory committee decided to invite Lord Gladwyn to be Chairman of the Campaign. He accepted, on condition that it was not run as a Federal Union project.[51]

This faced the federalists with a dilemma. Federal Union itself was actively promoting the idea of British membership of a federal Europe, and around this time had organised two meetings on the subject: one in November, addressed by F. M. Bennett, MP and John Hynd, MP; and a trade-union conference in February 1961, opened by Niall MacDermot, addressed by Bob Edwards, MP and attended by eighty delegates.[52] During the period when Lord Jellicoe was chairing the preparatory meetings, there had been no objections to the Campaign's being promoted by Federal Union, whose policy was explicitly to seek British membership without altering the Community's basic structure or weakening the 'federal aspirations of the Six'.[53]

Now the federalists who were going to put their energy into the Common Market Campaign had to decide whether to accept that its organisation would not have 'federal aspirations'. The risk to Federal Union was evident: many of its most capable people were now to be absorbed for two or three years in the work of another organisation without a federal objective. Given, however, the immediate objective of British entry into the Community, the gains from Gladwyn's leadership of the Campaign were obvious. After some agonising, Federal Union accepted Gladwyn's condition, realising that current British attitudes to federalism would reduce the effectiveness of the Campaign if Federal Union was overtly involved. It trusted (rightly, in the event) in Gladwyn's readiness to work with the federalists who would be active in the Campaign's Directing Committee. When the Committee was formally constituted, it did indeed include Norman Hart, John Leech, John Pinder, Findlay Rea and Tommy Thompson; the officers were Roy Jenkins, MP (Deputy Chairman), Peter Kirk, MP (Hon. Secretary), both Vice-Presidents of Federal Union, and John Diamond, MP (Hon. Treasurer), who had already shown himself friendly to the federalists. Bob Jarrett moved from Federal Union's office to run that of the Campaign.

In terms of immediate objectives, the federalists' compromise proved abundantly justified. The declaration in favour of British membership was rapidly completed and sent to a couple of hundred potential signatories, for the most part those known to be sympathetic through contacts with Federal Union, Britain in Europe and Europe House. The covering letter was signed by Gladwyn, Roy Jenkins, MP (for Labour), Peter Kirk, MP (for the Conservatives) and Mark Bonham Carter (who had been a Liberal MP during 1958–9). By the time of the public launch on 25 May 1961, there were

130 distinguished signatories.[54] Martin Maddan introduced a motion in similar terms in the House of Commons and there was a debate on the subject on 28 June. On 31 July, Prime Minister Macmillan announced the government's intention to negotiate terms for British accession to the EC Treaties.

It was a bold move, and not universally popular, even in Macmillan's own party. A few days before the announcement, the *Conservative News Letter* wrote that 'The Liberals call on the Government to apply forthwith to join the Common Market. It is foolish advice which the Government are wise to reject.'[55] In this atmosphere, the Common Market Campaign's declaration certainly had an important impact. It would be hard to contest the view that the list of its signatories and its impact on the press at least made it 'one of several predisposing factors' in Macmillan's judgement that he should go ahead.[56]

11 Hopes and Setbacks

THE COMMON MARKET CAMPAIGN

Harold Macmillan's announcement of Britain's decision to negotiate terms for membership of the European Community was the beginning of eighteen months of struggle for public support. Following the success of the Common Market Campaign's declaration, its Directing Committee had already held its first meeting on 19 June 1961. Two Vice-Presidents of Federal Union and five membets of FU's Regional Commission formed the Committee's hard core. As Executive Secretary, Bob Jarrett moved from Federal Union's cramped premises to two more pleasant rooms which Ota Adler had offered the Campaign rent-free up to June 1962.[1]

The Campaign immediately launched a monthly *Broadsheet*. It sent out two thousand copies of the first issue in July 1961; and in 1962 the circulation had risen to six thousand. Bill Rodgers was engaged as editor. He was soon to complete his stint as executive chairman of the Campaign for Democratic Socialism, supporting the policies of Hugh Gaitskell, then Leader of the Opposition; and he had some time available before becoming a Labour MP in 1962, then a Cabinet Minister in the 1970s, and later one of the four main founders of the Social Democratic Party. Rodgers played a key role among the Labour Europeans in the House of Commons during the entry negotiations in 1970–2. However, with his political career gathering pace, he had to give up editing the *Broadsheet*; and the task was taken over in July 1962 by Sir Anthony Meyer, who was later, as a Conservative backbencher, to remain a pillar of the European and federalist cause.

In addition to the *Broadsheet*, the Campaign distributed several pamphlets: two thousand copies of one produced by the *Daily Herald*; one thousand copies of the *Daily Telegraph*'s version; and, in summer 1962, a thousand copies of a Federal Union pamphlet by John Leech on the Commonwealth,[2] and a few thousand of a question-and-answer pamphlet by Norman Hart and Sir Anthony Meyer. Peter Kirk advised the Rank Organisation on a pro-Common Market film, first shown in September. Aware of the need to work outside London, the Campaign also set up regional committees in Glasgow and Manchester; and on the proposal of Roy Jenkins, it employed three regional organisers to drum up support in those constituencies whose MPs had been identified as uncommitted. One of them, Oliver Crawford, has been active in Britain's pro-European organisations ever since.

None of these activities was as impressive as the initial declaration; and the scale of the Campaign's budget was quite inadequate for a major effort of public relations. Expenditure for the whole period of one and a half years from the application to the veto was less than £10000 – no match for the resources poured into the activities of the Anti-Common Market League. The Campaign's strength lay, rather, in Gladwyn's influence among the Establishment and that of young and promising MPs such as Jenkins, Kirk and Maddan in their parties, together with the intellectual output and organising energy of the federalists. A number of those in and around Federal Union's Regional Commission had the knowledge and ability to write books about the Community and Britain's relations with it; and before the end of the negotiations in January 1963, there were more than half a dozen of such works, from authors who included Colin Beever, Uwe Kitzinger, John Lambert, Kim Mackay (this, sadly, his posthumous publication), Richard Mayne, John Pinder, Roy Pryce, and Dennis Thompson.[3] Harry Cowie, editor of *World Affairs* since 1958, continued to advocate a federalist approach to Europe.[4] Among the writers of booklets and reports were John Bowyer, Roger Broad, Norman Hart, John Leech, Anthony Meyer and John Pomian.[5] The research projects initiated by the federalists, resulting in *Britain and Europe* and *The Commonwealth and Europe*, had already provided convincing evidence that British membership of the Community would make economic sense. All this offered impressive underpinning for the favourable attitudes that came to predominate in business, the media, Whitehall, the Conservative Party and the Establishment in general. Unfortunately, among those less impressed were a doubting public and a suspicious Labour Party. Meanwhile, however, the federalists and the Campaign continued working in a fairly optimistic frame of mind.

The atmosphere at Britain in Europe was less expansive.[6] Although big business supported the government's application, it did not see the need for a special financial effort to support Britain in Europe. There were, to be sure, still 150 corporate subscribers at the end of 1961. But, after paying the fee of £11000 for the massive research project that had produced *The Commonwealth and Europe*, there was not enough to fund even the retrenched operation that had remained after the merger with Europe House in mid-1960. Jim Hunt, John Leech and former Ambassador Lingeman had to leave in the autumn of 1961 (although the two former continued to work hard in a voluntary capacity). Still, a respectable level of activity was maintained, with Val Schur – another of those who came from the Economist Intelligence Unit and was to find himself at home in FU's Regional Commission – as Executive Secretary. Martin Maddan and Tommy Thompson continued to be anchormen as Hon. Treasurer and Hon. Secretary. John Leech joined them on the Executive Committee. Liaison between Britain in Europe and the Campaign was facilitated, and the position of federalists on the governing bodies incidentally strengthened, by the co-optation of John Diamond and Peter Kirk on to Britain in Europe's Council, matched by Martin Maddan's co-optation by the Campaign. Although the budget was tighter than expected, expenditure was still as much as £12843 in 1962, and Britain in Europe's *Newsletter* and *Labour Bulletin*, as well as *Europe House Papers*, continued to be published. Britain in Europe also jointly sponsored some of the Federal Trust's series of conferences for business, which were organised at the rate of nearly one a month during the period of the negotiations. One, confidently entitled 'Inside the Common Market', attracted over 230 high-level participants, mostly from the larger companies. Speakers at this series included such figures from both sides of the Channel as Raymond Barre, Edward Heath, Roy Jenkins, Jean Rey, Jacques Rueff, Lord Shawcross and Robert Triffin. The Chairman and Deputy Chairman of the Stock Exchange were among the top speakers from the City. The younger generation was also represented, with David Howell and Christopher Layton; and David Barton recalls that at one of the conferences he found himself sitting next to a young French speaker whom Gladwyn had described as 'up-and-coming': his name was Valéry Giscard d'Estaing.[7]

Europe House lectures also continued, although, following the twenty that John Leech had organised in 1961, their frequency fell to about one a month in 1962. One of these was given by Gladwyn on the 'Prospects for a European Political Community' – with, recalling the salad days of the Federal Union Research Institute in 1939–40, Professor A. L. Goodhart of University College, Oxford, in the chair. But however eminent and intellectually challenging such activities may have been, Britain in Europe's resources were too little to make much mark on the general public or to produce an impressive riposte to the economic arguments of the only serious opposition among the business interest groups, the National Farmers Union. The Council of Management was well aware of the threat from the farmers' lobby, which had considerable influence among Conservative MPs, and in whose supposed interest the Ministry of Agriculture could hamper the accession negotiations from within the government machine. Following the precedents of *Britain and Europe* and *The Commonwealth and Europe*, a study of the agricultural effects of membership was commissioned in March 1962; but, in contrast with those two major studies, shortage of money and time constrained the project to a modest review, completed in two months by a single individual. When it was published towards the end of May, press attention was negligible. Unopposed by any weighty counter-argument, the NFU pursued its efforts to turn political and public opinion against the negotiations, and the Ministry of Agriculture continued to act as a brake within the government.[8]

A more successful effort was the work done by the Federal Trust and the Regional Commission among the lawyers. This had already begun in 1958, when the Regional Commission had seen the need for a commission of lawyers to advise on the role of a court in maintaining fair trade within a free trade area, and in September had set up a Legal Sub-Committee, with Dennis Thompson as convenor and John Bowyer and Donald Farquharson, then in the early stages of his distinguished legal career, as the other two members. The legal standing of the Federal Trust's Chairman, Sir John Foster, QC, MP, was also a substantial asset. By March 1959 Donald Farquharson was able to report that the commission was flourishing.[9] But it was Dennis Thompson who, from this starting-point, developed the effort to inform lawyers about the Community to the point where, by the time the accession negotiations began, those who mattered in the legal profession were both well informed and predominantly well disposed. Here, in his own words, is the story of how it was done:

> I was proposing to have a short holiday on the continent in 1957 and John Bowyer made the happy suggestion that I should go to Luxembourg (which then meant nothing to me) and visit the Coal and Steel Community. Richard Mayne, who was then working for the High Authority, treated me royally and introduced me to Michel Gaudet, then sitting behind a trestle table waiting to go to Brussels as the legal director-general designate of the EEC. He also took me to a session of the Court and arranged for me to have a discussion with the Advocate General Maurice Lagrange.

I immediately became an enthusiast for the Community and soon became busy with the Federal Trust and Federal Union. One of our concerns was to interest lawyers in the activities of the EEC, which was important to them as anti-competitive agreements made outside the Common Market with an effect inside were subject to the provisions of the Treaty of Rome. In order to get the support of lawyers the Federal Trust organised joint conferences together with the British Institute for International and Comparative Law and the School of Advanced Legal Studies. The British Institute comprised all lawyers interested in international law, whatever their views. Most of its members were sympathetic to the European ideas but there were also some who were not; but as they had no other body to join the prevailing attitude was a pro-European one. The President was Lord Denning and the two most active judges were Wilberforce and Diplock, both afterwards law lords, all of whom were favourable to Europe. I was privileged to introduce Gaudet to all three, and in this way the EEC legal service found an institutional link with Britain which it had been seeking. The Institute of Advanced Legal Studies was included in order to bring in the domestic lawyers not principally concerned with international affairs, but who none the less found themselves affected by the Treaty of Rome.[10]

The first of the joint conferences was a truly impressive occasion. Its chairman, Lord Diplock, welcomed Jean Rey, the EEC's Commissioner for External Relations, who led the Community's powerful delegation of speakers. These included Michel Gaudet, Director-General of the Joint Legal Services of the EC, Dr VerLoren van Themaat, Director-General for Competition in the EEC, Professor A. M. Donner, President of the Court of Justice, Dr E. N. van Kleffens, head of the Community's Delegation in the UK, as well as Jean Rey and Jean-François Deniau, the brilliant young official in Rey's Directorate-General who was soon to be leading the Commission's team of officials negotiating with Britain on the application for membership. The conference gave some 120 top British legal experts a masterly introduction to the problems of Community law on 29–30 September 1960, just a year before the negotiations eventually began; and a verbatim report was produced for wider dissemination.[11] A second joint conference, focusing on company law and tax, was held on 20–21 April 1961. Dennis Thompson's story continues from that point:

> One of the results of these conferences was that I was invited to become a part-time consultant to the Institute, on European and Common Market Law, and took part in a number of projects designed to promote the idea of British membership of the Community. In this we were greatly assisted by Norman Marsh, the Director of the Institute, who was also a keen European and who had the quality of being a most excellent showman.
>
> The most important activity of the Institute was the holding of the London–Leiden series of meetings (which still continue), started at the instance of Professor Samkalden of the Europa Instituut, Leiden, at which some twenty or thirty lawyers from eac country met every year to discuss recent developments in the EE(particularly in the Court of Justice. Wilberforce and Diplock we often present, and from the other side there came Judge Donner, tl President of the European Court, Gaudet and others from the Leg Service and a number of Dutch lawyers from practice and industry the Netherlands. The consequence was that when the first bid to jo Europe was made by the Macmillan government, the lawyers kne all about the Community. Wilberforce and Diplock were in the Lo Chancellor's delegation to Luxembourg to make arrangements f joining the Court . . .
>
> In retrospect it seems that I did more than I did, but whatever was achieved was due to the background that was given to me through the Federal Trust. This provided exactly the economic and political substance, as well as political certainty for my doings, which the other lawyers did not have, and which left the field largely open to myself. There were many possible objections that might have been raised by the lawyers against membership, such as the loss of legal sovereignty of Parliament, the inroads into the common law legal system ('the best in the world'), the domination of a foreign court in Luxembourg, and the making of regulations by the Commission. The only really informed opponent was Derek Walker-Smith in Parliament, but he never had much support from the Temple, owing I believe much to the effectiveness of the London–Leiden meetings.

This story illustrates how a few individuals who were well prepared intellectually were able to exercise considerable influence by organising suitable meetings as well as by lecturing and writing – for Dennis Thompson gave numerous lectures and was among those who rapidly wrote books when publishers saw the need in 1961–2.[12] He also bore out Ota Adler's observation that the reward for these disinterested efforts could come sooner than in heaven, for when Britain finally joined the Community he became a Director in the Competition Directorate-General; and on leaving the Commission he founded the *Journal of World Trade Law*, whose success enabled him to become a substantial benefactor of the Federal Trust.

THE FEDERALISTS' NETWORK

Meanwhile, back at the Regional Commission of Federal Union, resources were far more exiguous than in the Campaign for Britain in Europe, but it remained the place where the federalists' network met. One of its functions was to germinate new organisations to carry the federalists' ideas and policies to particular professions and groups. In the case of the lawyers, the work was done through the Federal Trust and in existing professional bodies. But a new British branch of the European Union of Teachers was formed;[13] and the Young European Management Association was established as the British section of the Jeunes Chefs d'Entreprise d'Europe. Its Chairman was Michel Montague, a member of Federal Union who was soon to become Chairman of Valor Ltd and, later, of the English Tourist Board and of the National Consumer Council; and the centre of gravity in the committee was located among three members of the Regional Commission, David Baker, Charles de Hoghton and Norman Hart. Similarly, John Bowyer was Chairman and Bob Jarrett Hon. Treasurer of the newly formed Young European Left.[14] The initiative for founding the Committee of European Student Associations came from the students themselves; but it was Federal Union, in the person of Bob Jarrett, that provided the necessary services and stability. Before long there were eight university clubs and a regular newsletter, *Europe Ahead*. In October 1960 the National Council was welcomed to a meeting at Cambridge by Hans Liesner, now a senior civil servant but then a young don and Vice-Chairman of the Cambridge Federal Union group of more than two hundred student federalists. In 1961 an Easter Seminar was organised by Diarmid McLaughlin of Cambridge University Federal Union, who later became Director of the Federal Trust and then a senior Community official in Brussels. A hundred and forty participants from 14 countries heard speeches by, among others, Professor Max Beloff, Roy Jenkins, MP, and Sir Roderick Barclay, then Deputy Under-

Secretary at the Foreign Office and later the British Ambassador to Belgium.[15] In January 1962 it was Karl Kaiser, now Director of the Foreign Affairs Institute in Bonn, who welcomed the Council to Oxford on behalf of the similar Strasbourg Group, which had been founded by Noël Salter in the late 1940s. Student European groups had sprung up in half a dozen other universities.

Other specialist organisations were also established by the federalists wearing their other hats. In 1962 the Federal Trust gave birth to the Wyndham Place Trust, with a religious outlook on federalist education and research. In the same year Britain in Europe established the European Educational Research Trust. The immediate purpose of this, as succinctly expressed by Jim Hunt in one of his last Executive Secretary's reports before leaving for a successful career as a banker, was 'simply to lay hands on the £250 offered by the Charles Henry Foyle Trust' at the time of the merger with Europe House. He did, however, immediately add that the new Trust could have a more important long-term function, which turned out to be right. Meanwhile, it began with a list of ultra-respectable Trustees, among whom the federalists included Lord Beveridge, still President of Federal Union, John Leech and Martin Maddan, MP.[16] Another of this new generation of organisations that was to have a key role in the future was the Labour Common Market Committee, which originated from the Campaign, and which worked very hard during the entry negotiations of 1961–3.

The Labour Committee was the only one of the specialist organisations to play a role of political importance at this time, although on this occasion the forces ranged against it proved too strong. All these bodies were the beginnings of an organisational infrastructure which became essential in the campaigns of the 1970s to get and keep Britain in the Community. Although in 1961–3 they lost the battle, federalists were acquiring the skills which enabled them to win the battles to come.

CHANNEL BRIDGES

Another of the federalists' strengths lay in their international links in Continental Europe, which helped to expose a series of British MPs to eminent and responsible Continental federalists. The need for such exposure was sharply evident from Tony Morris's report to the Regional Commission on a European Movement Congress held in

Rome in June 1957. The Establishment-oriented British Council of the European Movement had sent a delegation which included a number of MPs dangerously out of touch with their Continental colleagues, exacerbating the impression of British insularity that was to prove one of the obstacles against successful entry negotiations in 1961–3.[17] Attlee had earlier shown more vision when he explained why he was sending a delegation with a number of bright young Labour MPs to Strasbourg for the first meeting of the Council of Europe Assembly in 1949: 'I don't understand Europe, but in twenty years' time the party ought to have some people who do.'[18] Evidently the need was still great. But Roy Jenkins and Niall MacDermott, as well as the Rt Hon. Arthur Bottomley, were among those whom Attlee led in the Federal Union delegation to Wiesbaden early in 1959; and the federalists continued their efforts to bring British politicians into contact with Continental federalists and their thinking, as well as to remind Continentals that there was a growing number of British who would be able to work constructively with them in the Community.

Since the Paris conference of the Action Européenne Fédéraliste in 1957, Federal Union had been strengthening its links with the AEF, which brought together the federalist movements that supported the Monnet approach towards federation by building up the European Community, though with a more explicit commitment to the federal goal than Monnet usually made.[19] In March 1958, Martin Maddan, Norman Hart, Jim Hunt and Findlay Rea went to a smaller meeting organised by André Voisin for the French member organisation of AEF, at which Robert Schuman was the guest of honour at a banquet, and Voisin, who needed little convincing that Britain should be part of the European construction, championed the cause of British participation in the projected AEF activities.

By July, the Regional Commission had formed a Sub-Committee on AEF–FU relations.[20] In April 1959, Federal Union organised the two-day conference for the AEF on 'The New Europe and the Commonwealth', at which the speakers included Adler, Brugmans, Jenkins, Voisin and Jacques Tessier, a leading French trade unionist. Two former French ministers came to a repeat performance, this time on Euro-African relations, in June 1961, again in London. Here the British speakers were Maurice Foley, Norman Hart and Christopher Layton. In between, Sir John Foster, QC, MP led the Federal Union delegation to a demonstration in Berlin, at which Roy Jenkins was again one of the party.[21]

After entry negotiations began in the early autumn of 1961, th federal unionists were immersed in the campaign at home and ha little time for their connections on the Continent. Norman Hart, Joh Pinder and Tommy Thompson did find time, however, to attend th European Movement's Congress in Munich in June 1962. There the heard a Spanish delegation, including Salvador de Madariaga, who a an Oxford don had been active in the Federal Union Researc Institute during the war, assert their determination to bring Spai sooner or later into a democratic European union. The delegates wh returned to Spain were, on arrival, banished by the Franco regime t a remote island. It also became evident that a number of th delegates from the UK Council of the European Movement wer aligning themselves with the Gaullists in the French delegation. The doubtless took their cue from Macmillan, who already in his speec in the House of Commons on 2 August 1961, on the decision to ope negotiations, had gone out of his way to oppose the forces in Europ working towards a federal system and to support de Gaulle's concep of l'Europe des Patries.[22] In so far as this expressed a settle conviction, the federalists saw it as part and parcel of the misguide approach that had already cost Britain so dear since the time of th Schuman Plan. If it was intended to impress the General and secur his support for the negotiations, their outcome proved that it cut n ice, while at the same time it alienated the many Continentals powerful politicians as well as the general public – who wanted to se the Community develop in a federal direction, and who might hav been influential allies – most significantly in Germany.

While adhering to the more Monnetist AEF, and missing th experience of the Congress of the European People to whic Spinellists had been deeply committed,[23] Federal Union kept a lin open to Spinelli, and *World Affairs* published an article by him i which he argued that, provided the pluralist democracies could lear to deal with international problems by adopting federalist policie 'the future belongs not to tyrants, but to democrats'.[24] While puttin most of their energy into the campaign to support membershi moreover, the British federalists also explored the longer-ter implications for sovereignty. In November 1961, Federal Union ha organised a study conference on 'Sovereignty and the EC', addresse by John Hynd, MP, John Pinder and Tommy Thompson, and wit contributions by Richard Moore, Jock (later Lord) Bruce-Gardyn and John (later Lord) Vaizey. John Hynd, who had already foun himself in sympathy with Continental federalists in newly liberate

Paris in March 1945, at the conference which followed Spinelli's meetings with Resistance representatives in Geneva in 1944, posed a fundamental question which has been evaded by most British politicians to this day. 'Would we,' he asked, 'in this country really be content to see the sovereignty over such wide fields left to Ministers to decide in private and without parliamentary control?' Pressing farther into federalist territory, he affirmed the need for 'a common foreign policy controlled by an elected parliament'.[25]

Not long after this, John Pinder was writing in his *Britain and the Common Market* about the need for majority voting and democratic control by Community institutions over the taking of common decisions;[26] Richard Mayne's *The Community of Europe* sought to prepare the British for such developments by describing the Community as 'a continuous creation';[27] and Roy Pryce, having argued at the start of *The Political Future of the European Community* why the separate and sovereign nation-state was no longer viable, went on to draw the consequences of direct elections and a legislative role for the European Parliament, leading to a democratic United States of Europe.[28] Collectively, the Regional Commission decided in May 1962 to make a study of political integration.[29] But the entry negotiations were soon to reach their climax, and until the veto brought them to an abrupt halt in January 1963, attention was to be focused on the Campaign.

THE LABOUR PARTY, THE PUBLIC AND THE VETO

'So far so good' was a reasonable view for the federalists to take in the first half of 1962. Business and the Establishment were convinced that Britain should join the European Community; the government and the Conservative Party were on course; the bulk of the media were in support. But there was concern about the Labour Party. In Britain's polarised political system it seems hard for the Opposition not to oppose whatever the government does, even if this is in the country's general interest; and it is certainly hard for the governing party to avoid the temptation of seeking party political capital from such steps, even if this provokes the other side into outright opposition. Linked with the concern about the Labour Party was a worry about public opinion. Opinion polls showed that the 'poorer working class', where the Labour Party drew much of its support, were predominantly suspicious of the Community – a pattern that was to recur in 1970.[30] Aware of this danger, the Campaign agreed from the outset that a special effort should be made to seek support in the Labour Party.

At its first meeting, in June 1961, the Campaign's Directing Committee appointed a committee of three, Diamond, Hart and Jenkins, to organise a meeting at the Labour Party Conference that autumn. The following month, Jenkins reported that he had been conferring with Colin Beever about the establishment of a Common Market Committee within the Labour Party.[31] Beever and Hart had already been working for three years in Federal Union's trade-union affairs group, and it was only a few months since the successful FU conference for trade unionists. They and the two MPs, Jenkins and Diamond, had between them wide knowledge of the likely supporters in the Labour movement; and by September the Labour Common Market Committee (LCMC) had been founded, with Jenkins as Chairman, Diamond as Treasurer and Beever as secretary.[32] There were thirty-one members, the majority of them MPs, with – among those who had worked on Federal Union's Regional Commission – John Bowyer, Norman Hart, Roy Shaw (who was about to become Director of Federal Union and who was later to be a distinguished leader of Camden Council), and Shirley Williams, then Secretary of the Fabian Society and earlier one of the original members of the FU trade-union affairs group. The LCMC organised meetings, starting at the Party Conference, published a monthly *Newsbrief*, edited by Roger Broad from November 1961, and also produced a pamphlet by Broad and Norman Hart.[33]

The first few months were moderately reassuring. In a broadcast in May and a speech in the House of Commons in June, Gaitskell sounded favourable to British membership of the Community. Then in July he had talks with Spaak and other Continental socialists in Brussels and seems to have differed sharply from them about 'the nature of the European experiment',[34] i.e. about the Community's federal aspirations. This was followed in September by the Commonwealth Prime Ministers Conference, by which time Gaitskell was persuaded that membership was likely to be incompatible with Britain's Commonwealth obligations.[35] In a TV broadcast he attacked the federal idea and advocated that the Community be turned into a loose association – this to the 'consternation of many Socialists on the Continent'.[36] Finally at the Labour Party Conference, in October 1962, he came down squarely against membership.[37] There was no doubting the popularity of this stance among the majority of delegates at the Conference, and in this they reflected the opinions of Labour supporters in the country, who by then were dividing 36 per cent against membership, with only 27 per cent in favour.[38]

Throughout that year the polls showed the public to be generally favourable,[39] although by December *The Daily Telegraph* reported that Gallup had shown the public as a whole to be sharing the doubts of the Labour supporters. The same poll showed that the majority expected Labour to win the next election – not, given the stance of the Party Conference, a prospect likely to reassure Continentals who were negotiating about British entry.[40]

While the Campaign had been consolidating its support among the policy-makers, the opinion-formers and the better-educated, the Anti-Common Market League (ACML) made its impact at the other end of the spectrum.[41] It distributed a million copies of a *Common Market Quiz*,[42] which asked the recipients questions such as:

> Does Europe mean more to you than the British Commonwealth?
> Do you wish to give up British sovereignty and independence, to be ruled by a French/German/Italian majority from Brussels?
> Do you want food prices to rise – by as much perhaps as 5 shillings per head, per week?
> Do you want British farmers and farm-workers to grow less of our food?

These were the very issues – Commonwealth, agriculture and sovereignty – that became the most prominent in the House of Commons debates on the negotiations;[43] and the ACML followed the *Quiz* with 600000 copies of a leaflet on *Commonwealth or Common Market*, which was the most salient issue of all. Whatever the results of massive research on Commonwealth trade and whatever the prospects for relations between Britain and most of the Commonwealth countries over the longer term, the crude message of the ACML hit home, as did the relentless 'A Fact a Day' that appeared in the same vein throughout the negotiations in Beaverbrook's imperialist *Daily Express*, and the large advertisements that the League was well-enough funded to place in the newspapers. By the end of the negotiations, the League had organised thirty public rallies and gathered 30000 recorded members.

The League did not attempt to compete with the federalists as far as books and research were concerned. Nor could it match the Campaign among the Establishment and the quality press. But it distributed hundreds of thousands of leaflets where the Campaign distributed only thousands;[44] and its popular approach was remarkably effective – the more so since Macmillan's method was to manage his party and public opinion discreetly,[45] so that the Conservative Party organisation did not counter-attack effectively enough.

The other effect of Macmillan's 'backing into Europe',[46] intent on his method of managing domestic opinion and politics, was that the negotiations tended to be inward-looking: 'a Whitehall exercise', as Eric Roll, the most senior of the British officials stationed in Brussels for the negotiations, later put it, concluding that the final British negotiating position might, with a more outward-looking attitude, have been reached more quickly.[47] Until the summer of 1962, France was still embroiled in the Algerian war. Had the negotiations been concluded then, General de Gaulle might not have felt himself in a position to veto Britain. By the time the negotiations were nearing a conclusion, towards the end of the year, the General's hands were free in several respects.

In June 1962 Macmillan went to see de Gaulle at the Château des Champs; and it seems likely that de Gaulle then realised for the first time that the British government really wanted a European role for Britain and intended to make the concessions necessary for the negotiations to succeed.[48] He had already vetoed Britain's approach to Europe once, when he put a stop to the free trade area negotiations; and he was later to express his instinctive reaction to the idea of British participation when he told George Brown that two cocks could not live in the same farmyard and share a number of hens.[49] But in order to veto again without repercussions that would damage him politically, he needed to be sure of the support of Chancellor Adenauer as well as of the French electorate, who were to have their chance to pass judgement on his stewardship at the forthcoming elections in November.

The slow pace of the negotiations enabled him to secure his flank in Germany and his rear in Frence. Adenauer, with his experience of British behaviour over the Schuman Plan and the European Defence Community, was inclined to be suspicious of Britain's approach to Europe. But he for his part had to take account of the favourable attitude of many in German politics and much of public opinion. This attitude can hardly have been encouraged by the apparent dragging of British feet in the negotiations,[50] by Macmillan's explicit preference for de Gaulle's anti-federalist concept of l'Europe des Patries, or by the hostility of Gaitskell, who seemed increasingly likely to be the next Prime Minister. The British stance thus gave de Gaulle time and a suitable atmosphere in which to consolidate his alliance with Adenauer, with the help of a triumphal week-long visit to Germany in September.[51] Then, in November, with the negotiations still dragging on, de Gaulle won his elections with a big majority. He could safely put the knife in; and at his press conference on 14 January 1963, he duly announced his veto on British entry into the Community.[52]

BALANCE SHEET FOR THE FEDERALISTS

The negotiations which had seemed so promising had failed. There was no knowing when or even whether Britain would join the Community. In the event, a decade was lost. During it the British might have learned to work with their partners in the Community institutions during prosperous times – and, the federal unionists believed, Britian might thereby have become more responsive to the federalist approach. Yet, with hindsight, the federalists could count some impressive entries on the credit side to set against the heavy loss.

The negotiations themselves had been constructive. Solutions had been agreed with the Community for most of the technical problems, which could be taken off the shelf and used another time: this enabled the next negotiations to be quicker, and hence less vulnerable to political upsets on either side. Support among business and the Establishment was easier to summon up again. The federalists had also started to establish the infrastructure of specialist organisations which was an essential element in the success of the next campaign.[53] They had begun to widen their range of skills to deal with the problems which could now be seen as the Achilles heel of 1961–3: the Labour Party, the public, and the lack of resources. Those opposed to entry had been the first to take the European question to the people. The federalists were to repay them in their own coin in the 1970–2 negotiations and the referendum of 1975. As regards the Labour Party, the Campaign showed a sound sense of priorities for the future in allocating to the Labour Committee more than half of the nest-egg of some £4000 that remained after the negotiations had been broken off.[54]

Yet the federalists could be criticised – in particular for not having done more to confront the central issue of sovereignty. While Macmillan may have been impossible to shift from his preference for l'Europe des Patries – even if he could have been persuaded that it was impolitic to antagonise the federalists in the Community by so openly opposing their ideas – Gaitskell's mind was not closed, at least at the outset. While he said in the Commons debate on the decision to open negotiations that there was 'no question whatever of Britain entering into a federal Europe now', and that if the European Parliamentary Assembly were to be directly elected 'this would be a very long step towards a federal Europe', he also suggested that Britain's position might change 'twenty, fifty or a hundred years hence'.[55] But if a federal Europe might be acceptable for Britain twenty years hence (i.e., in the 1980s), it was at least arguable that steps should be taken in that direction. Even if there was no stopping Gaitskell's change of heart – and his widow later said that he might have changed back again[56] – there were many others who were sceptical about federalism yet open to arguments against national sovereignty and hence for moving towards a federal Europe.

This was indeed the idea behind Roy Pryce's book on *The Political Future of the European Community*. Michael Shanks and John Lambert took up the same theme in *Britain and the New Europe*, also published in 1962, which contained a chapter entitled 'Towards a United States of Europe'.[57] There they identified monetary union, security union and democratic control by the European Parliament as the major elements of such a federation. It was such thinking, beyond the customs union and the common agricultural policy, that was to give the federalists the key for a positive reaction to the consequences of the veto, as well as to the future of the enlarged Community in years to come.

12 Britain into Europe

On 22 January 1963, eight days after de Gaulle's veto on British entry into the Community, the Directing Committee of the Common Market Campaign met in Lord Gladwyn's flat in Whitehall Court. A framed letter in the General's handwriting stood on a side-table – in case anyone needed reminding of his existence. Lord Plowden suggested that the Campaign would have to close down as it would be very difficult to raise further funds. The federalists, on the contrary, were determined to fight on. Tommy Thompson, John Pinder, and John Leech all said so; and Martin Maddan, MP brought the welcome news that Britain in Europe wanted to continue, and perhaps to merge with the Campaign. Gladwyn, summing up, fell in with the federalists' proposals: to carry on by devising constructive pro-European policies while awaiting an opportunity to join; to combat xenophobic reactions in Britain; and to strengthen relations with the Europeans in the Community.[1]

JOINING FORCES

Martin Maddan's suggestion of merger made good sense. Britain in Europe had an income of over £10000 a year, based on corporate subscriptions, with which to pay for an office and a small staff. The initiative for founding both bodies had been taken by Federal Union's Regional Commission, whose members still occupied key positions in both. Norman Hart, John Leech, John Pinder, Roy Shaw and Tommy Thompson had no doubts about approving the merger at the last meeting of the Campaign's Directing Committee in March, along with Lord Gladwyn and the three MPs who were close to Federal Union – Jack Diamond, Roy Jenkins, and Peter Kirk.[2]

Within a month, the merger had also been approved by Britain in Europe's Annual General Meeting. Because the organisation's task had been to provide information to industry, apolitical industrialists predominated on its Council of Management. Apart from Martin Maddan as Hon. Treasurer and Tommy Thompson as Hon. Secretary, the only Federal Unionists on the Council at that time were Colin Beever and John Leech. With the merger, they were joined by Norman Hart, Uwe Kitzinger, Sir Anthony Meyer, John Pinder, and

Roy Shaw, as well as five Members of Parliament: Roy Jenkins, who became a Vice-President; Jack Diamond, Douglas Houghton and Peter Kirk, who joined the Executive Committee; and David Jones, a Conservative who, like Jenkins, Kirk and Maddan, was a Vice-President of Federal Union, and who became a member of the Council. Lawrence Robson, who had chaired Britain in Europe for over three years, now became Deputy Chairman to make way for Lord Gladwyn as Chairman, while Martin Maddan and Tommy Thompson continued as Hon. Treasurer and Hon. Secretary respectively. Two more Federal Unionists, Val Schur and Robert Jarrett, were General Secretary and Executive Secretary, while Sir Anthony Meyer together with Hugh Beesley continued to give voluntary help as they had for the Campaign.[3]

Although the federalists were again well placed in key positions the political line taken by the new merged body was less to their taste. Gladwyn was not willing to try to preach federalism to the British Establishment. He told the AGM that Britain in Europe, with the new political role brought to it by the Campaign, should aim for a political union that was less than a federation though more 'organic than a simple confederation'. This meant, he said, the use of Community techniques. But the policy statement which he had drafted, and which was approved by the AGM, called for 'the entry of the UK into a European Economic and Political Community . . . [and] for Britain's participation in a European Ministerial, Political and Defence Council . . . ; an independent political Commission to advise this Council . . . ; and greater powers for the existing European Parliament.'[4] A purely advisory Commission of this sort would lack the powers of the EEC Commission; and the whole proposed framework was intergovernmental, not federal, even if the 'greater powers' for the European Parliament, which then had almost none was a modest concession to the federalists. Gladwyn had, however worked loyally with the federalists throughout the campaign and they acquiesced in this policy for the new Britain in Europe. They still had Federal Union to fall back on, as well as time ahead in which to press for a policy closer to their aims.

THE CAMPAIGN FOR A EUROPEAN POLITICAL COMMUNITY

In Federal Union the reaction to the veto was vigorous and un equivocal. De Gaulle was clearly out to block Monnet's Community road towards federation, as well as Britain's chance to embark on it. The General should be countered by asserting the Monnet method and the federal goal. The editorial of the next issue of *World Affairs* was entitled 'Europe against de Gaulle': a 'statement of hope, not of fact' as the editorialist put it.[5] Britain, he argued, could change the balance of forces in Western Europe by adopting as its aim a federal Community with majority voting and European parliamentary control of the executive. In a book with the same title as the editorial, published for the Federal Trust later in the year and launched at a reception in the House of Commons with a few words from Roy Jenkins, John Pinder went into more detail. A political Community with federal institutions, he maintained, should control not only economic policy but also foreign policy and defence; the Economic Community and the Defence Community would be the two elements of a Political Community; Britain could relaunch Europe by aiming for such a Political Community, taking its first step in defence if de Gaulle persisted in debarring it from the EEC. These two elements of the EPC would be put together as soon as the veto was at last lifted.[6] This idea, like Gladwyn's, identified defence as the way round de Gaulle's roadblock, but the federalists insisted that intergovernmentalism was not enough if the Defence Community was to be effective and France's five partners were to be weaned away from their dependence on de Gaulle. Monnet, too, saw possibilities in the field of defence: when Britain failed to seize the opportunity, however, he tried to promote a mixed Allied deterrent, to be called the multilateral force, or MLF, which might have both Atlantic and European contingents; but this too failed to attract enough support.[7] When these more pragmatic proposals came to nothing, the federalists had some cause to feel that their preference for the longer-term radical strategy was the best on offer.

In pursuit of this longer-term strategy, Federal Union continued to cultivate its links with Continental federalists. In July 1963 a delegation comprising Sir Anthony Meyer, then chairing the Regional Commission, John Leech, Tommy Thompson and John Wakeham, by then Federal Union's Hon. Treasurer, went to a meeting of the Federal Committee of the Action Européenne Fédéraliste in Flanders, amid impressive public demonstrations in Bruges, Ghent, and Tielt. In October, Gladwyn led a delegation of Federal Unionists to an AEF conference in Luxembourg, again with Tommy Thompson and John Wakeham, but this time with Ota Adler, David Baker, Roy

Shaw, Julian Critchley, MP and Patrick McNally as well.[8] In the previous month, Gladwyn had tried out his own ideas on the international European Movement.[9] He had had a polite hearing, but his intergovernmental proposals were not what federalists on the Continent wanted to hear.

Even to these ideas, the British were less receptive still. In his presidential address to Britain in Europe's 1964 AGM, Gladwyn referred to some success on the Continent . . . but little success in this country. However, if 1963 had been politically barren for Britain in Europe, its educational and information activities had continued unabated. It had organised nine business conferences jointly with the Federal Trust: the speakers had included Edward du Cann, MP, William Rees-Mogg and Peter Shore, MP, as well as Max Kohnstamm, the Vice-President of Monnet's Action Committee for the United States of Europe. The Europe House lectures had gone ahead, with a politically brighter spot when François Mitterrand and Charles Hernu, who was to become Minister of Defence in Mitterrand's socialist government in the 1980s, served on a panel under Roy Jenkins's chairmanship. A new *Quarterly Review* was launched; and small grants were obtained from the Foreign Office, for exchange visits across the Channel, and from the EEC Commission, for educational work such as teachers' conferences on the Community. Britain in Europe also developed its role as a co-ordinating centre for special-interest organisations, for example enabling the Labour Committee to continue as an independent body using the services of Britain in Europe's secretariat, including those of Bob Jarrett as Secretary.[10]

A year later, in March 1964, Gladwyn returned to the charge, proposing that Britain in Europe set up a Political Committee, to include both 'those who believe in a Federal Europe and those who prefer a more pragmatic approach'.[11] By April John Pinder had drafted a policy declaration, not surprisingly more compatible with the federalists' thinking than the previous policy statement. This was just as well, for it was now that Federal Union was considering a split between its European and its world groupings. For the Europeans, a home in the better-funded Britain in Europe had its attractions, if 'the terms were right'. One such condition was precisely a suitable policy declaration. A second was that there should be a place for those individual members of FU who were European federalists. A third was that the new organisation should be affiliated to the AEF.

These conditions were met; and in June 1966 Britain in Europe and

Federal Union launched the Campaign for a European Political Community, which quickly produced a newsletter, a speakers' service, and regional groups in Birmingham, Manchester and Scotland. The Labour government had just made clear that it wanted to join the European Community,[12] so the atmosphere was receptive for the new Campaign's first big political venture, a declaration calling for British membership of the EEC and the creation of a European Political Community to include responsibilities for foreign policy and defence. This was signed by some 400 eminent people, including 150 MPs. The first political director of the Campaign, Roy Hattersley, MP, who had recently been part-time Director of Conferences for the Federal Trust and was later to become Deputy Leader of the Labour Party, was in his element organising such activities, but had to give it up the following year, when he obtained a post in the government; he was replaced by Donald Anderson, MP. At the Campaign's 1967 AGM Lord Gladwyn was elected Chairman; the Deputy Chairmen were Ota Adler, Jo Grimond, MP, Lord Harlech and Christopher Mayhew, MP; the Joint Treasurers were David Barton and Martin Maddan, MP, and the Joint Secretaries Norman Hart and Peter Kirk, MP. In addition to the Federal Unionists among the officers, the Committee included Christopher Layton, Sir Anthony Meyer, John Pinder, Noël Salter, Tommy Thompson and John Wakeham. The Conservatives, now in opposition, were represented not only by Harlech, Meyer and Wakeham, but also by Tufton Beamish, MP, Eldon Griffiths, MP, Ben Patterson and Lena Townsend; and, although the Labour Party's leaders serving in the government were mostly precluded, there was nevertheless a strong contingent from the Labour Committee, including MPs such as Tam Dalyell, Stanley Henig, Evan Luard, Kevin McNamara, Francis Noel-Baker, Charles Pannell, Ivor Richard, George Strauss, Alan Lee Williams and Sam Silkin.[13]

THE LABOUR COMMITTEE FOR EUROPE

By summer 1963, with the dowry from the Common Market Campaign and the secretarial services from Britain in Europe, the Labour Committee had converted itself from an *ad hoc* group occasioned by the negotiations for entry to a solid organisation on a permanent footing. This was reflected in its change of name from the Labour Common Market Committee to the Labour Committee for Europe –

recently again renamed the Labour Movement in Europe. Roy Jenkins was the Chairman, Jack Diamond the Hon. Treasurer, and Colin Beever remained the anchorman as Hon. Secretary. Shirley Williams and Bill Rodgers, by now an MP, continued to be involved as members. Others from the House of Commons included such federalists as Bob Edwards and the brothers John and Harry Hynd, while among the new blood were Tony Crosland, whose allegiance later proved less than unshakeable, John Strachey, a reformed character since writing his anti-federalist polemic in 1940,[14] and Herbert Morrison, who had said 'the Durham miners won't wear it' on being informed of the Schuman Plan in 1950, but who by 1954 had admitted to the Council of Europe's Assembly that 'our earlier approach was . . . too conservative' and envisaged that a series of agreements might be 'built up into . . . at any rate the beginning of federal governmental and parliamentary institutions in Western Europe'.[15] On the Committee too, to refute Morrison's earlier allegation of narrow provincialism, was the Durham miners' leader, Sam Watson, together with the other eminent miners' leaders, W. E. Jones and Sir Will Lawther, and Geoffrey Drain, who was to become Secretary General of the National Association of Local Government Officers, then Deputy Chairman of the European Movement in the 1980s. Federal Union was represented by John Bowyer, Norman Hart, Uwe Kitzinger and Roy Shaw.

The Labour Committee for Europe set about organising conferences, the first a high-level European one in Oxford, jointly with *Socialist Commentary*; arranging visits to Brussels; and publishing a new quarterly, *Europe Left*, which, like *Newsbrief* before it, was edited by Roger Broad. That same year Colin Beever published two studies on trade unions and Europe.[16]

The Labour Committee for Europe's efforts soon bore fruit. When Labour won the general election in 1964, no fewer than twenty of its members were in the government, five of them in the Cabinet.[17] In contrast with Labour's mood when Gaitskell had spoken to the Party Conference only two years before, the parliamentary party was reassuringly European. The Committee itself, with this exodus of senior people, had to appoint new officers: Austin Albu, MP (Chairman); Norman Hart and Shirley Williams, now an MP and soon to take over as Chairman of the Committee on Albu's appointment as Minister of State (Deputy Chairmen); Francis Noel-Baker, MP (Hon. Treasurer); and ensuring continuity, Colin Beever again as Hon. Secretary. Surprisingly soon, the Committee found itself supporting a Labour government's attempt to join the Community.

After the Labour government had strengthened its position following new elections in March 1966, George Brown and George Thomson, who had a quarter of a century before been chairman of Federal Union's Dundee branch, were given special responsibility for relations with Europe. George Brown became Foreign Secretary in August; and by the end of the year, he and the Prime Minister, Harold Wilson, began a series of visits to the capitals of Community countries in order to find out how they would react to a fresh application for membership.[18] Wilson's apprenticeship under Beveridge in the Federal Union Research Institute may now have stood him in good stead, for he slipped remarkably readily into his European role, telling the Council of Europe in Strasbourg, for example, that the alternative to the building of Europe would be 'industrial helotry' under American domination.[19] Even James Callaghan, as Chancellor of the Exchequer, admitted that 'the argument about sovereignty is rapidly becoming outdated',[20] an observation he might have done well to anticipate in 1962 and remember in 1971: on both occasions he helped the Labour Party to adopt a backward-looking posture.

In May 1967 the government delivered in Brussels its formal application for EC membership; and this time de Gaulle avoided the formality of negotiations by announcing his veto in five days flat. At the Labour Party Conference later that year, Labour nevertheless voted two to one in favour of the government's effort to join the Community, showing the effects that the Labour Committee for Europe had achieved – as well as the magnetic attraction of government policies for the party in power in Britain's confrontational political system.

GEORGE BROWN AND THE FEDERALISTS

In March 1968 George Brown was replaced by Michael Stewart as Foreign Secretary, thus becoming liberated from government office; and this was the occasion of an encouraging episode for British federalists.

In July, the Federal Trust organised a weekend conference bringing together some forty people from France, Germany and Italy as well as Britain to discuss ideas about new policies for Europe, at Sussex University's 'White House' conference centre in the leafy setting of the Isle of Thorns, near Harold Macmillan's home. John Pinder wrote a substantial paper for it, entitled 'The time has come for a more radical European policy', in which he argued that Britain should propose a European Political Community, its scope to include foreign policy and security, defence technologies and monetary policy, with institutions that would become federal by the end of a transitional period. The EEC would continue and would merge with the EPC once the veto on British entry was removed. The proposal was designed to outflank the General's impregnable position in the EEC, and his veto on British membership, by launching a community and eventually federal project in important fields where the EEC was not yet active.[21]

Altiero Spinelli, who was then a frequent participant at the Federal Trust's conferences, responded enthusiastically. Encouraged by this, the British federalists, now including Ernest Wistrich who had taken over at Britain in Europe and the Campaign for a European Political Community, and had participated in the White House meeting, decided to see if George Brown could be persuaded to promote the idea. Full of generous European impulses and, it may be surmised, still smarting from having his initiative for joining the Community rebuffed by de Gaulle, he was enthusiastic, and agreed to visit Brussels, Bonn, Paris, and Rome to explore the potential support. He went with Wistrich to Bonn, and with Pinder to Brussels (to see people in the Commission as well as the Belgian government), Paris (including a day with Monnet, Hirsch, Mayne and Uri at Monnet's farmhouse retreat near Paris), and Rome.

It was in Rome in November 1968 that George Brown really connected. Spinelli arranged meetings for him with the principal party leaders, as well as with the half dozen most important members of the government assembled at a lunch hosted by President Saragat, whom Brown harangued on the need for Italy to take the initiative in proposing a Political Community, to which Britain could respond. But it was his meeting with the veteran socialist leader, Pietro Nenni, that turned out to be seminal. Brown began, as at other meetings, by urging an initiative in the fields of defence, foreign policy, technology and money. Nenni expressed complete agreement and stressed that the Labour Party and the Italian Socialist Party should work together to this end. A few days later the prevailing government crisis was resolved by reshuffling jobs in the Italian government and, according to Spinelli with whom Nenni had a long talk, Brown's words were 'strongly in his mind' when he decided to accept the post of Foreign

Minister, in which he would be able to follow up these ideas with the Labour government. Immediately afterwards, Nenni asked Spinelli to become his adviser on European affairs.[22]

When he had completed his explorations inside the Community, George Brown delivered a speech on 6 March 1969 to a well-filled Grand Committee Room in the House of Commons at a meeting organised by Britain in Europe. He proposed negotiations to establish a European Political Community, with powers in the fields of foreign policy, defence, money and technology. There should be no veto in the Council; the European Parliament should have 'effective power over the instruments by which policy is made and executed'; and the executive, 'a Commission with stature and authority', should be controlled jointly by the Council and Parliament.

This degree of federalist precision about the institutions doubtless owed something to John Pinder, who drafted the speech; in a version published in two long articles in *The Guardian* of 7 and 8 March, the institutional detail was curtailed. But Brown had worked for hours on successive versions of the speech and was in full agreement with all that was in it. Next Sunday *The Observer* reported that the British government would not rebuff such proposals if they came from a Community member government, and that Italy was 'the favoured nation', particularly in view of the Italian state visit, due in the following month, when President Saragat was to visit London with Nenni.[23] The Foreign Secretary, Michael Stewart, while necessarily prudent, was sympathetic to George Brown's European ideas: with Roy Jenkins, the two of them later shared the presidency of the Labour Committee for Europe, and Stewart had ensured the help of embassies, provided correctly if warily, during Brown's Continental travels. The machinery was ready for an Anglo-Italian declaration during the State visit; and on the Italian side at least, the talk was of preparing a 'new Messina'.

But at the very moment when the two governments' representatives were working on the declaration, with Spinelli, who was accompanying Nenni, ever alert to promote the federalist cause, the news came through that de Gaulle had resigned after losing a referendum on regional decentralisation within France. So the focus of the Anglo-Italian Declaration of 28 April 1969 was swiftly shifted to the prospective enlargement of the Community. As a significant vestige of the discussions on political union, however, it retained a commitment to support direct elections to the European Parliament.[24] Those federalists who gave time to George Brown's apparently abortive travels are perhaps justified in thinking that the Anglo-Italian Declaration made it easier for the Labour government to accept direct elections at a time in the 1970s when the Party was hesitant about Europe.

EUROPEAN LINKS

The White House weekend meeting in July 1968 was one of a dozen or so that the Federal Trust organised between 1966 and 1970, three Anglo-Italian, three Anglo-French, one Anglo-German, one Anglo-Belgian, and five multilateral with participants from Britain and various Community countries.[25] They were held in a variety of environments calculated to lift the spirits: several at the White House; two at the conference centre sponsored by the Foreign Office at Wiston Park looking out at Chanctonbury Ring on the South Downs; two at Great Fosters, Egham, a Tudor hunting-lodge converted into a hotel; one at Saint George's conference centre alongside Saint George's Chapel inside the walls of Windsor Castle; and one in the impressive surroundings of Ditchley Park, where Churchill had stayed during the war.

The Ditchley Park meeting was the first, in February 1966. Somewhat ambitiously, it set the scene with a discussion on 'The Future of Europe'. The Continental participants included Georges Berthoin, who had introduced David Howell to the British federalists and was generally most helpful to them in those years; René Foch, a grandson of the great Maréchal Foch of World War I, now working at the Commission (where he was a colleague of Heinrich von Moltke, also a grandson of a famous World War I leader; he also took part in a Federal Trust conference); Schelto Patijn, who was to make his name as the Dutch MEP who became the European Parliament's rapporteur on direct elections; Fernard Spaak, son of Paul-Henri Spaak and later a Director-General in the Commission; and Altiero Spinelli, who took part in half the conferences of the series. There were also a few Americans: Miriam Camps, who in the US State Department had been 'present at the creation' of post-war European policy and whose books (written at PEP, Chatham House and the Council on Foreign Relations) established her as a leading authority on Britain's relations with the Community;[26] Leon Lindberg, who had been prominent in developing the neo-functionalist theory of Community evolution;[27] and Joe Slater, of the Ford foundation, who liked what he saw so much that he helped fund a number of the Federal Trust's activities in the next few years.

The British participants included a number of regulars. All ten authors of the previous year's special issue of the *Journal of Common Market Studies* were among them, including François Duchêne, David Howell, Christopher Layton, Richard Mayne, John Pinder and Roy Pryce, as were David Barton, Norman Hart, Roderick MacFarquhar, Diarmid McLaughlin (who became the Federal Trust's Director in 1966) and Tommy Thompson. These weekends enabled them to make friends with some of the brightest Continentals who were already becoming influential in the Community, and to acquire a feel for Community problems, policies and institutions that stood them in good stead during later efforts to join the Community and then to encourage constructive British attitudes within it. They also helped other British people to acquire some of the same experience. Like the regulars, the more occasional British participants came from many walks of life. The politicians who were either then or subsequently MPs included Peter Hordern, John MacGregor, Christopher Mayhew, Sir Anthony Meyer, Gerry Reynolds, Ivor Richard and Christopher Soames; future MEPs included Ben Patterson and Derek Prag; future ambassadors included John Robinson, John Thomson and Robert Wade-Gery; among the journalists were Ian Davidson of the *Financial Times* and Stephen Hugh-Jones of *The Economist*; academics included David Coombes, Geoffrey Denton (later Director of the Federal Trust and then of Wilton Park), Tim Josling, Uwe Kitzinger, John Marsh, Roger Morgan and Michael Steed. The intermingling of these with like-minded people from the Community built a solid basis of knowledge and generated a powerful brew of ideas.

The first encounter after Ditchley was at Poigny-la-Forêt, near Paris, where the Federal Trust group were invited in September 1966 by the Club Jean Moulin, a hive of constructive, radical, non-party political thinking. Etienne Hirsch and Pierre Uri, from Monnet's select group of advisers, were leading members and favoured the developing relationship with the Federal Trust. Among the Frenchmen who took part in one or more of the meetings, in addition to Hirsch and Uri, were Michel Albert, Michel Crozier, Simon Nora, Michel Rocard (later French Prime Minister), Robert Toulemon, and Marc Ullman of *L'Express*. The German participants included Peter Corterier, a member of the SPD Executive Committee; Karl-Heinz Narjes, then Chef de Cabinet to Commission President Walter

Hallstein and later himself a member of the Commission; Christoph Bertram and Christoph Sasse, both distinguished intellectuals; Graf Brühl, later the Federal Republic's Permanent Representative in Brussels; Franz Froschmaier and Karlheinz Neunreither, both to become Directors General in the Community institutions. Spinelli brought bright young members of the staff of his Istituto Affari Internazionali, including Cesare Merlini and Riccardo Perissich, and last but far from least his wife Ursula, who had shared his federalist work from Ventotene onwards. The Belgian group, led by former Prime Minister Théo Lefevre, included Alain Camu, from the Prime Minister's Cabinet, Guy Spitaels who was to become leader of the Socialist party, no less than two Secretaries-General of trade-union internationals – J. Kulakowski and T. Rasschaert – and Jacques Vandamme, then a Director in the Commission and later to be the Chairman of TEPSA, the Federal Trust's own international network of sister organisations, which emanated from these meetings. The Rt Hon. Christopher Soames, who came to the Anglo-Belgian meeting, seemed shocked that such important foreigners should spend their time with a less senior group of British; but the important foreigners seemed pleased to have found British with whose ideas they had an immediate rapport.

The discovery by these Continentals that there were a number of British people – not only the explicit federalists but also less committed politicians, officials, journalists, academics and businessmen – who could share their thinking was evidently quite a surprise after so many years of mutual incomprehension; and it must have influenced their attitude towards the successful British application to enter the Community that followed the departure of General de Gaulle. One striking example of such an effect occurred when Spinelli, by then a member of the EC Commission, chose Christopher Layton, with whom he had participated in several of these meetings, as his Chef de Cabinet even before Britain joined the Community.

The Federal Trust's series of weekend meetings is a good example of the British federalists' links with people and organisations inside the Community. Others were the relationships with Continental socialists fostered by Norman Hart and others in the Labour Committee for Europe, and the contacts made by Tommy Thompson and other Conservatives with their political counterparts across the Channel. Meanwhile, the British had a hand in a significant development in the relationships among the federalist organisations themselves.

Until Spinelli established his institute in the mid-1960s and began coming to the Federal Trust's conferences, the British federalists' links had for about a decade been with the Action Européenne Fédéraliste: contacts with the Spinellist international, the Mouvement Fédéraliste Européen, had been few and far between. But Spinelli's interest had been excited by the Federal Trust, and he may have passed the word to the MFE, because a British delegation was invited to an MFE conference in Trieste in October 1968. The delegation included Ernest Wistrich, temperamentally inclined to find common ground, who thought these differences between AEF and MFE were old history and suggested that a joint conference be held in London.

Almost exactly a year later, the conference was duly held in the well-equipped building of the International Coffee Organisation in Berners Street, well attended by delegates from both AEF and MFE. The conference was welcomed by Lord Gladwyn and opened by George Brown under the chairmanship of Professor Albertini, the President of the Italian section of the MFE. Brown made a very European speech, federalist to the extent of advocating the creation of European Ministers responsible to the European Parliament. He was followed by Nicholas Ridley, MP, who as a Cabinet Minister in the Thatcher government earned a reputation for expressing his opinions unvarnished. He said that the Council of Ministers, with the veto abolished, should become a European Senate; and, characteristically, that we must now approach federalism through the front door, not the back door. Then came Brugmans and Wistrich, from the AEF, and Hirsch and Spinelli, from MFE. Pinder summed up, identifying a wide measure of agreement between the two sides, and taking up Albertini's practical proposal that an informal group be appointed to plan future action.[28]

Wistrich turned out to have been right. People from the two sides, who had worked separately since their split in 1956, now found that their differences had dwindled with the years. Before long, co-operation in the informal group had broadened into a general desire to reunite. The AEF and MFE merged at a Congress at Nancy in 1972. Tommy Thompson chaired the statutes committee which defined the legal structure for the merged organisation and Etienne Hirsch became its first President. Some regret that it was named the

Union of European Federalists instead of the European Union of Federalists, as the federalists' international had originally been called a quarter of a century before. But what's in a name? The federalists were reunited in a single organisation; and in 1972, as in 1947, the British federalists had played a significant part in creating it.

FROM BRITAIN IN EUROPE TO THE EUROPEAN MOVEMENT

Britain in Europe had remained active in the years after the veto. In 1965, the Executive Secretary Bob Jarrett was able to report a quickening of interest in Europe, together with signs of a change in the attitude of the Labour government.[29] In mid-1966, as has been seen, the Campaign for a European Political Community was launched, sharing an office with Britain in Europe. But Jarrett was beginning to feel that he should move on. He resigned in June 1967, the month after the Labour government's application to join the Community was immediately vetoed; and Ernest Wistrich, an energetic, sanguine, 'sunny, imaginative, capable man',[30] who had sold his timber company to pursue a Labour political career, but just missed winning a seat in the 1966 election, was appointed Britain in Europe's Director. He had never been a member of Federal Union. But his wife Enid had once belonged to the students' branch at the London School of Economics and her advice had been sought by the Regional Commission on public administration aspects of the Community institutions;[31] and it turned out that he himself was a committed federalist.

During the lull between the first veto and the second application, corporate subscriptions had been hard to sustain. Britain in Europe's budget had fallen off to a rate of some £7000 a year, of which £2500 was the Foreign Office grant for exchanges across the Channel.[32] More money was needed. In line with the government's new European policy, Lord Chalfont tripled the Foreign Office grant. But the breakthrough came with a dinner chaired by Lord Gladwyn, with Valéry Giscard d'Estaing as the guest of honour, when £25 000 was raised. The next year, Wistrich went for bigger money, even if this time most of it was to be for related educational work through the European Educational Research Trust (EERT).

The starting-point was an invitation to Tommy Thompson to visit Lyon where M. Gordiani was arranging meetings for youth groups, under the exchange programme which the French and German governments were financing to the tune of several million pounds a year. Thompson, who had worked on similar projects for the European Youth Campaign in Paris in the early 1950s, and was the first Briton for several years to become involved with the current programme, returned to London convinced of the importance of such work. He initiated an effort to persuade government and industry of the need to finance youth programmes.[33] Britain in Europe, and Wistrich, got to work on the project. Jeffrey Archer, who has since become famous in more than one capacity, organised a very successful fund-raising dinner at the Guildhall in July 1969, with speeches from both Wilson and Heath, as Prime Minister and Leader of the Opposition respectively. The target was half a million pounds, and £450000 was in fact raised, mostly in the form of covenants to the EERT, but with substantial money for Britain in Europe itself.

While Britain in Europe was gathering financial strength and, together with the Campaign for a European Political Community, humming with activity, the UK Council of the European Movement, as it was then called, was at a low ebb. Sir Edward Beddington-Behrens, who had led it for many years, died towards the end of 1968. While Sir Edward had never had much time for the federalists, the Executive Committee now became open to the idea of a merger which had been mooted by Britain in Europe. After discussions between Lord Gladwyn, for Britain in Europe, and Duncan Sandys, MP for the European Movement, the two bodies moved towards a merger which was consummated in July 1969, under the new name of the British Council of the European Movement. Lord Harlech was the first Chairman, Sir Geoffrey de Freitas, MP was Deputy Chairman and Gladwyn and Sandys were Vice-Chairmen. Martin Maddan, MP was an Hon. Treasurer and David Howell, MP an Hon. Secretary. The General Purposes Committee included Ota Adler, Norman Hart, John Hynd, MP, Peter Kirk, MP, Christopher Layton, John Pinder. Ernest Wistrich and Denis Walwin Jones, who had been Director of the UK Council, became joint directors. But when Walwin Jones resigned in February 1970, the merger 'became in effect a takeover by the newer and more vigorous organisation'.[34]

The individual members of the Campaign, many of them former members of Federal Union, became members of the United Europe Association, which also contained some individuals formerly affiliated to the UK Council. The Association had the same officers as the British Council of the European Movement; and by June 1973 the distinction between Association and Movement was removed and the individual membership was transferred to the European Movement itself. The individual membership was first affiliated to the AEF, then, after the AEF and MFE merged in 1972, to the resulting Union of European federalists.

The crux of the matter for the federalists, when deciding their attitude towards the merger between Britain in Europe and the UK Council, would be the policy and principles of the new organisation. The old European Movement under Beddington-Behrens had 'tended to follow rather than lead government policy even in 1961'.[35] As late as November 1960, when the federalists were already busy with preparations for the Common Market Campaign, Beddington-Behrens had actually organised a prestige conference on how to consolidate the European Free Trade Association. Nor had Duncan Sandys' resistance to the federalists during the formation of the European Movement been forgotten. Yet the federalists were well placed during the merger negotiations. Tommy Thompson was still Hon. Secretary of Britain in Europe and Ernest Wistrich its Director. Ota Adler, David Barton, Norman Hart and John Pinder were on the Council of Management. Lord Gladwyn, it was true, preferred the Community institutions without their reform into a federal structure: but his views had moved on since 1963. A book he published at that time supported direct elections to the European Parliament; and he wanted the Community method, rather than a purely inter-governmental organisation, to be applied to foreign policy and defence, with the aim of creating a West European entity powerful enough to give the Americans confidence that they could withdraw their forces provided that the Russians did the same.[36]

Already before the merger, the British Council of the European Movement had, at a meeting in which Ota Adler, Sir Anthony Meyer, John Pinder and Tommy Thompson participated, adopted a resolution which showed how much ground the federalists had gained in the more generally communautaire circles that the Movement also encompassed. It called for a United States of Europe, whose institutions must embrace foreign policy and defence, as well as economic matters. They should be based on the principles of the Treaty of Rome, and their decisions should be taken by majority vote. There should be a democratically elected European Parliament with adequate powers.[37] 'Adequate' was perhaps a weasel word. For the federalists, it would not be legitimate to give the Community wide powers in economic policy, foreign policy and defence, without real control by the European Parliament, shared with a chamber of states which could be the Council of Ministers voting by majority; and the resolution should have made this clear to the British people, whose leaders had for too long preferred to evade the issue of national sovereignty. But direct elections, majority voting and 'adequate powers' seemed an acceptable minimum; and the fact that the two latter points went beyond what might reasonably be construed as 'the principles of the Treaty of Rome', which the resolution had also endorsed, could be written off as one of the customary costs of political compromise. So at least the federalists could reason when they approved the merger, in the interests of establishing a more powerful organisation and with the hope of firming up its policy later.

The British Council of the European Movement was duly set up in July 1969, with its membership organisation affiliated to the AEF; and the Movement's General Purposes Committee expressed its 'general acceptance' of the aims of the political declaration of the newly reunited Union of European Federalists in January 1973 – though the doubts of some members were reflected in the Committee's rider that within the British Movement there was 'full room for divergent views about our objectives and methods of achieving them'.[38] In the Executive Committee Duncan Sandys explained why he now felt he could go along with words which he had opposed so toughly in the past: federalism had become the usual word to describe the common objectives for the Community; but the specific form of a new type of European federalism and the steps towards its creation were a matter for debate within the European Movement.[39] Weasel words again or a genuine conversion? Despite a real rapprochement with the federalists, some equivocation doubtless still remained. The European Movement in Britain was to live with such ambiguity for the next two decades, during much of which time its energies were consumed by the battle for public support over joining and staying in the Community. The next phase of this battle was about to begin; and there is no doubt that the regenerated European Movement, with the federalists now in key positions, played a significant part in ensuring victory.

INTO THE COMMUNITY: ENSURING CONSERVATIVE SUPPORT

In April 1969 de Gaulle resigned from the French Presidency and on

9 November he died, coincidentally on Monnet's eighty-first birthday. Three weeks later the new President, Georges Pompidou, went to meet the heads of government of France's five Community partners in The Hague, and agreed to the principle of the Community's enlargement. The Labour government took its application off the shelf where it had been since 1967. The Community agreed to open negotiations in Luxembourg on 30 June 1970, and the relevant departments in Whitehall prepared all the necessary papers, which were approved by their Ministers, ready for the final Cabinet decision to hand the British negotiating position to George Thomson, who was to lead the negotiation on the British side.[40]

At the general election on 18 June 1970, Labour lost to the Conservative Party led by Edward Heath. A committed European, he had made his maiden speech in the House of Commons debate in June 1950 on the invitation to take part in the negotiations on the Schuman Plan. In it he had appealed to the government to go into the Schuman Plan to develop Europe and co-ordinate it in the way suggested.[41] Now, within ten days of forming his government, he had Geoffrey Rippon, MP in Luxembourg, leading the negotiation in the place of George Thomson, and evidently on the basis of the documents already approved by the outgoing Labour Ministers. Thus began the negotiation that finally achieved British membership of the Community on 1 January 1973.

The federalists saw the opening of negotiations as a great step towards British participation in a Community that they believed would eventually become a federation. They recalled the chief obstacles to success on the British side in 1961–3: doubts among the general public and the effect of these on a Labour Party that tended, when in Opposition, to oppose. There was clearly still a lot of work to be done, for throughout 1970 the opinion polls were showing around three times as many against joining the Community as were in favour.[42] This time, too, the Conservative government had a majority of only twenty-eight over the opposition parties. The 'anti-marketeers' among Conservative MPs numbered considerably more than this. Another lesson from 1961–3, moreover, was the danger of allowing worries about the management of party as well as public opinion to fix the government's attention too intently on safeguarding its domestic rear, at the expense of the negotiations themselves. It was up to federalists to focus on attitudes in the Conservative Party as well as in the Labour Party and the public.

Federalists of Conservative persuasion had already begun their preparations in the previous year, when they feared that the logic of opposition might strengthen the hand of the Conservative Antis should the Labour government have another chance to apply for entry, as de Gaulle's weakening position, and eventually his resignation in April 1969, had made increasingly likely. These preparations were far enough advanced for the European Forum to be founded, with a mission similar to that of the Labour Committee for Europe on the other side, in the month after de Gaulle resigned.[43] David Baker, now an Alderman, was the founding Chairman, flanked by two other former members of Federal Union's Regional Commission, Tommy Thompson as Vice-Chairman and Martin Maddan, MP as Hon. Treasurer; and the Forum was run from the office of Britain in Europe – soon to become the office of the merged European Movement – at Chandos House in Buckingham Gate. Activities in the first year included arranging speakers for Conservative meetings, drafting constituency motions for the 1970 Party Conference, establishing a study group on the sensitive issue of the Common Agricultural Policy, drawing up guidelines for questions in the House of Commons, organising dinners there, and holding conferences with Centre-Right parties in the Community, particularly in France.

Tommy Thompson had in the past worked closely with André Voisin, the President of the AEF's French affiliate, including the preparation of the spectacular conference at Wiesbaden in 1959. Between them they did much to bring together Conservatives and people from the like-minded parties in France (then called the 'majority parties', because they provided the majority for the government in the Assemblée Nationale), in order to increase mutual understanding for European problems and to pave the way for British membership of the Community. The operation was facilitated by the International Committee of the Conservative Party, then headed by Lady Diana Elles, later to become Baroness Elles and a Vice-President of the European Parliament; and it prospered to the point where a Liaison Committee was set up to consolidate the links between the Forum and the French majority parties. Since the coming negotiations were to hinge on the understanding between Heath and Pompidou, and since this could have been harder to achieve if their respective supporters had not felt at ease with each other, the work of the Liaison Committee was particularly important. Here again, the federalists' European links were a considerable asset in bringing the British back towards the Continental mainstream.

The Forum's first Annual General Meeting, soon after the Conservative victory in the June 1970 election, already counted fourteen MPs among those present. With the negotiations getting under way, the Forum's role had rapidly increased. Its name was changed to the more self-explanatory title of Conservative Group for Europe (CGE). In view of the forthcoming battle in Parliament, moreover, it seemed necessary to bring more MPs into the Forum's direction. David Baker stood down as Chairman in favour of Tufton Beamish, MP; and in all there were ten MPs among the officers and committee members, although Tommy Thompson remained Vice-Chairman until 1973, after the negotiations had been successfully completed. With Maddan still as Treasurer and Baker still active, the federalists continued to play an important part; and the now quasi-federalist European Movement gave the Group the resources to enable it to function effectively, providing over two thirds of the income of some £6500 in 1971/2. With this the CGE intensified its activities. Of particular interest for federalists was an address to the Young Conservatives by Hans Nord, who had established a Federal Union branch in the Netherlands soon after the war and was one of the founders of the European Union of Federalists in 1946–7; he was now Secretary-General of the European Parliament. More directly germane to the eventual House of Commons decision on the negotiations, the CGE (underpinned by the European Movement) provided the infrastructure for the operation run by Norman St John-Stevas, MP to muster support among Conservative MPs, which eventually whittled down the Conservative vote against entry to a manageable thirty-two, with two abstentions.

THE CAMPAIGN FOR ENTRY

The balance of three to one against in the opinion polls was a legacy of resentment at de Gaulle's second veto. Until May 1967, when he announced it, there had for two years been an equally large majority in favour of joining the Community.[44]

The federalists reasoned that the tide of opinion could surely be turned again; indeed it had to be done if the debacle of 1961–3 was not to be repeated. Ernest Wistrich and the officers of the European Movement discussed with Labour Ministers the need for a public relations campaign to this end early in 1970, when the Wilson government was preparing to revive its application. When Wilson was replaced by Heath in June, the new government picked up these discussions along with the negotiating dossiers; and it was soon agreed that the government would co-operate with the campaign.[45]

This time, in contrast with 1961–3, the federalists were determined not to let the campaign be outgunned by the Antis through lack of resources. Thanks to the Guildhall dinner, the income of the European Educational Research Trust was some £75000 in 1969/70, and a little less in each of the following two years. While this was sizeable, the EERT was a charitable trust whose money could be used only for apolitical activities such as youth exchanges and seminars. The annual income of the European Movement itself was less than half as much, up to the financial year 1971/2. Then, given a fair wind by Heath, the EM managed to raise an additional sum of some £850000 from two or three big donations. Expenditure rose in 1971/2 to £644374. The Antis decried the unfairness of this; but they had not mentioned fairness when they had the resources to distribute nearly two million leaflets in 1961–3. This time the boot was on the other foot. There was to be no shortage of money for the pro-entry campaign.

Nor was there a lack of intelligence in planning it. The first step was the analysis of a survey of public opinion, undertaken by Social and Community Planning Research.[46] The conclusions drawn by the European Movement not only provided a framework for the campaign, but were also of intrinsic interest to federalists. Of the eight themes identified as likely to find favour with the public, three were bread-and-butter issues (living standards, social welfare, social security), against four which related to political union (British participation in decision-making, strength through unity, peace and security, and Britain's world role), with one somewhere between (trade-union links). The emphasis of the arguments in the political union category was, to be sure, on British influence within it; and given the popular character of the campaign, it was natural that this aspect should be stressed. But federalists could note, for future reference, that these concerns could equally become the basis of an eventual campaign for federal institutions.

In order to persuade the public that British economic problems and political influence required Community membership, the European Movement (EM) established a Campaign Group which met weekly during the critical year leading up to the approval of entry by the House of Commons at the end of October 1971. The Group was led by Ernest Wistrich, who directed the staff of enthusiasts, mainly young, many of them federalists or sympathisers, like Stanley Henig and Alan Lee Williams, who had lost their Labour seats in the Commons in the June elections. Norman Hart looked after the public relations for the Labour Committee for Europe and Roland Freeman for the Conservative Group for Europe, both combining partnership in their public relations firms with membership of their respective party group and, in Norman Hart's case, with his record of holding many offices in Federal Union and its successor organisations. Philip Zec, who had been the *Daily Mirror*'s famous wartime cartoonist and then Editor of the *Sunday Pictorial*, brought his remarkable talents to the team.

The specialist groups, most of them initiated by the federalists during the 1960s, had flourished and proliferated. Several were accommodated in Chandos House, where they were serviced by Wistrich's staff: the United Europe Association, the Campaign for Europe, the European Luncheon Club; the European Educational Research Trust; the British Section of the Council of European Municipalities; the Conservative Group for Europe, the Labour Committee for Europe, the Trade Union Committee for Europe; Young European Left, the Young European Management Association, the Committee of European Student Associations. These and a number of others, such as the Liberal European Action Group, together comprised a vast hive of activity, centred on the European Movement.

In addition to these closely related organisations, the EM liaised closely with the government's own co-ordinating group, which normally met in the Foreign Office; and the EM's relationships with the media went into top gear with its 'media breakfasts'. At these a varying group of Movement people and media people met at weekly intervals in the Connaught Hotel.

The EM's reach was enormously enhanced through these relationships with the associated organisations, the government and the media. But it generated an immense output on its own account. Whereas in 1962 the Common Market Campaign had been outdone by the 237 meetings organised by the Anti-Common Market League, this time the Antis' effort was exceeded by up to four thousand meetings organised by the EM, 700 in July 1971 alone. Six and a half million items of literature were distributed, including a tabloid called *The British European*, whose issue of July/August 1971 rose to one million copies. The tabloid's style, which owed much to Philip Zec's experience at the *Mirror* and the *Pictorial*, did not suit everyone: a committed pro-Community MP returned a consignment of the fourth issue protesting that it was 'totally unsuitable for Beckenham'.[47] The campaign was not, indeed, short on razzmatazz. Students demonstrated outside the House of Commons with flaming torches and a jazz band. A pop group called The Unity made a disc of the campaign song, 'Got to get in to get on'. Advertisements were supported by signatories as diverse as Petula Clark, Jilly Cooper, Jimmy Greaves, Yehudi Menuhin (who had spoken at Federal Union meetings after the war), Mary Quant, Henry Cooper, the heavy-weight champion, and Jack Solomons, the legendary boxing promoter. The Liberal European Action Group inserted, alongside one of the Antis' advertisements in *The Times*, their own counter-advertisement: 'Also against the Common Market: Communist Party of Great Britain, the League of Empire Loyalists, the National Front, the IRA, the Right Honourable Enoch Powell, MP, the Union of Soviet Socialist Republics'. Evidently the federalists and their friends were no longer confined to the decorous and the highbrow.

That did not mean that they had abandoned the world of books and studies where they had won such an ascendancy in the past. On the contrary, about a dozen books favourable to British entry had been produced by 1972, almost all by authors who had been involved in the work of the Federal Trust or of Federal Union and its successors.[48] As for studies and high-level seminars, the Federal Trust ran five study groups and organised twenty one-day or two-day meetings in 1971. One of these was held in May, timed to bring the results of studies to bear at a critical juncture in the negotiations.

A few weeks earlier, Andrew Shonfield, Director of Chatham House, had observed signs of a loss of nerve about the negotiations among Permanent Secretaries of key departments in Whitehall. He asked John Pinder what could be done; and the result was a two-day Federal Trust Conference, chaired by Sir Alex Cairncross, until recently the Economic Adviser to the Treasury, attended by some fifty leading academic, business and government economists, and put together with extraordinary speed by Diarmid McLaughlin, the Director of the Trust. The key was the existence of half a dozen major studies on the chief topics at issue in the negotiations – agriculture, the balance of payments, industry, macroeconomic effects, taxation, trade – undertaken by economists known to the Federal Trust and by then virtually completed but not yet published. These were the basis for a set of papers providing a comprehensive assessment of what was at stake for the British economy, which fortunately for the federalists added up to a resounding endorsement of the economic case for membership. Samuel Brittan, whose influential weekly articles in the *Financial Times* had for some months been located on the fence, was convinced enough to come down the following week unequivocally on the side of entry; and other economists from the government and from journalism were impressed in a similar way.

The conference papers were edited by John Pinder and published as a book three months later.[49] But by then there had been a meeting of minds between Heath and Pompidou in Paris; the negotiations had been completed, and the opinion polls, thanks in no small measure to the efforts of Wistrich and his team at the European Movement, had returned to a fairly even balance between for and against. The focus of the drama shifted to the House of Commons, which was to vote in October on the principle of entry on the terms negotiated.

THE LABOUR COMMITTEE AND THE VOTE ON 28 OCTOBER

The Conservative majority in the Commons was substantially less than the number of Conservative MPs who appeared likely to vote against; so the Treaty of Accession could not be ratified without Labour votes. Yet the Labour Party Conference, shortly before the crucial Commons debate on 28 October on the decision to enter on the terms negotiated, voted by five million to one million to reject entry on those terms. How many Labour MPs would vote against Conference? Clearly, the spadework of the Labour Committee for Europe over the years, as well as during the negotiations, was now going to be put to the test.

Until 1970, the Labour Committee for Europe, originating 'by Federal Union out of the Campaign for Democratic Socialism', had been doing a quiet but effective job on a budget of £2–3 thousand a year.[50] By early 1971, however, its membership list included ninety MPs. It organised ten rallies in September 1971, to counter the seventeen rallies organised by the National Executive Committee, which had by then come down on the other side; and it arranged a meeting at the Party Conference where the speakers included Roy Jenkins who, because of his leading role in favour of British membership, was precluded from speaking in the Conference itself. Meanwhile the Trade Union Committee for Europe had been founded in 1970, with Tom Bradley of the Transport Salaried Staffs

Association as its Chairman, Alan Lee Williams as Secretary and Geoffrey Drain among the most active members.

The Labour Committee for Europe thus provided a basis for the mobilisation of Labour MPs' support, led by Roy Jenkins and organised by Bill Rodgers. In the event they secured 69 votes for entry and 20 abstentions in the vote on 28 October, bringing the majority in favour to 112. This result also owed much, of course, to the Conservative Group for Europe, whose missionary work in the Conservative Party had facilitated the task of the government whips. But the true heroes of the occasion were the Labour Europeans and above all Roy Jenkins. The federalists could justly feel some satisfaction that Rodgers had originally become involved through being first editor of the Common Market Campaign's *Broadsheet* in 1962 and an early member of the Labour Committee, while Jenkins's commitment dated from his initial exposure to Community affairs as Vice-President, then Vice-Chairman of the National Council, of Federal Union.

When Britain joined the European Community on 1 January 1973, the government gave a magnificent banquet in Hampton Court for those who had been involved in the campaign for entry. The veterans of Federal Union's Regional Commission were well represented, together with many of their more recently acquired federalist friends. Edward Heath took care that a number of the federalists who had been most deeply involved were admitted to the Order of the British Empire in the New Years Honours (some thought it would on this occasion have been more aptly called the Order of Britain in Europe). But there was little inclination to dwell on past achievements. The federalists wanted to make sure that Britain became a constructive member of the Community, willing to develop it into the federal structure they had always envisaged, with majority voting in the Council, a proper share of power for the European Parliament, and responsibility for foreign policy and defence as well as for trade and economic policy. Net assets of some £200000 still remained with the EM in April 1973, enough to finance such work for some time ahead. But the Labour Party which had opposed entry became the government in March 1974; and the European Movement found that it had on its hands another battle for public support over the principle of membership.

In the run-up to the election, Harold Wilson had already seen a referendum as a means of avoiding a Labour Party split. In this he succeeded for the time being, although Roy Jenkins was unable to stomach the device and resigned the recently acquired position of Deputy Leader of the Labour Party – a harbinger of the more serious split that was to come in the 1980s. Having won the election on this basis, the Wilson government proceeded to 'renegotiate the terms' of membership, and having gained a few largely cosmetic improvements, put the question whether to accept or reject membership to the electorate, with a government recommendation to accept, but at the same time leaving the Labour Party members, MPs and Ministers free to campaign against.

The situation looked dangerous because, after becoming more favourable when the Treaty of Accession was ratified, the public had now shifted on to the newly joined Community the blame for the jump in prices that followed the oil shock at the end of 1973; and in mid-1974, a year before the referendum, the polls showed two to one in favour of withdrawal. Although the common agricultural policy was to blame for only a small part of the rise in prices, the Antis scented an advantage arising from their stress on the question of food prices during the entry campaign. It was clear that the federalists and the European Movement, instead of trying to build for the future had to hit the campaign trail again.

This time there was no help from the government. But Wistrich and the European Movement now had the experience of the recent entry campaign to their credit, and they lost no time before launching a repeat performance.[51] Planning began in May 1974, a good year before the referendum. During the summer, seven million leaflets were distributed to half the households in the country, seeking helpers for the campaign. As a result some 12000 volunteers set up 475 local campaign groups. Specialist groups were established on a yet wider scale than last time, ranging from Christians for Europe to Communists for Europe – a *jeu d'esprit* that was quite embarrassing for the official, and still far from Eurocommunist, Communist Party. There were rallies, demonstrations and stunts as before. A significant new development was the substantial number of information campaigns conducted by companies, helped by pro-European trade unionists, among their employees.

The enthusiasm generated amongst the pro-Europeans was, in Wistrich's words, 'quite astonishing'. Long-standing party political opponents worked harmoniously for the common cause. This applied equally at the national level where the campaign was led by Roy Jenkins down to the 475 local groups which were deliberately formed to ensure an all-party balance in their direction.[52] The result was another famous victory. The two-to-one against was swung round to a vote of two-to-one in favour of continued membership. The European Movement was again left with a substantial nest-egg and with a lot of new members from among the volunteer helpers.

Unfortunately, this was still not the last of the battles about British membership. Soon after going into opposition again, the Labour Party reverted to its hostile stance; the 1980 Party Conference voted massively for unconditional withdrawal. One result was to stimulate the creation of the Social Democratic Party, which contained many of the Labour Europeans, from Roy Jenkins, Bill Rodgers and Shirley Williams to federalist stalwarts such as Colin Beever, Norman Hart and Ernest Wistrich. Meanwhile the Labour Party was committed to withdraw if it should win the 1983 general election.

The European Movement is an all-party organisation; and it could not oppose any of Britain's democratic parties as such. But it could campaign against a policy of withdrawal from the Community; and so it did. Yet another campaign was launched on the question of membership: the fourth, counting the Common Market campaign of 1961–3. This time the emphasis was more on information about the risk to jobs in the export industries.[53] Opinion polls towards the end of 1982 showed, once again, a majority for withdrawal. Once again, the EM's campaign contributed to swinging public opinion round until there was, according to polls at the time of the June 1983 election, another two-to-one majority for staying in. Had Labour won, this would have given a strong argument to those who wanted to avoid withdrawal. As it was, the anti-Europe policy was itself a major cause of Labour's defeat. Being a prime reason for the split with the SDP, this policy contributed to the formation of the Alliance, which split the non-Conservative vote almost equally with the Labour Party. The Labour Party later gradually distanced itself from its commitment to withdrawal. The series of membership campaigns has, it seems, at last been concluded with Britain inside the Community for good.

By the mid-1980s, then, the British federalists and the organisations they had created had won three great campaigns to secure public support for Community membership. They had raised over £5 million, and distributed some fifteen million pieces of literature. Popular campaigning on this scale was unprecedented among the European federalist movements.

But for too much of the time the price had been a narrow focus on the question of British membership of the European Community, to the detriment of broader thinking and of action to develop the Community in a federal direction.

It was not that the effort of persuasion over the years had no effect: by 1987, one-quarter of the British wanted the Community to become a federation or a 'single country'; and 52 per cent were in favour of the evolution of the EC to a United States of Europe.[54] The proportions in the six founder member countries, however, were higher. The British federalists could well feel that much had been achieved. But much still remained to be done.

13 Towards Federation?

Even while the European Movement had been engaged in the series of campaigns to ensure British membership of the European Community, the Federal Trust – which as an educational charity had to steer clear of the political battle – had begun to turn its attention to questions about the Community's long-term development. To do such forward thinking, the Trust came to rely more on research and study groups than on the conferences through which it had disseminated knowledge about the Community in the 1960s. But the Trust avoided isolation from the pragmatic contemporary British mainstream by focusing many of its studies on specific Community policies or institutions rather than on more general ideas about the European Union of the future.

STEPS TO MONETARY UNION

The Trust had established itself in the field of European and international monetary policy long before it entered its period of study groups and policy studies. Three major conferences in the 1960s attracted a galaxy of finance ministers, bank governors, and international economic super-stars. The British speakers included Lord Cromer, Jack Diamond, Harold Lever, Reginald Maudling, Eric Roll, and Andrew Shonfield. Among the Continentals were Raymond Barre, Robert Triffin, Pierre Uri, and Jacques Rueff, former Governor of the Banque de France and adviser on monetary matters to President de Gaulle. Rueff had taken part in the meeting between Frenchmen and British Federal Unionists in Paris in the spring of 1940; and at a dinner after the conference in May 1965 there was a memorable exchange between Triffin, the federalist, adviser to Monnet and convinced protagonist of a European currency and central bank, and Rueff as adviser to de Gaulle and a latter-day defender of the gold standard. Thus the Trust had the connections required to set up an effective study group on international and European monetary policies when the time seemed ripe. De Gaulle's resignation as President of France opened up the potential for new European developments in which Britain could play its part.

When President Georges Pompidou accepted the principle of the

Community's enlargement at his meeting with the heads of government of the other five member states in December 1969, this was part of a deal that also included the principle of economic and monetary union. In 1970 the Commission published the Werner report,[1] which recommended the early establishment of a modest exchange rate co-ordination among the Community currencies and the permanent fixing of parities by 1980, or the replacement of the existing currencies by a European currency, with scant attention paid to the intermediate steps. But the plan was soon wrecked in the currency upheavals of that period, amid recriminations among the member states. Concerned that Britain, on joining the Community, should be able to participate in constructive steps towards economic and monetary union, the Federal Trust set up a study group in 1971 to think of ways to achieve it.

The group was chaired by Charles Villiers, Chairman of Guiness Mahon merchant bankers, and the joint rapporteurs were Giovanni Magnifico, the Banca d'Italia's representative in London, and John Williamson, who had recently moved from the Treasury to be Professor of Economics at the University of Warwick. Magnifico, who had an inventor's creative energy, was generating the idea of a parallel currency which would develop alongside the existing currencies for both private and official uses. Williamson, in full sympathy with this approach, was able to clarify it and expound it in terms that made sense to all who interested in the subject. Their report, *European Monetary Integration*, published in 1972, stimulated thinking on both sides of the Channel, and reassured some of those on the Continental side that the people on the island side were capable of focusing their minds on subjects other than the Community budget and the price of butter. Magnifico and Williamson were, moreover, among the first to foreshadow some of the developments and major proposals of the 1980s: a European reserve fund; a European currency unit; an intervention role to stabilise its exchange rate with the dollar; encouragement of its use in the private sector, with the reserve fund as lender of last resort; and harmonisation of member states' monetary policies.[2] The idea was tested out with a group of sympathetic specialists from Britain's prospective Community partners at a weekend meeting at the Conference Centre at St George's, Windsor in October 1971; and the report was launched at a conference jointly sponsored by the *Financial Times*, the *Investors Chronicle* and the Federal Trust in February 1972, when the speakers included the Chancellor of the Exchequer and the Governor of the Banca d'Italia.

The momentum was maintained for a time, with study groups leading to the publication in 1974 of three reports on the implications of monetary integration.[3] But currency storms, economic troubles and the British renegotiation and referendum distracted attention from further steps through most of the 1970s. After 1974, the Trust turned more towards work on industrial, employment and social policies, until Roy Jenkins as President of the Commission successfully initiated the European Monetary System in 1979, in particular enlisting the support of Germany and France. With Britain four years later still outside the System's central feature, its exchange rate mechanism, the Trust returned to the subject with a new study group chaired by David Howell, by now a former Cabinet Minister. The group's report, written by David Lomax of the National Westminster Bank and published by the Trust in 1984, bore the title *The Time is Ripe* – reflecting the government's stated policy that sterling would enter the mechanism when the time was ripe. The report's conclusion was that the arguments which had led the government to regard the time as unripe were no longer valid.[4] Yet despite another prestigious Federal Trust conference to launch the report[5] and a convergence of financial, industrial, and Whitehall opinion on the view taken by the Trust's group, the government still persisted in keeping its distance from the Community's monetary integration. Reasoning that a broader and longer view might be better understood, the Trust reconstituted the study group, again under David Howell's chairmanship, to consider steps beyond the exchange rate mechanism and towards economic and monetary union. The new report, *Paving the Way: Next Steps for Monetary Cooperation in Europe and the World*, by John Young of Lloyds Bank, was published in 1987. It considered different routes to monetary union and the relevance of the Deutsche Bundesbank and the US Federal Reserve Board system to the constitution of a European central bank.

AGRICULTURE AND THE BUDGET

The Federal Trust was likewise one of the first to suggest a shift in the Community's agricultural policy from price support to income support. Already in 1958 the Trust was holding conferences on agriculture and the Community, and in 1965 one of its conference speakers was Sicco Mansholt, the Dutch Commissioner who had by then triumphantly succeeded in establishing the common agricultural policy – but was afterwards, unfortunately, less successful in his efforts to reform it. By the later 1960s, the Trust had identified such reform as crucial for both Britain and the Community as a whole; and in 1969 it set up a study group on the subject, with John Marsh as its rapporteur. In 1970, he produced his report on *A New Agricultural Policy for Europe*.[6] The report's main proposal, to shift the policy from price support to income support, was then seen as original and, by many Continentals, as impossible. But the Trust stuck to its theme, with conferences at intervals in the 1970s and early 1980s; and income support is now a respectable idea which is becoming part of Community policy for reforming agriculture and the budget.[7]

Not all the Federal Trust's studies could be devoted to long-term strategic thinking. The rapid deployment of new results of economic research on Britain and the Community seemed necessary, for instance, at a critical point in the negotiations in spring of 1971. Later, when agriculture and the budget were at the heart of controversies both between Britain and its Community partners and regarding the Labour Party's policy of withdrawal, Geoffrey Denton, then Director of the Trust, wrote reports on the Community budget and on the economics of British membership 'revisited'.[8] But it was the exception for the Trust's work to be so closely geared to throwing light on immediate political crises. The Trust's experience showed that good ideas and significant new constellations of facts do not usually commend themselves immediately to politicians, but that patient persistence can work. A similar degree of faith and hope was certainly appropriate to ideas about European institutions.

INSTITUTIONS

It is not true, as is sometimes alleged, that British federalists have tried to ignore the Community's institutions. In 1970 the Federal Trust set up a study group on direct elections to the European Parliament, followed in 1971 by one of the Community institutions more generally. It organised three conferences on the subject before Stanley Henig produced the study group's report, published in the *Journal of Common Market Studies* in 1974.[9] The report of the next study, on the Presidency of the EC Council, was written by Geoffrey

Edwards and Helen Wallace and published in 1977.[10] Meanwhile the Trust had applied itself to the practical problems of presidency, organising a weekend discussion near Dublin in January 1975, where an Irish group led by the then foreign Minister Dr Garret FitzGerald, which was preparing for the first Irish presidency later that year, probed the knowledge of the Federal Trust's team. FitzGerald declared the occasion 'enormously useful'; and pre-presidential colloquia have since become a feature of the programme of TEPSA (Trans-European Policy Studies Association, the Federal Trust's European network), in relation to a number of member countries, including the Federal Republic of Germany in 1987, Spain in 1988 and France in 1989.

Direct elections to the European Parliament were not only, in the federalists' view, democratically necessary: they were also an essential building block for a federal constitution. A Federal Trust study group broached the subject in 1970, with Michael Steed as rapporteur; this made one of the first comparisons of the various systems that could be used by the Community; and a report on the subject was published in 1972.[11] In September 1974, when Britain was again preoccupied with its internal quarrel about membership, President Valéry Giscard d'Estaing told Jean Monnet that he wanted the Community to fix a date for direct elections to the European Parliament.[12] The Union of European Federalists played a significant part in securing support for direct elections in several countries, paving the way for the final decision to hold them.[13] In July 1977, after much lobbying by the European Movement, the House of Commons approved elections by 394 votes to 147.[14] In the three years before the first direct elections in June 1979, the Federal Trust held a score of seminars, organised for the most part in conjunction with universities, in places as far apart as Aberdeen and Reading, Edinburgh and Exeter, Birmingham and Belfast, to help prepare the public for this new experience. Papers were prepared on the issues likely to feature in the elections and on the parties' preparations for them; and after the elections were over, the Trust published a report to help the drawing of conclusions for future use.[15]

One consequence of the elections was that Altiero Spinelli, convinced of the need for a European Union with federal characteristics, persuaded many Members of the newly elected European Parliament to support the drawing-up of a Draft Treaty for a European Union, for the Parliament to present to the member states. MEP members of the European Movement in Britain who, from federalist conviction, played an important part in creating the Draft Treaty included Christopher Jackson and Derek Prag. In 1986, after Spinelli's death, the MEPs established an inter-party federalist group to continue to promote the European Union project. Bill Newton-Dunn was one of the half a dozen founder-members. The British European Movement at successive Annual Congresses passed resolutions supporting the European Union project. Since Spinelli had derived his ideas from the early literature of Federal Union and its Research Institute, the Federal Trust could hardly fail to react to his initiative. The report of a Trust study group was published as a New Europe paper, *Towards European Union*, and discussed at the Congress of the European Movement in 1983; Vernon Bogdanor wrote a report for a joint group of the Federal Trust and the European Centre for Political Studies; and Roy Pryce, who became the Trust's Director in 1983, led a study for TEPSA that resulted in a book on *The Dynamics of European Union*, in which he argued for a better understanding of the forces that might promote the project.[16]

The intergovernmental conferences set up by the European Council to deal with European Union gave birth, not to any such Union, but to the Single European Act. In a paper for discussion in the Federal Trust and TEPSA, John Pinder analysed the difference between the existing Community, the Single European Act, a European Union, and a European federation.[17]

The Single Act gave the Community a better chance to complete its internal market. To take the Community from there to European Union, three main elements would be required: economic and monetary union; public finance union, or Community tax powers sufficient for an adequate budget; and co-decision by the European Parliament and the Council, creating a two-chamber legislature instead of the monocameral legislation by government representatives as at present. If integrated security forces were placed under the Union institutions, it would become a European federation. Pinder's conclusion was that the transition from Community to Union would need reforms that were not hard to envisage in practical political terms and quite likely to be undertaken in the 1990s.

ONE EUROPE IN ONE WORLD

While its sense of the practicable led the Federal Trust to concentrate its work for some three decades mainly on the European Community, the world federal ideal that had also motivated Federal Union was never forgotten. Increasingly, however, the Trust's interest in world order was expressed through study of the Community's role in the world: as the founding Congress of the European Union of Federalists had put it in 1947, 'One Europe in One World'.

In the world as it is, composed of sovereign states and dominated by the superpowers, the peoples of the Community have to accept responsibility for their security; and the Trust included the theme of a common European foreign and defence policy from the outset of its 'era of study groups' in the late 1960s. To keep the balance between studying the problems of living in the world as it is and looking at ways to improve its political structure, the Trust was soon also occupied with studies of the prospects for a European Security Conference and for East–West relations in general.

Sir Bernard Burrows was a key figure in all this work. A schoolfriend of one of the founders of Federal Union, Derek Rawnsley, and always sympathetic to the federal idea, he had ended his distinguished diplomatic career in 1970 as the Permanent British Representative to the North Atlantic Council. Attracted to the Trust's work on foreign policy and defence, he became a member of its Council in 1972, and its Director-General from 1973 to 1975. Since then he has remained a Consultant to the Trust. Working conditions at the Trust were hardly ambassadorial: the sharing of tiny offices and rickety desks, the constant coming and going and ringing of telephones. But all this he accepted without complaint; and he achieved a tremendous amount. 1971 saw two conferences, on West European defence co-operation and on joint arms procurement in Europe; in the next year came Burrows's first book, written with Christopher Irwin, Deputy Director of the Trust, on a common European defence policy.[18] Later in the 1970s the European Movement asked the Trust to square the circle: that is, to study the idea of a European defence force or other means of defence co-operation and if possible to reconcile all shades of opinion on the subject. Burrows again chaired a working party; and the report, published in 1979, was able to show a wide measure of agreement that defence co-operation among the countries of Western Europe should be strengthened, although views diverged about the Community's role. Burrows then wrote another book, with Geoffrey Edwards, and organised a conference on 'European Defence Co-operation: Prospects and Limits' in 1983, with Andrew Tyrie who joined the Trust's Council a year later.[19]

Here again, the drip effect of many years of work on new ideas by bodies such as the Federal Trust, combined with shifts in the surrounding landscape, began to move the rock of opinion about the structure of West European defence. Influential voices on the Continent began to speak for defence integration in a European Security Community.[20] In 1987, the Trust established a new group, chaired by Sir Michael Palliser, former Permanent Under-Secretary at the Foreign and Commonwealth Office and a Patron of the Trust, to examine the idea of a European Security Community, Europe's role in East–West relations, and its contribution to peacekeeping in other regions of the world. The group's report, *A Step Beyond Fear: Building a European Security Community*, by Christopher Layton, envisaged a common security and foreign policy and pooled defence forces in the framework of European Union, with democratic accountability to the European Parliament jointly with the Council. The European Union would thus become the partner of the United States as the European pillar of the Atlantic Alliance. As such it could carry its full weight in negotiations to seek a common security relationship with the Soviet Union and to reform the United Nations into a more effective peacekeeper – a kind of world Community of regional Communities, as a stage on the way to the more distant prospect of world government.[21]

The Trust's concern with other regions of the world was not coincidental. From the 1950s onwards it had arranged conferences and publications about developing countries and, from the time of the first negotiation for British entry into the Community, about relations between the Community and the Commonwealth.[22] In the mid-1970s Uwe Kitzinger wrote a paper for the Trust on *Europe's Wider Horizons* and gave the first Federalist Lecture, organised by the Trust in memory of Noël Salter, who had died in 1974, and held in Chatham House, on 'European Ideals: Third World Realities'.[23] In 1986 John Leech chaired a study group on Community policy towards third world countries, whose report was discussed at a conference organised in Brussels by the Trust with backing from the Commission.[24]

Both these study groups, on European security and East–West relations, and on Community relations with the third world, were aspects of a new impulse in the Federal Trust towards work on problems of world order and institutions. The main source of this impulse was Christopher Layton, back in London after over a decade in Brussels, first as Chef de Cabinet to Spinelli when the latter was the Commissioner for Industrial Affairs, then as a Commission official, helping to germinate the Esprit project for joint Community research. Layton saw the need to stimulate a process in the wider world similar to that which had initiated the post-war unification of Europe. The Trust welcomed the idea, and combined its interests in European unity and world order in a study group on 'Europe's contribution to world order', with Layton as rapporteur. The combination of European and world interests was reflected in the sponsorship of the group, which included the Wyndham Place Trust and the One World Trust as well as the Federal Trust, and in its membership, which included both committed Europeans and world federalists. The report was published under the evocative title *One Europe: One World*, and is the basis for a wide-ranging project, animated by Christopher Layton, with activities in a number of European countries and with the aim of action relating to the world as a whole.[25]

FEDERALISM

The federalists who are the subject of this book were not the slaves of an 'ism', least of all those active in the Federal Trust. But the Trust has seen the need also to look at the wide canvas on which it works and consider what pattern the whole may comprise. In the 1960s it held conferences on federalism and the European Community.[26] In the 1970s, with pressure for devolution in the United Kingdom, the focus shifted to ideas of intranational federation;[27] and, with the trend to centralisation in the 1980s, a study of the case for local autonomy was made by a group with Vernon Bogdanor of Brasenose College, Oxford, as rapporteur.[28] The application of federal principles both within and among nation-states, as well as in economic and social life, was considered in a series of New Federalist Papers in the mid-1970s by sixteen authors associated with the Trust; and the whole set was edited into a book and published for the Trust by Macmillan.[29] This was followed by a weekend conference at which one of the founders of Federal Union, Charles (by now Sir Charles) Kimber, joined academics and politicians (including Tom Ellis, MP, Stanley Henig, Professor David Marquand, Robert Oakshott, and Professor Maurice Vile) in animated discussion of federalism. To consolidate this work, the Trust started a study group on the subject in 1985, and in 1986 held a conference at Leicester University, organised jointly with Murray Forsyth, at which leading academic specialists presented papers on the current relevance of both intranational and multinational federalism. In 1988, in response to a Federal Trust initiative, a Centre for Federal Studies was set up by the University of Leicester, with Murray Forsyth as its joint Director.

The renewed attention now paid to federalism as a whole is in part a response to an inevitable question. After four decades of the Federal Trust and nearly half a century after the foundation of the Federal Union Research Institute, after over 200 conferences, 100 publications and some 50 study groups, what has all this activity achieved? It has not made federalism clearly understood in Britain, let alone a popular cause. But this does not imply that the work on federalism has failed; rather that the Trust has concentrated on specific areas within the federalist canvas and has not stressed the idea as a whole or the word that denotes it.

Where the Trust has concentrated its activity on practical issues its ideas have often become generally accepted, if after long delay. British industry has come to accept the European Community as a legitimate context for its activity; the Trust's ideas on the Community's agricultural, budget and monetary policy have been widely adopted; and its work on European security has foreshadowed the reawakening of interest in West European security integration.

Now that the Community has regained its dynamism, the Trust has been producing a coherent set of proposals for its development into a European Union with federal institutions. Trust study groups have considered the need not only for completing the single market, but also for a European federal bank at the centre of an economic and monetary union, for a common security policy based on common defence forces, for a common foreign policy aiming to establish a world framework for peace, and for federal institutions with co-legislation by the European Parliament and the Council voting by majority, and enough executive power for the Commission to become a democratically accountable European government; in short, the Federal Trust, like Federal Union and its Research Institute half a century ago, is creating a new design for a federal Europe in a peaceful, uniting world.

Such work requires committed people; and such people are, indeed, the essence of the Federal Trust. Those who came together in the 1950s and 1960s and are still active in the Trust have already been named. Douglas Sanders has been on the governing body ever since he helped found the Federal Trust in 1945, with Ota Adler providing the first Trust covenant. Members of the staff have also shown great consistency; Eileen Usher, Penny David and Judy Keep have spanned almost three decades as Executive Secretaries. Some of the Trust's leading figures have gone on to distinction in other contexts: for example, the Rt Hon. David Howell, John MacGregor, MP, now a Cabinet Minister, who was the Trust's Honorary Treasurer in the 1970s, and Lord Justice Farquharson. Others have come into the Trust's work after distinguished careers elsewhere, such as Sir Bernard Burrows and Sir Donald Maitland, former Ambassador and Permanent Under-Secretary who became the Trust's President in 1987; yet others, after major contributions as federalists in the European Movement.

Most important for the future, a new generation of younger members has joined the Council since 1984. The Trust, like Federal Union itself, intends to keep working until federal principles are sufficiently recognised as a basis for political action, in Europe, inside the United Kingdom, and in the world at large.

But action needs activists. The question that now faces Federal Union is whether it should continue to work within existing parties and organisations, or try to revive the popular movement which it created at its beginnings in the crisis years on the eve of World War II. It is a dilemma that only the new generation of pioneers can resolve.

14 Envoi

Federal Union has always been ahead of its time.

In World War II, it looked ahead to peace aims which differed markedly from those of Versailles in 1919. In its treatment of the German problem, notably, it helped steer public opinion away from revenge and towards reconciliation.

It founded the first avowedly popular federalist movement in Europe, working both on a European and on a world plane.

Its intellectual contribution was recognised and used by Continental federalists whose influence helped shape the European Community.

As the Community developed, Federal Union performed the bulk of the work of persuasion and education which helped prepare official and public opinion in Britain for future membership.

It has pressed unceasingly to develop the European Community into a more efficient and democratic body, and one firm and united enough to offer a new role to the countries of Eastern Europe.

In the Atlantic area, it put forward two of the basic ideas which led to the formation of the OECD.

In world affairs it helped to shape and articulate pressure for the reform of the United Nations and for an international peacekeeping force.

Its members and sympathisers are still at work. They are pressing not only for the completion of the European Community as a European Union with federal institutions, but also for greater stability and peace in a wider Europe and a wider world.

Despite much more hopeful signs in East–West relations, the same conditions of international anarchy that prompted the formation of Federal Union in 1938 still exist today, especially outside Europe. The threats of destruction and ecological disaster that they pose are infinitely greater. Purely national action cannot meet these challenges. So federalists must still reiterate the same message: that unfettered national sovereignty is outdated and a barrier to peace, that free men must unite and submit their arguments and their force to the rule of law, and that the federations which they form must provide the nucleus of a world order pledged to maintain peace and ensure justice.

If the road is long, all the more reason to hurry.

Notes and References

Introduction

1. *Federal News*, no. 120, February 1945, p. 16, citing *The Times*, 18 January 1945.
2. Quoted in Carl van Doren, *The Great Rehearsal* (London and New York: Viking Press and Cresset Press, 1948) p. 164.
3. Patrick Ransome, 'Federal Government', *Fortnightly Review*, October 1939, p. 417.
4. Lord Lothian (Philip Kerr), *The Ending of Armageddon* (Federal Union, 1939) p. 3; reprinted in Patrick Ransome (ed.), *Studies in Federal Planning* (London: Macmillan, 1943) p. 5.
5. *Ibid*, p. 5.
6. Lionel Robbins, *The Economic Causes of War* (London: Jonathan Cape, 1939) p. 105.
7. *Ibid*, p. 104.
8. Ransome, *op. cit.* (n. 3, *supra*) p. 418.
9. H. N. Brailsford, *The Federal Idea* (Federal Union, 1939) p. 10.
10. W. B. Curry, *The Case for Federal Union* (Harmondsworth: Penguin Books, 1939) p. 128.
11. Lionel Robbins, 'Economic Aspects of Federation', in M. Chaning-Pearce (ed.), *Federal Union: A Symposium* (London: Jonathan Cape, 1940) p. 167; reprinted in Federal Tract No. 2 (London: Macmillan, 1941) p. 3, and in Ransome, *op. cit.* (n. 3, *supra*) p. 77.
12. W. Ivor Jennings, *A Federation for Western Europe* (Cambridge University Press, 1940) chapters V, VI.
13. K. C. Wheare, *What Federal Government Is*, Federal Tract No. 4 (London: Macmillan, 1941) p. 18; reprinted in Ransome, *op. cit.* (n. 3, *supra*) p. 32.
14. *Federal Union* (Federal Union pamphlet, 1940).
15. R. W. G. Mackay, *Federal Europe* (London: Michael Joseph, 1940) p. 137; revised and republished as *Peace Aims and the New Order* (London: Michael Joseph, 1941) p. 147.
16. Harold Wilson, 'Economic Aspects of Federation', p. 2, in Federal Union Research Institute, *First Annual Report 1939–40*.
17. Robbins, *op. cit.* (n. 6, *supra*) p. 98.
18. Cf. Konni Zilliacus: 'World Government and World Peace', in Ransome, *op. cit.* (n. 3, *supra*).
19. Jennings, *op. cit.* (n. 12, *supra*) p. 23.
20. Mackay, *op. cit.* (n. 15, *supra*) p. 24.
21. Cf. Curry, *op. cit.* (n. 10, *supra*) p. 140.
22. Jennings, *op. cit.* (n. 12, *supra*) pp. 3, 29; Mackay *op. cit.* (n. 15, *supra*) pp. 90, 91.
23. William Beveridge, *Peace by Federation?*, Federal Tract No. 1 (Federal Union, 1940).

24. R. J. Mackay in Chaning-Pearce, *op. cit.* (n. 11, *supra*) p. 143.
25. Curry, *op. cit.* (n. 10, *supra*) p. 105.
26. C. E. M. Joad, 'The Philosophy of Federal Union', in Ransome, *op. cit.* (n. 3, *supra*) p. 50.
27. G. W. Keeton, 'The Federation and India', in Chaning-Pearce, *op. cit.* (n. 11, *supra*) p. 194.

1 Against the Tide

1. David Davies, *The Problem of the Twentieth Century: A Study in International Relationships* (London: Ernest Benn, 1930).
2. *Federal Union News*, no. 98, April 1943, p. 5.
3. Derek Rawnsley, in *Federal Union News*, no. 23, Feb–March 1940.
4. Harold Macmillan, *The Middle Way* (London: Macmillan, 1938).
5. Nigel Forman, 'The European Movement in Great Britain 1945–1954' (University of Sussex, unpublished thesis, 1966) p. 62.
6. Alexander Hamilton, John Jay and James Madison, *The Federalist Or, The New Constitution*, first published in New York journals, 1787–88 (London: J. M. Dent, 1911). Lord Acton, 'Nationality', in *The History of Freedom and Other Essays* (London: Macmillan, 1907); James Bryce, *The American Commonwealth* (London and New York: Macmillan, 1888); A. V. Dicey, *Introduction to the Study of the Law of the Constitution* (London: Macmillan, 1885); Edward A. Freeman, *History of Federal Government in Greece and Italy* (London: Macmillan, Bury, 2nd edn. 1893); J. S. Mill, *Considerations on Representative Government* (London: Parker, 1861), ch. xvii; J. R. Seeley, 'United States of Europe', *Macmillan's Magazine*, vol. 23, 1871, pp. 436–48; H. Sidgwick, *The Elements of Politics* (London: Macmillan, 1891) and *The Development of European Policy* (London: Macmillan, 1903); W. T. Stead, *The United States of Europe* (London: *Review of Reviews* Office, 1899).
7. Michael Burgess, 'Empire, Ireland and Europe: A Century of British Federal Ideas', in Michael Burgess (ed.), *Federalism and Federation in Western Europe* (London: Croom Helm, 1986) p. 127.
8. Dicey, *op. cit.* (n. 6, *supra*, 9th edn. 1939) p. 179.
9. See Burgess, *op. cit.* (n. 7, *supra*) pp. 137–8. Lionel Curtis set out his federalist faith in *The Commonwealth of Nations: an enquiry into the nature of citizenship in the British Commonwealth and into the mutual relations of the several communities thereof* (London: Macmillan, 1917) and subsequently in *Civitas Dei* (London: Allen & Unwin, Vol. I, 1934, Vols II and III, 1937, revised edn. 1950). F. S. Oliver's book was *Alexander Hamilton: An Essay on American Union* (London: Macmillan, first edn. 1906, reprinted 1931).
10. See, for example, Norman Angell, 'The International Anarchy', in Leonard Woolf (ed.), *The Intelligent Man's Way to Prevent War* (London: Gollancz, 1933); H. N. Brailsford, *Towards a New League* (New Statesman Pamphlet, 1936); G. D. H. Cole, *War Aims* (New Statesman Pamphlet, 1939); Bertrand Russell, *Which Way to Peace?* (London: Michael Joseph, 1936); H. G. Wells, *After Democracy:*

Addresses and Papers on the Present World Situation (London: Watts, 1932); Leonard Woolf, 'Introduction', in Woolf, *ibid*. Some of Laski's writings on federalism are cited in n. 11, *infra*. Other academic works included S. C. Y. Cheng, *Schemes for the Federation of the British Empire* (New York: Columbia University Press, 1931); D. G. Karve, *Federation: A Study in Comparative Politics* (London: Oxford University Press, 1932); A. P. Newton, *Federal and Unified Constitutions* (London: Longmans Green, 1923).

11. Harold J. Laski, *A Grammar of Politics* (London: Allen & Unwin, 1938, first edition 1925) pp. 270–1. Other relevant works included his *Studies in the Problem of Sovereignty* (Oxford University Press, 1917); *The Foundations of Sovereignty and other Essays* (London: Allen & Unwin, 1921); and *Nationalism and the Future of Civilisation* (London: Watts, 1932). For the New Europe Group, see Walter Lipgens, *A History of European Integration 1945–1947: The Formation of the European Unity Movement* (Oxford: The Clarendon Press, 1982) pp. 161–2. One of the Group's leading members, Niall MacDermot, was later a Vice-President of Federal Union.
12. Harold J. Laski, 'The Economic Foundations of Peace', in Leonard Woolf (ed.) (*op. cit.* in n. 10, *supra*) p. 536.
13. Laski, *op. cit.* (n. 11, *supra*), Preface to the third edition.
14. See John Pinder, 'Prophet not without Honour: Lothian and the Federal Idea', *The Round Table*, April 1983, revised and reprinted in John Turner (ed.), *The Larger Idea: Lothian and the Problem of National Sovereignty* (London: The Historians' Press, 1988); Andrea Bosco, 'Il pacifismo non basta', in Giulio Guderzo (ed.), *Lord Lothian. Una vita per la pace* (Florence: La Nuova Italia Editrice, 1986), with an English version entitled 'National Sovereignty and Peace: Lord Lothian's Federalist Thought', in Turner (ed.), *ibid.*; and Andrea Bosco, *Lord Lothian: Un pioniere del federalismo 1882–1940* (Milan: Edizioni Universitarie Jaca, 1989). Among Lothian's principal writings are: Philip Kerr (later Lord Lothian) and Lionel Curtis, *The Prevention of War* (New Haven: Yale University Press, 1923); Philip Kerr, in 'World Problems of Today', in the Earl of Birkenhead, General Tasker H. Bliss and Philip Henry Kerr, *Approaches to World Problems* (New Haven: Yale University Press, 1924); and *Pacifism is not Enough* (1935, see n. 15, *infra*).
15. P. H. Kerr (Marquess of Lothian), *Pacifism is not Enough (nor Patriotism Either)* (London: Oxford University Press, 1935, reprinted with a preface by Sir William Beveridge, 1941).
16. This book is still seen in Italy as a federalist classic. See, for example, Andrea Bosco, 'Lord Lothian e la nascita di Federal Union', *Il Politico* (Pavia), 1983, no. 2, pp. 271–304; and 'La dottrina politica di Lord Lothian', *Annali della Fondazione Luigi Einaudi* (Turin, 1984) pp. 519–73; and 'Il pacifismo non basta', *op. cit.* (n. 14, *supra*). See also the preface by Giulio Guderzo, and Luigi Vittorio Majocchi, 'Perche un convegno su Lord Lothian', in Guderzo, *op. cit.* (n. 14, *supra*). See also the several Italian translations of Lothian's writings (of which half a dozen examples are given in Chapter 6, n. 19, *infra*).

17. Lionel Robbins, *Economic Planning and International Order* (London: Macmillan, 1937).
18. Lionel Robbins, *The Economic Causes of War* (London: Jonathan Cape, 1939). Also deemed a classic by Italian federalists (see Ch. 6, n. 19).
19. Ramsay Muir, *The Expansion of Europe: The culmination of modern history* (London: Constable, 1922; 6th edition 1939).
20. *International Affairs*, vol. XVIII, no. 3, pp. 849–50.
21. A. L. Rowse, *A Cornishman Abroad* (London: Jonathan Cape, 1976) p. 142.
22. Sir Charles Kimber, letter to John Pinder, 29 February 1980.
23. *The Times*, 13 July 1938, quoted in Daniel George and Rose Macaulay, *All in a Maze* (London: Collins, 1938) pp. 462–3.
24. Sir Charles Kimber tape, 1976.
25. Her own comment in her autobiography, *In a World I Never Made* (London: Allen & Unwin, 1967) p. 97.
26. Lionel Curtis, letter to Miss M. M. Wingate, 24 October 1944.
27. Kimber *op. cit.* (n. 22, *supra*). See also Charles Kimber, 'Federal Union', *The Federalist* (Pavia), December 1984, p. 204.
28. Clarence Streit, *Union Now: a Proposal for a Federal Union of the Democracies of the North Atlantic* (London and New York: Jonathan Cape and Harper, 1939). The first chapter was published by Federal Union as a pamphlet entitled *America Speaks* (undated, but certainly in 1939).
29. Conversation with John Roberts, 1980.
30. Kimber tape, 1976, and 'Federal Union', *op. cit.* (n. 27, *supra*) p. 203.
31. Kimber tape, 1976.
32. RIIA Archives 8/603, pp. 4, 14.
33. RIIA Archives 9/18 f, p. 7.
34. W. B. Curry, *The Case for Federal Union* (Harmondsworth: Penguin Books, 1939).
35. *Ibid*, p. vii.
36. Kimber, *op. cit.* (n. 22, *supra*).
37. Curry, *op. cit.* (n. 34, *supra*) pp. 24, 27.
38. Lothian Papers, GD40/17/395 (Edinburgh, Record Office), cited in Bosco, 'Lord Lothian e la nascita di Federal Union', *op. cit.* (n. 16, *supra*) p. 288.
39. Curry *op. cit.* (n. 34, *supra*) pp. 17, 28–9.

2 At War

1. Margaret Richards, *Memorandum*, 6 July 1976.
2. Christine Dowson on F. L. Josephy tape, 1979.
3. *Federal Union News*, no. 11, 2 December 1939; Alexander Hamilton, John Jay and James Madison, *The Federalist Or, The New Constitution* (London: J. M. Dent, 1911; first published 1787–8); Lionel Curtis, *Civitas Dei* (London: Allen & Unwin, Vol. I, 1934, Vols II and III, 1937, revised edn. 1950); Clarence Streit, *Union Now: A Proposal for a Federal Union of the Democracies of the North Atlantic* (London and

New York: Jonathan Cape and Harper, 1939).
4. W. B. Curry, *The Case for Federal Union* (Harmondsworth: Penguin Books, 1939).
5. *Federal Union News*, no. 12, 9 December 1939. *The Road to Oxiana* was first published by Macmillan, London, in 1937.
6. *Federal Union News*, no. 17, 13 January 1940.
7. *Federal Union News*, no. 21, 10 February 1940, and no. 90, August 1942, p. 12.
8. C. R. Attlee, *Labour's Peace Aims* (London: Peace Book Co., 1940), reprinted in C. R. Attlee, Arthur Greenwood and others, *Labour's Aims in War and Peace* (London: Lincolns-Prager, 1940); the study group document was 'European Order and World Order' (London: Labour Party, 2 January 1940; located in Labour Party Library).
9. *Report of the Proceedings of the 73rd Annual Trades Union Congress*, pp. 81, 82.
10. G. D. H. Cole, *Europe, Russia, and the Future* (London: Gollancz, 1941) pp. 54–63, 125–32.
11. H. N. Brailsford, *The Federal Idea* (Federal Union, 1939).
12. *Philosophy and Living*, Vol. II (Harmondsworth: Penguin Books, 1939) p. 429. *First and Last Men. Story of the Near and Far Future* was published in London by Methuen in 1930. For Federal Union, Stapledon wrote 'Federalism and Socialism', in M. Chaning-Pearce (ed.), *Federal Union* (London: Jonathan Cape, 1940).
13. Sir Charles Kimber tape, 1976, and conversations of John Roberts with Dr B. G. Whitmore (17 November 1979) and Mrs M. M. Shaw-Zambra (Monica Wingate).
14. C. E. M. Joad, *The Testament of Joad* (London: Faber & Faber, 1937) p. 97.
15. *Federal News*, no. 115, September 1944, p. 6. (Note: the title was changed to *Federal News* as from issue no. 109 in March 1944.)
16. Margaret Richards, letter to Sheila Barton, 1976.
17. *Federal Union News*, no. 28, 30 March 1940.
18. Ota Adler tape, 1980.
19. Viscount Samuel, 'Introduction', in Royal Institute of International Affairs, *World Order Papers*, First Series (London: RIIA, 1940) pp. 7–13.
20. *Report of the League of Nations Union General Council*, November–December 1940; papers at the British Library of Political and Economic Science, LSE.
21. In William Teeling (ed.), *After the War* (London: Sidgwick & Jackson, 1940).
22. *Federal Union News*, no. 25, 9 March 1940.
23. Geoffrey Vickers, 'Purpose and Force – The Bases of World Order', in *World Order Papers*, *op. cit.* (n. 19, *supra*) p. 173.
24. In *Information*, 5 April 1940.
25. *Federal Union News*, no. 22, 17 February 1940.
26. See Walter Lipgens, *A History of European Integration 1945–1947: The Formation of the European Unity Movement* (Oxford: Clarendon Press, 1982) p. 145. The request was repeated to the Home Secretary

and the incident was quoted in several Federal Union leaflets.

27. Dr R. Edgar Hope-Simpson, letter of 30 May 1980.
28. D. N. Pritt, *Federal Illusion? An Examination of the Proposals for Federal Union* (London: Frederick Muller, 1940) pp. 31, 36, 97–101.
29. John Strachey, *Federalism or Socialism* (London: Gollancz, 1940) p. 221.
30. W. B. Curry, *op. cit.* (n. 4, *supra*) p. 29.
31. C. E. M. Joad, *Why War?* (Harmondsworth: Penguin Books, 1939) p. 179.
32. *Federal Union News*, no. 1, 5 September 1939.
33. Quoted in *Federal Union News*, no. 9, 19 November 1939.
34. *Federal Union News*, no. 20, 3 February 1940.
35. *Federal Union News*, no. 25, 9 March 1940.
36. Quoted in N. and J. Mackenzie, *H. G. Wells* (London: Weidenfeld & Nicolson, 1973) p. 435.
37. Kimber tape, 1976.
38. *Federal Union News*, no. 40, 29 June 1940.
39. *Federal Union News*, no. 46, 10 August 1940.
40. Mackenzie, *op. cit.* (n. 36, *supra*) p. 434.
41. Forty years on, D. W. Sanders recalled with pride that he had served on the sub-committee which drafted the aims 'for the principle of federal order and the society we wanted'. Douglas Sanders tape, 1980.
42. Charles Kimber, 'Federal Union', *The Federalist* (Pavia), December 1984, p. 202.
43. Josephy tape, 1979; *Federal Union News*, no. 24, 2 March 1940.
44. Minutes, 28 February 1940. Members present included Jennings, Joad, Josephy, Kimber, Ransome, Rawnsley, and Wootton (in the chair).
45. National Council Minutes, 31 March 1940; W. Ivor Jennings, *A Federation for Western Europe* (Cambridge University Press, 1940).
46. *Federal Union News*, no. 31, April–May 1940.
47. Jennings, *op. cit.* (n. 45, *supra*) p. viii. The conferences are described in Chapter 3 of the present volume.
48. *Federal Union News*, no. 14, 23 December 1939.
49. Wilson Harris, 'Federal Union Examined – I', *The Spectator*, 15 March 1940, p. 354.
50. F.O. 371, vol. 24298, C 4444/9/17, minute by Orme Sargent, 28.2.40, cited in Peter Ludlow, 'The Unwinding of Appeasement', in Lothar Kettenacker, *Das 'Andere' Deutschland im Zweiten Weltkreig* (Stuttgart: Klett Verlag, 1978) p. 41. Information about this incident has been drawn from this source and from Peter Ludlow, 'Français et Britanniques dans le Drôle de Guerre', *Actes du colloque franco-britannique tenu à Paris du 8 au 12 Décembre 1975* (Paris: Editions du Centre National de la Recherche Scientifique, 1979).
51. Jennings, *op. cit.* (n. 45, *supra*); R. W. G. Mackay, *Federal Europe* (London: Michael Joseph, 1940); Sir William Beveridge, *Peace by Federation?,* Federal Tract No. 1 (Federal Union, 1940); M. Chaning-Pearce (ed.), *Federal Union: A Symposium* (London: Jonathan Cape, 1940).
52. This, and the other citations in the following paragraphs (except where

otherwise stated), are from Jean Monnet, *Memoirs* (translated by Richard Mayne. London: Collins, 1978) pp. 22, 24, 28, 29, 35.

53. Winston S. Churchill, *The Second World War*, Vol. 2 (London: Cassell, 1948) pp. 180–1. Sir John Colville, who was Assistant Private Secretary to Churchill at the time, has confirmed Churchill's recollection of the Cabinet's reaction: 'It was a marvellous idea and I have never seen such enthusiasm', cited in Michael Charlton, *The Price of Victory* (London: BBC, 1983) p. 37.
54. Peter Ludlow, 'The Unwinding of Appeasement', *op. cit.* (n. 50, *supra*) p. 30.
55. Sir John Colville, *The Fringes of Power: Downing Street Diaries 1939–1955* (London: Hodder & Stoughton, 1985) pp. 30, 159, 161.
56. Executive Committee Minutes, 19 June 1940.
57. Executive Committee Minutes, 6 November 1939.
58. Josephy tape, 1979.
59. Margaret Richards, *Memorandum*, 6 July 1976.
60. *Federal Union News*, no. 50, 14 September 1940.
61. Board Minutes, 10 January 1941.
62. Board Minutes, 27 May 1941.
63. National Council Minutes, 12–13 April 1941.
64. Board Minutes, 7 August 1941, and 6 February 1942.
65. For two successive Birmingham constituencies, 1945–50 and 1950–9.
66. National Council Minutes, 11–12 October 1941.
67. Board Minutes, 7 August 1941.
68. National Council Minutes, 17 October 1942.
69. *Federal News*, no. 111, May 1944, p. 9.
70. Margaret Richards, *Memorandum*, 6 July 1976.
71. *Federal Union News*, no. 96, February 1943, pp. 3, 4.
72. Executive Committee Minutes, 12 September 1944. Hoyland's book was completed in 1943 and published by Federal Union in 1944.
73. Executive Committee Minutes, 31 May 1944.
74. National Council Minutes, 15 January 1944 and 13 January 1945.
75. National Council Minutes, 5 May 1944.
76. National Council Minutes, 9 July 1945.

3 Peace Aims

1. John Middleton Murry, 'Pre-Conditions of Federal Union', in M. Chaning-Pearce (ed.), *Federal Union: A Symposium* (London: Jonathan Cape, 1940) pp. 158–9.
2. A brief history of the Federal Union Research Institute appears in John Pinder, 'Federal Union 1939–41', in Walter Lipgens (ed.), *Documents on the History of European Integration, Vol. 2: Plans for European Union in Great Britain and in Exile 1939–1945* (Berlin and New York: de Gruyter, 1986) pp. 26–155.
3. 'Economic Aspects of Federal Union', p. 1, in Federal Union Research Institute, *First Annual Report 1939–40* (FU Archive), duplicated, 142 pp. The Constitutional Conference added Eire and Switzerland, and the Chairman (Beveridge) and others stressed 'the importance of

including the Dominions' ('Report on Conferences on the Constitutional Aspects of Federal Union', p. 1, FURI, *ibid.*)

4. *A Federation for Western Europe* (Cambridge University Press, 1940) p. viii.
5. Extensive extracts from the works of federalist authors of the period can be found in Pinder, *op. cit.* (n. 2, *supra*).
6. Lord Lothian, *The Ending of Armageddon* (Federal Union, June 1939) pp. 3–5; reprinted in Patrick Ransome (ed.), *Studies in Federal Planning* (London: Macmillan, 1943) pp. 1–3.
7. Patrick Ransome, 'Federal Government', *Fortnightly Review*, October 1939, p. 418.
8. Lionel Robbins, *The Economic Causes of War* (London: Jonathan Cape, 1939) pp. 104–5.
9. C. E. M. Joad, *The Philosophy of Federal Union*, Federal Tract No. 5 (London: Macmillan, 1942) pp. 13–17; reprinted in Ransome, *op. cit.* (n. 6, *supra*) pp. 49–53.
10. Lionel Robbins, 'Economic Aspects of Federation', in Chaning-Pearce, *op. cit.* (n. 1, *supra*) p. 167; reprinted in Federal Tract No. 2 (London: Macmillan, 1941) p. 3, and in Ransome, *op. cit.* (n. 6, *supra*) p. 77.
11. J. B. Priestley, 'Federalism and Culture', in Chaning-Pearce, *op. cit.* (n. 1, *supra*) pp. 98–9.
12. Sir John Boyd Orr, 'Federalism and Science', in Chaning-Pearce, *op. cit.* (n. 1, *supra*) p. 103.
13. K. C. Wheare, *What Federal Government Is*, Federal Tract No. 4 (London: Macmillan, 1941) pp. 3–4, 9–17; reprinted in Ransome, *op. cit.* (n. 6, *supra*) pp. 17–18, 23–31. Wheare's book on *Federal Government* was written for the Royal Institute of International Affairs and published in London by the Oxford University Press in 1946.
14. *Ibid*, pp. 22–4, and 36–8 respectively.
15. Sir William Beveridge, *Peace by Federation?*, Federal Tract No. 1 (Federal Union, 1940) pp. 18, 19.
16. Jennings, *op. cit.* (n. 4, *supra*) pp. 19–20, 25–6, 83.
17. Otto Kahn-Freud, 'Memorandum on the Constitutional Aspects of Federal Union', p. 1, in FURI, *op. cit.* (n. 3, *supra*).
18. 'Report on First Conference: Economic Aspects of Federation', in FURI, *ibid*.
19. Harold Wilson, 'Economic Aspects of Federation', in FURI, *ibid*, pp. 4–5.
20. Lionel Robbins, 'Interim Report on Economic Aspects of the Federal Constitution', in FURI, *ibid*, pp. 4–5.
21. James Meade, 'Economic Problems of International Government', in FURI, *ibid*, pp. 9–13.
22. Lionel Robbins, *op. cit.* (n. 10, *supra*) pp. 176–7.
23. Lionel Robbins, *op. cit.* (n. 8, *supra*) p. 98.
24. See F. A. von Hayek, 'Economic Conditions of Inter-State Federation', *New Commonwealth Quarterly*, September 1939, reprinted as a chapter in F. A. Hayek, *Individualism and Economic Order* (London: Routledge & Kegan Paul, 1976, first edition 1949).

25. Harold Wilson, *op. cit.* (n. 19, *supra*) p. 2.
26. Barbara Wootton, *Socialism and Federation*, Federal Tract No. 6 (London: Macmillan, 1942); reprinted in Ransome *op. cit.* (n. 6, *supra*) pp. 295–8.
27. R. H. Tawney, *Equality* (London: Allen & Unwin, 1931; citation from third edition 1938) p. 280.
28. R. W. G. Mackay, *Federal Europe* (London: Michael Joseph, 1940) pp. 136–9; revised and republished as *Peace Aims and the New Order* (Michael Joseph, 1941) pp. 146–9.
29. Barbara Wootton, *op. cit.* (n. 26, *supra*) pp. 294–5.
30. Board Minutes, 4 March 1941.
31. *Op. cit.* (n. 6, *supra*).
32. *Federal Union News* no. 21, 10 February 1940.
33. *Federal Union* (Federal Union pamphlet, 1940).
34. Board Minutes, 3 October 1941.
35. Board Minutes, 2 January 1942.
36. Printed in full in *Federal Union News*, no. 88, June 1942, pp. 1–16.
37. *New World*, March 1969.
38. Sir Charles Kimber, *Memorandum*, 29 February 1980.
39. *Federal Union News*, no. 104, October 1943, p. 1.
40. *Ibid*. The issue of *Federal Union News*, which opened with Joad's analysis also carried five anonymous articles on alternative approaches: on 'Global Federation', advocating a 'nucleus federation' of democracies from whatever part of the world: 'Commonwealth Union', with 'Allies in Western Europe' invited to join at the outset and USA membership hoped for later, as a step towards world federation; 'Union with Europe', with the British Dominions joining should they wish; 'Anglo-American Union', to include if possible Europe's 'Atlantic Democracies' from the outset and to be open to accession by other democracies; and 'Against any immediate Nucleus Federation', advocating the functionalist approach to world federation, which was clearly influenced by David Mitrany, the founder of the functionalist school, whose best known work on the subject, *A Working Peace System* (London: Royal Institute of International Affairs, 1943), was published in the same year as the article.
41. *Federal Union News*, no. 108, February 1944, p. 11.

4 Postwar Debate

1. Conversation between John Roberts and Monica Wingate.
2. Frederick L. Schuman, *The Commonwealth of Man: An Enquiry into Power Politics and World Government* (London: Robert Hale, 1954) p. 432.
3. *Federal News*, no. 135, June 1946, p. 11; *ibid*, no. 140, November 1946, p. 9.
4. *Federal News*, no. 116, October 1944, p. 9.
5. *Federal News*, no. 128, November 1945, p. 13.
6. *Federal News*, no. 126, September 1945, p. 11.
7. Walter Lipgens, *A History of European Integration 1945–1947: The*

Formation of the European Unity Movement (Oxford: Clarendon Press, 1982) p. 310.

8. Accounts of the Luxembourg Conference, with slightly varying statistics of participation, are given in *Federal News*, no. 139, October 1946, pp. 7–8; *Federal News*, no. 140, November 1946, pp. 6–8; F. L. Josephy, 'Full Steam Ahead', *Federal News*, no. 141, December 1946, pp. 2–6; Henri Koch-Kent, *Vu et entendu vol. 2: années d'exil 1940–1946* (Luxembourg: Koch-Kent, 1986) pp. 368–70; Finn Laursen, *Federation and World Order*, Vol. II (Copenhagen: World Federalist Youth, 1972) pp. 2–9, 103–4; Lipgens, *ibid*, pp. 310–14.
9. Board Minutes, 27 May 1941.
10. R. W. G. Mackay, *Let's Not Make the Same Mistake Twice* (Federal Union, not dated, probably May 1941).
11. Board Minutes, 13 June and 3 September 1941.
12. Board Minutes, 3 July 1942.
13. Executive Committee Minutes, 3 September 1943, 1 December 1944, and 9 July 1945.
14. *Federal Union News*, no. 29, 6 April 1940.
15. *Federal Union News*, no. 88, June 1942, pp. 1–6.
16. *Federal News*, no. 116, October 1944, p. 13.
17. Emery Reves, *The Anatomy of Peace* (New York: Harper, 1945; London: Allen & Unwin, 1946; Harmondsworth: Penguin Books, 1947).
18. F. L. Josephy, 'The Federal Implications of the Atom', *Federal News*, no. 126, September 1945, pp. 1–2.
19. The Annual General Meeting in September 1945 voted in favour of both 'a restatement of Federal Union policy, stressing the imperative need for a World Federal Government and indicating immediate steps towards its achievement' and 'the advocacy of a democratic federation in Europe' (*Federal News*, no. 128, November 1945, p. 12).
20. F. L. Josephy, *op. cit.* (n. 8, *supra*) pp. 4, 5.
21. *Ibid*, pp. 2, 6.
22. Cited in Laursen, *op. cit.* (n. 8, *supra*) p. 9.
23. R. Edgeworth Johnstone, letter to *Federal News*, no. 145, June 1947, p. 17.
24. The Movement was subsequently again renamed, this time the World Association for World Federation, thus managing to retain the acronym as WAWF.

5 World Federalism?

1. Sir William Beveridge, *The Price of Peace* (London: Pilot Press, March 1945); and *Federal News*, no. 135, June 1946, p. 14.
2. *Hansard*, 23 November 1945; Col. 785.
3. Quoted from speech in Newcastle, February 1946, in *Federal News*, no. 149, August 1947, p. 6.
4. *Ibid*, p. 9.
5. *Federal News*, no. 149, August 1947. *The Plan in Outline for World Government by 1955* was issued by the Parliamentary Group for World

Government on 6 June 1947. See Finn Laursen, *Federalism and World Order*, Vol. II (Copenhagen: World Federalist Youth, 1972) pp. 17–23, which cites among others *Common Cause* (Chicago), August 1947. See also Henry Usborne, *Prescription for Peace: The Case of a Minimal and Neutral Federation of Middle-World Nations ('Minifed')* (Evesham: 'Minifed Promotion Group', 1985) pp. 105–6. *The Plan in Outline* was republished in 1948 by the Crusade for World Government.

6. Usborne, *ibid*, pp. 83–4.
7. Frederick L. Schuman, *The Commonwealth of Man* (London: Robert Hale, 1954) pp. 436–7.
8. Usborne, *op. cit.* (n. 5, *supra*) p. 104.
9. Otto Nathan and Heinz Norden (eds), *Einstein on Peace* (New York: 1960; London: Methuen, 1963) pp. 421, 463.
10. Sources on the Montreux Congress include JKK (Keith Killby), 'World Federalists Confer', *Federal News*, no. 151, October 1947; Finn Laursen, *op. cit.* (n. 5, *supra*) pp. 23–34; Walter Lipgens, *A History of European Integration 1945–1947: The Formation of the European Unity Movement* (Oxford: Clarendon Press, 1982) pp. 585–90. The delegates from Federal Union included Ota Adler, Victor Collins, MP, Norman Hart, Jo Josephy, Keith Killby, Gordon Lang, MP, Henry Usborne, MP and Monica Wingate.
11. J. Simey, *Continental Congress* (Exeter: privately printed, 1947).
12. Monica Wingate, *World Federalist* (Littlehampton), December 1978, p. 7.
13. Conversation between John Roberts and Monica Wingate.
14. Laursen, *op. cit.* (n. 5, *supra*) pp. 124–6. When running the World Student Federalists office in Paris following its establishment there in October 1948, Norman Hart edited a symposium by leading federalist writers, including Alexandre Marc, Sir John Boyd Orr, Abbé Groues Pierre and Henry Usborne, MP, entitled *Basis of Federalism* (Paris: World Student Federalists, 1949), which included expositions of the main approaches to world government then current among world federalists: functional, parliamentary, peoples' convention and UN reform, as well as chapters on regional and integral federalism. He also met there Vivian Symon, who soon became Vivian Hart and was to be President of Jeunesse Fédéraliste Européenne and subsequently a committed member of Federal Union.
15. *Federal News*, no. 155, February 1948; and conversation between John Roberts and Monica Wingate.
16. Garry Davis, *My Country is the World: The Adventures of a World Citizen* (London: Macdonald, 1962).
17. Laursen, *op. cit.* (n. 5, *supra*) pp. 45–63.
18. *Federal News*, no. 193, May 1951, p. 2. See Laursen, *op. cit.* (n. 5, *supra*) pp. 74–102.
19. Boyd Orr, with Scottish humour, confided to Ota Adler that he had accepted a peerage because, living as he did in the North of Scotland, it was the only way he could get a free train journey to London (Ota Adler on FU meeting tape, 1980).

20. Douglas Robinson tape, 1980.
21. Grenville Clark, *A Plan for Peace* (Dublin, New Hampshire: privately printed, 1950). His subsequent development of this work, together with Louis B. Sohn, included *Peace through Disarmament and Charter Revision: Detailed Proposals for Revision of the United Nations Charter* (Dublin, New Hampshire: 1953; Supplement, 1956) and *World Peace through World Law* (Cambridge, Massachusetts: Harvard University Press, 1958).
22. *United Nations Reform: Proposals for a Federal United Nations*, prepared by the Joint Commission on UN Charter Reform (Federal Union and The Crusade for World Government, 1953).
23. John Pinder, *UN Reform: Proposals for Charter Amendment*, with Foreword by J. E. S. Simon, QC, MP (Federal Union, 1953). The most recent American work was Clark and Sohn, *op. cit.* (n. 21, *supra*) 1953.
24. *Federal News*, no. 222, April–May 1954, p. 11. The other members of the deputation were David Barton, Martin Maddan, Douglas Robinson, Monica Wingate, and John Pinder (the latter being the source of the cited recollection).
25. *Federal News*, no. 225, October–November 1954, pp. 9–12, 15.
26. *Federal News*, no. 229, Summer 1955, p. 3; and letter from Monica Wingate to Ota Adler, 13 January 1980.
27. *Federal News*, no. 229, Summer 1955, p. 3; *World Affairs*, no. 231, January–February 1956, pp. 9–10. (*Federal News* had been renamed *World Affairs* following no. 230 of October–November 1955.)
28. *World Affairs*, no. 237, January–February 1957, pp. 3–4.
29. *World Affairs*, no. 239, July-August 1957, pp. 43–4, 58.
30. *Proposals for a Permanent United Nations Force* (Federal Union, 1957, second impression 1957, third 1960). The report was summarised in *World Affairs*, *loc. cit.*
31. *World Affairs*, *ibid*, p. 58.
32. *PUNF for Peace* (Federal Union, not dated, 1958) p. 7.
33. *A World Security Authority?* (London: Conservative Political Centre, 1958). The ten Conservative MPs, all closely connected with Federal Union or the Parliamentary Group, were C. Wilson Black, A. D. Dodds-Parker, John Foster, R. Reader Harris, John Hay, Vice-Admiral John Hughes-Hallett, Martin Maddan, I. J. Pitman, David Price and John Tilney; the relevant extract from Sandys's speech was reprinted on pp. 38–9.
34. Annual General Meeting Minutes, 1958, 1959.
35. Federal Union Research Institute, *First Annual Report 1939–1940*, 'Editorial Note', p. 3.
36. *A World Investment Convention?* (London: Parliamentary Group for World Government, 1959), reproduced in *World Affairs*, no. 247, Summer 1959, pp. 35–42.
37. *World Affairs*, no. 249a, Spring 1960, pp. 27–8, printed an excerpt from Lord Hailsham's speech of 9 March.
38. *World Affairs*, no. 250, Summer 1960, pp. 51–3.
39. *Keeping the Peace* (London: Wyndham Place Trust, 1962); citations from p. 14.

40. *Hansard* (Lords), 20 February 1963, Col. 1425, cited in Rolf Paul Haegler, *Histoire et idéologie du mondialisme* (Zürich: Europa Verlag, 1972) p. 188.
41. *Op. cit.* (n. 39, *supra*) p. 27.
42. Letter from Monica Wingate to Ota Adler, 13 January 1980.
43. *Law not War* (Federal Union, 1961) p. 1.
44. Federal Union Annual Reports 1961–2, 1962–3.
45. Bertrand Russell, *Has Man a Future?* (Harmondsworth: Penguin Special, 1961).
46. *Barnet Press*, 24 November 1961; and *Hansard*, 2 March 1955, Col. 2181.
47. John C. de V. Roberts, *Disarmament in Fifteen Years* (Federal Union, 1964), and *Disarmament is Not Enough* (Association of World Federalists, 1981).
48. *Federal News*, no. 104, October 1943, pp. 12, 15. See also Chapter 3, n. 40, above.
49. See David Mitrany, *A Working Peace System – An Argument for the Functional Development of World Organisation* (London: Royal Institute of International Affairs, 1943; reprinted by National Peace Council, 1946, and, with other papers by Mitrany, in Chicago: Quadrangle, 1966). The original pamphlet was reviewed by Patrick Ransome in *Federal News*, no. 105, November 1943, pp. 4–5.
50. 'The Functional Approach to World Government', in Hart, *op. cit.* (n. 14, *supra*) p. 36.
51. *World Prosperity: Can we build it together?* A statement of Federal Union's policy on economic development (Federal Union, October 1956), reproduced in *World Affairs*, no. 236, November–December 1956, pp. 20–2.
52. *World Affairs*, no. 251, Autumn 1960, p. 98.
53. *Report of Session on Economic Development*, Congress of World Association of World Federalists in Vienna, 10–15 July 1961 (Amsterdam: WAWF, 1961).
54. *World Affairs*, no. 261, Autumn 1963, pp. 12–15.
55. Brochure published by World Parliament Association (London, 1962).
56. *World Federalist* (The Hague), October 1963, p. 59.
57. Ota Adler tape, 1980.
58. *Federal News*, no. 193, May 1951, p. 4.
59. See successive issues of *The Federalist* (Pavia) since it first appeared in English in July 1984.
60. Christopher Layton, *One Europe: One World – A first exploration of Europe's potential contribution to world order*, Special Supplement No. 4 to the *Journal of World Trade Law*, 1986. Further editions are cited in Chapter 13, n. 25, below.

6 Groundwork in Europe

1. Ivor Jennings, *A Federation for Western Europe* (Cambridge University Press, 1940). For details regarding its genesis, see its preface, pp. vii–ix, and Patrick Ransome, 'Editorial Note', p. 3, in Federal Union Research Institute, *First Annual Report 1939–40*. The paper for the

London Institute of World Affairs was published in the Institute's Proceedings, 1938.
2. *A Federation for Western Europe*, *ibid*, pp. 6, 11, 28.
3. In *Economic Planning and International Order* (London: Macmillan, 1937); the citation is from a reference to this earlier book in his *The Economic Causes of War* (London: Jonathan Cape, 1939) p. 10.
4. *The Economic Causes of War*, *ibid*, p. 109.
5. H. N. Brailsford, *The Federal Idea* (Federal Union, 1939) pp. 15–16.
6. Robbins, *The Economic Causes of War*, *op. cit.* (n. 3, *supra*) pp. 107–8.
7. Harold Wilson, 'The Economic Aspects of Federation', p. 4, in FURI, *op. cit.* (n. 1, *supra*).
8. Duncan Wilson, 'The History of Federalism', in M. Chaning-Pearce (ed.), *Federal Union: A Symposium* (London: Jonathan Cape, 1940) p. 55. He was also, with his wife Elizabeth Wilson, co-author of *Federation and World Order* (London: Thomas Nelson & Sons, 1939).
9. R. W. G. Mackay, *Federal Europe* (London: Michael Joseph, 1940) p. 118; and revised and republished as *Peace Aims and the New Order* (Michael Joseph, 1941) p. 128.
10. 'Anglo-French Economists' Conference', FURI, *op. cit.* (n. 1, *supra*); and letter of 19 August from Jean Laloy to John Pinder.
11. FURI, *op. cit.* (n. 10, *supra*).
12. Barbara Wootton, *In a World I Never Made* (London: Allen & Unwin, 1967) p. 98; *Federal Union News*, 11 April 1940.
13. Letters to John Roberts from A. A. Evans, adviser to a research group set up by the Circle, 28 May and 9 June 1980.
14. F. L. Josephy, *Europe – The Key to Peace* (Federal Union pamphlet), October 1944, quoted in Nigel Forman, 'The European Movement in Great Britain 1945–1954' (University of Sussex, unpublished thesis, 1966).
15. F. L. Josephy tape, 1979.
16. Walter Lipgens (ed.), *Documents on the History of European Integration. Vol. 1: Continental Plans for European Union 1939–1945* (Berlin and New York: de Gruyter, 1985) pp. 661–5, 672–82, citation from p. 680; and Walter Lipgens, *A History of European Integration 1945–1947: The Formation of the European Unity Movement* (Oxford: Clarendon Press, 1982) pp. 56–8. The latter book gives some details about the Socialist Vanguard Group (p. 162). One of the German participants in the Geneva meetings, Hilda Monte, had also been an exile in London, in touch with Federal Union members; H. N. Brailsford had indeed written an introduction for her book, *The Unity of Europe* (London: Gollancz, 1943). For reference to Spinelli's autobiographical accounts of the Geneva meetings, see n. 22, *infra*.
17. Josephy, *op. cit.* (n. 14, *supra*).
18. Altiero Spinelli, *Come ho tentato di diventare saggio: Io, Ulisse* (Bologna: Il Mulino, 1984) pp. 307–8. See also Spinelli, *L'Europa non cade dal cielo* (Bologna: Il Mulino, 1960) p. 15; this section of the book was the Italian version of an article by Spinelli published in *Preuves* (Paris), October 1957. See also Michael Burgess, 'Federal Ideas in the

European Community: Altiero Spinelli and "European Union", 1981–84', *Government and Opposition*, Summer 1984, p. 346; and 'Intervista con Altiero Spinelli', in Spinelli, *Il progetto europeo* (Bologna: Il Mulino, 1985) pp. 201–3. Robbins's *Economic Causes of War*, translated by Spinelli, was published as *Le cause economiche della guerra* (Turin: Einaudi, 1944).

19. The translations of British federalist literature into Italian have included Norman Bentwich, 'Il problema coloniale e la soluzione federale', in *La Federazione Europea* (Florence: La Nuova Italia, 1948); Lord Lothian (Philip Kerr), 'La fine di Armageddon', *Comuni d'Europa* (Rome), July–August 1962; Lothian, 'L'anarchia internazionale', in Mario Albertini, *Il federalismo e lo Stato federale: Antologia e definizione* (Milan: Giuffre, 1963) and *Il federalismo: Antologia e definizione* (Bologna: Il Mulino, 1979), and in Sergio Pistone (ed.), *Politica di potenza e imperialismo* (Milan: Franco Angelo Editori, 1973); Lothian, *Il pacifismo non basta* (Bologna: Il Mulino, 1986); Lionel Robbins, *Le cause economiche della guerra* (Turin: Einaudi, 1944); Robbins, *L'economia pianificata e l'ordine internazionale* (Milan: Rizzoli, 1948); Robbins, *La base economica dei conflitti di classe* (Florence: La Nuova Italia, 1952); Robbins, 'L'anarchia internazionale e l'economia liberale' and 'L'anarchia internazionale e l'economia socialista', in Albertini, *op. cit.*; Robbins, 'L'economia della sovranita territoriale' and 'La causa ultima dei conflitti internazionali', in Pistone, *op. cit.*; Robbins, *Il federalismo e l'ordine economico internazionale* (Bologna: Il Mulino, 1985); K. C. Wheare, *Del governo federale* (Milan: Comunita, 1949); Barbara Wootton, *Socialismo e federazione* (Lugano: Nuove Edizioni di Capolago, 1945; Milan: La Fiaccola, 1945), in *La Federazione Europea* (Florence: La Nuova Italia, 1948) and in part as 'Il fallimento internazionale del socialismo', in Albertini, *op. cit.* Among other Italian sources which pay particular attention to the Federal Union literature are: Mario Albertini, Andrea Chiti-Batelli, Giuseppe Petrilli, *a cura di* Edmondo Paolini, *Storia del federalismo europeo* (Turin: Edizioni RAI, 1973, pp. 21, 38–40, 134–5, 138–42); Andrea Chiti-Batelli, *L'unione politica europea* (Rome: Senato della Republica, 1978) pp. 30–7, 72–5; Lucio Levi, *Federalismo e integrazione europea* (Palermo: Palumbo, 1978) pp. 39–46; Edmondo Paolini, *L'idea di Europa* (Florence: La Nuova Italia, 1979) pp. 46–50; Francesco Rossolillo, 'La scuola federalista inglese', in Sergio Pistone (ed.), *L'idea dell'unificazione europea dalla prima alla seconda guerra mondiale* (Turin: Fondazione Luigi Einaudi, 1975); Altiero Spinelli, 'The Growth of the European Movement since World War II', in C. Grove Haines (ed.), *European Integration* (Baltimore, Johns Hopkins Press, 1957) pp. 38–42. See also numerous articles in *Il Federalista*, which has been published triannually in Pavia for the last 28 years, and since 1984 had also been published in English, as *The Federalist*, and in French, as *Le Fédéraliste*.

20. Published in *Problemi della Federazione Europea* (Rome: Edizioni del Movimento Italiano per la Federazione Europea, 1944), and reprinted under the same title (Bologna: Centro Stampa del MFE Bologna,

1972), and in Altiero Spinelli, *Il progetto europeo* (Bologna: Il Mulino, 1985). An English translation of most of the Manifesto is printed in Walter Lipgens (ed.), *Documents on the History of European Integration, Vol. 1* (*op. cit.* in n. 16, *supra*) pp. 471–84; and the whole Manifesto with related documents has been published in English in Altiero Spinelli and Ernesto Rossi, *The Ventotene Manifesto* (Ventotene: Altiero Spinelli Institute for Federalist Studies, 1988; distributed in UK by Federal Trust).

21. Walter Lipgens, *A History of European Integration 1945–1947* (*op. cit.* in n. 16, *supra*) p. 109.
22. Walter Lipgens, 'Transnational Contacts', in Lipgens, *op. cit.* (n. 20, *supra*) pp. 661, 673, and 'Intervista con Altiero Spinelli', *op. cit.* (n. 18, *supra*) p. 209. See also Spinelli, 'European Union and the Resistance', in Ghita Ionescu (ed.), *The New Politics of European Integration* (London: Macmillan, 1972) pp. 6, 7. The Geneva meetings are also described in a posthumously published second part of Spinelli's autobiography, *Come ho tentato di diventare saggio: La goccia e la roccia* (Bologna: Il Mulino, 1987) pp. 67–71.
23. Extract from Einaudi's diary, cited in Riccardo Faucci, *Einaudi* (Turin: UTET, 1986) p. 321.
24. Board Minutes, 2 January 1942.
25. Letter to *The Times Literary Supplement*, 4 September 1943, reproduced in *Federal Union News*, no. 105, November 1943, p. 13.
26. *Federal Union News*, no. 108, February 1944, p. 11.
27. Report on Annual General Meeting of 23/4 September 1944, in *Federal News*, no. 116, October 1944, p. 13.
28. *Federal News*, no. 118, December 1944, pp. 1–2, 6–7. See also Lipgens, *op. cit.* (n. 21, *supra*) p. 148.
29. Robbins, *op. cit.* (n. 6, *supra*) pp. 105–6.
30. Mackay, *op. cit.* (n. 9, *supra*) p. 90.
31. Jennings, *op. cit.* (n. 1, *supra*) p. 30.
32. W. B. Curry, *The Case for Federal Union* (Harmondsworth: Penguin Books, 1939) p. 189.
33. Mackay, *op. cit.* (n. 9, *supra*) p. 106.
34. Federal Union meeting tape, 1980.
35. H. C. Usborne, in *Federal Union News*, no. 103, September 1943, p. 2; and anonymous authors in *Federal Union News*, no. 104, October 1943, pp. 2, 11.
36. Executive Committee Minutes, 21 December 1944, 9 July 1945.
37. 'Italians Demand European Union', *Federal News*, no. 107, January 1944, p. 2.
38. 'European Resistance Calls for Federation', *Federal News*, no. 116, October 1944, pp. 1, 2, 11. *Federal News* incorrectly reported that the meetings were held 'in a town in occupied Europe'.
39. Mary Saran, 'Paris Conference on European Federation', *Federal News*, no. 123, June 1945, pp. 9–11.
40. Lipgens, *op. cit.* (n. 21, *supra*) p. 126; Spinelli, *La goccia e la roccia*, *op. cit.* (n. 22, *supra*) pp. 79–83.
41. Spinelli, *ibid*, pp. 83–5, and 'European Union and the Resistance', *op.*

cit. (n. 22, *supra*) p. 8; Edmondo Paolini, *Altiero Spinelli: Appunti per una biografia* (Bologna: Il Mulino, 1988) pp. 40–4.

42. George Orwell, 'Towards European Unity', *Partisan Review*, July/August 1947, cited in Jeremy Moon, *European Integration in British Politics 1950–1963: A Study of Issue Change* (Aldershot: Gower, 1985) p. 72.
43. Lipgens, *op. cit.* (n. 21, *supra*) p. 129.
44. *Ibid*, p. 310.
45. *Ibid*, pp. 136, 406, 634. See also *Federal News*, no. 131, February 1946, pp. 11–12, and no. 136, July 1946, pp. 8–9, regarding the Belgian section.
46. F. Clemminck, 'Why I am a Federalist', *Federal News*, no. 132, March 1946, p. 11. The soldier's name was Maitland. See also *Federal News*, no. 121, March 1945, p. 18, and no. 124, June 1945, p. 19.
47. Lipgens, *op. cit.* (n. 21, *supra*) pp. 136–42 and chs II 2 and III 4. Nord was to strengthen his personal links with British federalists by marrying Margaret Dru, the secretary of FU's Golders Green branch (see *Federal News*, no. 190, February 1951, p. 7). He later became the Secretary-General of the European Parliament and then, as a Liberal MEP, one of its Vice-Presidents.
48. *Ibid*, pp. 303–10.
49. *Ibid*, pp. 305, 312, 634.
50. *Ibid*, p. 23, see also pp. 305–6. The impact of the Dutch federalists on the Hertenstein Programme is also underlined in Hendrik Brugmans, *Wij, Europa; Een halve eeuw strijd voor emancipatie en Europees federalisme* (Amsterdam and Leuven: Meulenhoff and Kritak, 1988) p. 172.
51. See also Ch. 4 in the present book and, for sources of information on the conference, Ch. 4, n. 8.
52. See Jean-Pierre Gouzy, *Les Pionniers de l'Europe Communautaire* (Lausanne: Centre de Recherches Européennes, 1968) pp. 34–5. Both sides of the argument are recorded in Finn Laursen, *Federalism and World Order*, Vol. II (Copenhagen: World Federalist Youth, 1972) pp. 4–8.
53. Lipgens, *op. cit.* (n. 21, *supra*) p. 362.
54. *Ibid*, pp. 314–16.
55. *Ibid*, pp. 362–9.
56. Accounts of the meeting, 12–15 April 1947, are given in Lipgens, *ibid*, pp. 369ff., and in *Federal News*, no. 147, June 1947, pp. 8–12, which are the sources for the information given here.
57. *Federal News*, *ibid*, p. 9.
58. *Ibid*, p. 12.
59. Accounts of the EUF's First Congress, 27–30 August 1947, are given in Lipgens, *op. cit.* (n. 21, *supra*) pp. 569ff.; in Denis de Rougement, 'The Campaign of the Congresses', in Ionescu, *op. cit.* (n. 22, *supra*); and in *Federal News*, no. 151, October 1947, pp. 9–11, and no. 152, November 1947, pp. 5–7. These are, except where other references are cited, the sources for the information given here.
60. John Pomian (ed.), *Joseph Retinger: Memoirs of an Eminence Grise*

(London: Chatto & Windus, 1972) p. 215.

61. Lipgens, *op. cit.* (n. 21, *supra*) p. 42. An evaluation of the work of this personalist group and its relationship with federalism is to be found in Ferdinand Kinsky, 'Fédéralisme et personnalisme', *L'Europe en formation*, no. 190–192, January–March 1976.
62. de Rougement, *op. cit.* (n. 59, *supra*) p. 12.
63. de Rougement's speech was published as 'L'attitude fédéraliste', *Revue Economique et Sociale* (Lausanne), October 1947.
64. 'True democracy must be a pyramid of solidarities from bottom to top . . . But federalism makes liberty the very principle of this organisation . . . the cause of European federation has deliberately been set within a world perspective . . . federalism on every plane and at every stage of human society from the bottom to the top.' From Montreux general policy resolution, reproduced in *Federal News*, no. 152, November 1947, p. 5; also in Andrew and Frances Boyd, *Western Union* (London: Hutchinson, undated – 1948 or 1949) pp. 141–8.
65. *Federal News*, *ibid*, p. 6.
66. Lipgens, *op. cit.* (n. 21, *supra*) p. 581. Spinelli's speech to the Congress is reproduced in full in Altiero Spinelli, *Il progetto europeo* (Bologna: Il Mulino, 1985) pp. 141–9.
67. *Federal News*, no. 157, October 1947, p. 11.
68. Pomian, *op. cit.* (n. 60, *supra*) p. 215.
69. de Rougement, *op. cit.* (n. 59, *supra*) p. 13.
70. See Altiero Spinelli, 'European Union and the Resistance', *op. cit.* (n. 22, *supra*).
71. *Federal News*, no. 133, April 1946, pp. 3–4.
72. *The Times*, 24 September 1946; reprinted in *Federal News*, no. 140, November 1946, pp. 5–6.
73. Lipgens, *op. cit.* (n. 21, *supra*) p. 325.
74. *Federal News*, no. 182, June 1950, p. 5.
75. The declaration and the names of the committee members were printed in *Federal News*, no. 143, February 1947, pp. 1–2.
76. Lipgens, *op. cit.* (n. 21, *supra*) pp. 327–8.
77. *Federal News*, no. 144, March 1947, p. 3. On page 2 of the same issue, the report on the Council meeting of 26 January stated that 'Europe has always divided the Council', although 'a group favouring federalism in Europe has always been strongly represented'.
78. Brugmans wrote on 21 January 1947, in the letter to which Josephy replied on 27 January (see n. 76, *supra*), that he and his group would 'have to fight the Churchill movement', on the grounds that the federalist movement would fall if a 'Western bloc' appeared to be its aim (Lipgens, *op. cit.* in n. 21, *supra*, p. 365).
79. Lord Plowden, cited in Michael Charlton, *The Price of Victory* (London: BBC, 1983) p. 84.
80. Lord Garner, cited in Charlton, *ibid*, p. 62.
81. Plowden, *loc. cit.* (n. 79, *supra*).
82. Lipgens, *op. cit.* (n. 21, *supra*) pp. 326–7.
83. Letter from Duncan Sandys, cited in Lipgens, *ibid*, p. 669.
84. Beveridge, like Curtis, did support the European Federal Pact (*Federal*

News, no. 182, June 1950, p. 5) but world federalism remained his chief commitment. Robbins, however, in the preface to a new edition of *The Economic Causes of War* (New York: Fertig, 1968), later expressed his regret about his post-war 'failure to realise the potentialities both of the creation . . . of a United Western Europe and of the part that could be played in it by Great Britain' and went on to reaffirm his commitment to the ringing call for the United States of Europe with which he had concluded his book in 1939 (in the passage cited earlier, to which n. 4, *supra*, refers).

85. *Op. cit.* (n. 60, *supra*) p. 216.
86. Conversation of Ota Adler with John Pinder, 1986.
87. Lipgens, *op. cit.* (n. 21, *supra*) p. 361.
88. Paolini, *op. cit.* (n. 41, *supra*) pp. 45–51; Sergio Pistone, 'Il ruolo del Movimento Federalista Europeo negli anni 1948–1950', in Raymond Poidevin (ed.), *Histoire des débuts de la construction européenne*, Groupe de Liaison des Historiens auprès des Communautés, Actes du Colloque de Strasbourg, 28–30 Novembre 1984 (Brussels, Bruylant, 1986) p. 287.
89. Spinelli, *op. cit.* (n. 66, *supra*) pp. 148–9; also quoted in Lipgens, *op. cit.* (n. 21, *supra*) p. 598.
90. Gouzy, *op. cit.* (n. 52, *supra*) pp. 56, 60.
91. Brugmans at the EUF Central Committee meeting on 15 November 1947, cited in de Rougement, *op. cit.* (n. 59, *supra*) p. 18.
92. The term 'unionist' was then used in contrast with federalist, to denote supporters of a loose association or an intergovernmental Europe (see, for example, Sandys's own use of Union of Europe, cited in Lipgens, *op. cit.* in n. 21, *supra*, p. 669). It is ironic that, since Spinelli and the European Parliament started to describe their more federalist proposals as a European Union, there has been a tendency in Britain to attribute long-standing federalist connotations to the word (for example in Christopher Tugendhat, 'How to get Europe moving again', *International Affairs*, Summer 1985, p. 421).
93. Accounts of the Congress of Europe are given in de Rougement, *op. cit.* (n. 59, *supra*) pp. 17ff.; Gouzy, *op. cit.* (n. 52, *supra*) pp. 46ff.; Pomian, *op. cit.* (n. 60, *supra*) pp. 214ff.; and, as regards the preparations for the Congress, Lipgens, *op. cit.* (n. 21, *supra*) pp. 657ff.
94. Pomian, *ibid*, p. 222.
95. See F. L. Josephy's obituary for Mackay in *World Affairs*, no. 249a, spring 1960, p. 47.
96. See de Rougement, *op. cit.* (n. 59, *supra*) p. 24, and Pomian, *loc. cit.* (n. 94, *supra*).
97. See *Federal News*, no. 143, February 1947, p. 1, and Lipgens, *op. cit.* (n. 21, *supra*) pp. 328, 605.
98. *Hansard*, 18 March 1948, Cols 2303–3; Mackay's speech on it is in *Hansard*, 5 May 1948, Cols 1280–92.
99. Cited in Jeremy Moon, *op. cit.* (n. 42, *supra*) pp. 73–4.
100. Alan S. Milward, 'The Committee of European Economic Cooperation (CEEC) and the Advent of the Customs Union', in Lipgens, *op. cit.* (n. 21, *supra*) pp. 557–8; and Milward, *The Reconstruction of*

Western Europe 1945–51 (London: Methuen, 1984) pp. 235–6.
101. Paul-Henri Spaak, *The Continuing Battle: Memoirs of a European 1936–66* (London: Weidenfeld & Nicolson, 1971) pp. 144–5, 203.
102. Cited in Charlton, *op. cit.* (n. 79, *supra*) p. 76.
103. Henry Usborne, *Prescription for Peace* (Evesham: 'Minifed' Promotion Group, 1985) pp. 83–4.
104. See, for example, Sir Roderick Barclay, cited in Charlton, *ibid*, p. 79; and Retinger's notes, in Pomian, *op. cit.* (n. 60, *supra*) p. 220.
105. See Moon, *op. cit.* (n. 42, *supra*) pp. 72–4.
106. Mayhew cited in Charlton, *op. cit.* (n. 79, *supra*) p. 77.
107. Pomian, *op. cit.* (n. 60, *supra*) p. 223; and Gouzy, *op. cit.* (n. 52, *supra*) p. 58.
108. Gouzy, *ibid*, p. 47; and Lipgens, *op. cit.* (n. 21, *supra*) p. 620. the texts of both resolutions are given (in German) in Walter Lipgens, *45 Jahre Ringen um die Europäische Verfassung: Dokumente 1939–84* (Bonn: Europa Union Verlag, 1986).
109. Josephy, *op. cit.* (n. 95, *supra*) p. 47.
110. Lipgens, *op. cit.* (n. 21, *supra*) p. 147.
111. Cited in Gouzy *op. cit.* (n. 52, *supra*) p. 65; see also Pomian, *op. cit.* (n. 60, *supra*) p. 244.
112. Cited in Charlton, *op. cit.* (n. 79, *supra*) p. 75.
113. Pistone, *op. cit.* (n. 88, *supra*) pp. 285–7 and 300–3. Except where otherwise stated, the following paragraph too is based on this source and on Gouzy, *op. cit.* (n. 52, *supra*) pp. 64–7 and 81.
114. E. G. Thompson, 'Frontier Incident – For Peace', *Federal News*, no. 186, October 1950, p. 4. Tommy Thompson, who had previously played a leading part in Federal Union's Cambridge University Branch, worked for three years for the European Youth Campaign before returning to London in 1954 and joining Federal Union's Executive Committee (*Federal News*, no. 227, February–March 1955, p. 15).
115. Gouzy, *op. cit.* (n. 52, *supra*) p. 68.
116. *World Affairs*, no. 253, Summer 1961, p. 42. The book was R. W. G. Mackay, *Towards a United States of Europe: An analysis of Britain's role in European Union* (London: Hutchinson, 1961).
117. Spaak, *op. cit.* (n. 101, *supra*) p. 219.
118. Pomian, *op. cit.* (n. 60, *supra*) p. 244.
119. Spaak was to write that, while the European army initiative was Churchill's, it was 'the most audacious among the deputies' who added the provision for a European defence minister and democratic control (*op. cit.* in n. 101, *supra*, p. 217). In any case, Churchill did not demur, and continued to sponsor the resolution.
120. The citations are from Spaak, *ibid*, pp. 219–20, and Charlton, *op. cit.* (n. 79, *supra*) pp. 137, 146, 151.
121. Gouzy, *op. cit.* (n. 52, *supra*) pp. 83–4.
122. Spaak, *op. cit.* (n. 101, *supra*) pp. 221–5.
123. Gouzy, *op. cit.* (n. 52, *supra*) p. 85.
124. Cited in Lipgens, *op. cit.* (n. 21, *supra*) p. 670.

7 New Thinking: The Federal Trust Begins

1. See Federal Union Research Institute, *Second Annual Report 1940–1941* (London: 1941), duplicated, 76pp.
2. Patrick Ransome (ed.), *Studies in Federal Planning* (London: Macmillan, 1943).
3. Much of the following information is to be found in *Working for a Better World: The Federal Trust 1945–1990* (Federal Trust, 1990), a report on the first four and a half decades of the Trust's work.
4. Douglas Sanders tape, 1980.
5. See Ch. 5, p. 69 and n. 39.
6. R. W. G. Mackay, *The Economic Aspects of European Federation* (Oxford: Blackwell for the Federal Trust, 1952); and *Whither Britain?* (Oxford: Blackwell for the Federal Trust, 1953). The Trust was later responsible for the posthumous publication of Mackay's last book, *Towards a United States of Europe* (London: Hutchinson, 1961).
7. Sanders tape, 1980.
8. *Journal of Common Market Studies*, July 1965. The ten were: John Bowyer, François Duchêne, David Howell, John Lambert, Christopher Layton, Richard Mayne, John Pinder, Roy Pryce, Noël Salter, and Dennis Thompson.
9. See, for example, *The Times*, 12 July 1965; *The Daily Mirror*, 13 July 1965.
10. Sir Cecil Weir, *The First Step in European Integration: The European Coal and Steel Community*, 1957; Paul Bareau, *Europe: The Next Steps Towards a Supermarket*, 1957; Georg Schwarzenberger, *Atlantic Union, a Practical Utopia?*, 1957; the Rt Hon. Patrick Gordon Walker, *Britain and the Commonwealth: Expanding or Contracting?*; Barbara Ward (Lady Jackson), *Forty Years on: Britain in the Second Half of the Twentieth Century*, 1959. All these were published by the Federal Trust.
11. Roy Pryce, *The Political Future of the European Community* (London: John Marshbank for the Federal Trust, 1962).
12. John Pinder (ed.), *The Economics of Europe: What the Common Market Means for Britain* (London: Charles Knight for the Federal Trust, 1971); Stuart Holland, *The Price of Europe: A Reassessment*, with a Preface by Sir Alec Cairncross (London: SGS Associates for the Federal Union, 1971).
13. Uwe Kitzinger, *Diplomacy and Persuasion: How Britain Joined the Common Market* (London: Thames & Hudson, 1973) pp. 291–2.
14. Geoffrey Denton, John Dodson, Tim Josling, Marcus Miller, *The Economics of Renegotiation* (Federal Trust, 1975). Another report produced in time for the referendum was that of a study group chaired by Tim Josling and written by him and Simon Harris, *The CAP and the British Consumer* (Federal Trust, 1975).
15. *Report of the Study Group on the Role of Public Finance in European Integration*, the MacDougall Report (Brussels: Commission of the EC, April 1977).

16. Geoffrey Denton, *The British Problem and the Future of the EEC Budget* (Federal Trust, 1982), and Denton, *The Economy and EEC Membership* (Federal Trust, 1983).

8 The Birth of the European Community

1. Alan Milward, 'The Committee of European Economic Cooperation (CEEC) and the Advent of the Customs Union', in Walter Lipgens, *A History of European Integration 1945–1947: The Formation of the European Unity Movement* (Oxford: Clarendon Press, 1982) p. 568.
2. Jean Monnet, *Memoirs* (London: Collins, 1978) pp. 279ff.
3. Cited in Michael Charlton, *The Price of Victory* (London: BBC, 1983) p. 83.
4. Monnet, *op. cit.* (n. 2, *supra*) pp. 278–81.
5. Milward, 'The Committee of European Cooperation' (*op. cit.* in n. 1, *supra*) p. 550. In his later work, *The Reconstruction of Western Europe 1945–51* (London: Methuen, 1984) pp. 162–3, 468. Milward shows that officials in the French Ministry of Foreign Affairs began in 1948 to promote the idea of 'a Franco-German economic association'. This does not appear to detract from Monnet's role in creating the Community institutions.
6. 'Speech to the Inaugural Session of the High Authority of the ECSC, 10 August 1952', in Jean Monnet, *Les Etats-Unis d'Europe ont commencé* (Paris: Robert Laffont, 1965) pp. 55–8.
7. Altiero Spinelli, *Diario europeo: 1948–1969* (Bologna: Il Mulino, 1989) p. 142.
8. Bernard Donoghue and G. W. Jones, *Herbert Morrison: Portrait of a Politician* (London: Weidenfeld & Nicolson, 1973) p. 481, cited in Jeremy Moon, *European Integration in British Politics: A Study of Issue Change* (Aldershot: Gower, 1985) p. 5.
9. *Hansard*, 5 May 1948, Col. 1317.
10. Record by Sir R. Makins of a conversation between Sir S. Cripps and M. Monnet on 10 May 1950, CE 2338/2141/181, Foreign Office, 15 May 1950. See also Richard Lamb, *The Failure of the Eden Government* (London: Sidgwick & Jackson, 1987) pp. 60–1, which refers to *Documents on British Policy Overseas*, Series Two, Vol. I, 1950, 1952, HMSO, 1985, Cab 134/224.
11. Record by Sir R. Makins, *ibid*.
12. Cited in Charlton, *op. cit.* (n. 3, *supra*) pp. 102–3.
13. See, for example, citations in Charlton, *ibid*, pp. 92, 99, 102–3, 116.
14. In the early 1950s the Conservative government and the Labour opposition both adopted the habit of using the term 'federalism' as a pejorative description of developments on the Continent in which they did not want to participate. See Moon, *op. cit.* (n. 8, *supra*) p. 128.
15. Moon, *ibid*, p. 124.
16. *Ibid*, pp. 91–2, 129, 149. The 1948 resolution which approved the proposal for a constitutional assembly was moved by Wilfred Roberts, and Miss Josephy supported it 'with characteristic vigour' (*Federal News*, no. 158, May 1948).

17. Moon, *ibid*, pp. 98–9.
18. Personal recollection, John Pinder: Miss Josephy was saying that the federalists were 'the only British who are not crazy'.
19. Monnet recounted his part in the launching of the EDC proposal in his *Memoirs* (*op. cit.* in n. 2, *supra*) ch. 14.
20. Federal Union's Annual General Meeting in May 1952 urged the British government to negotiate full membership (*Federal News*, no. 207, July/August 1952, p. 6) and this was reiterated at the AGM in May 1954 (*Federal News*, no. 223, June/July 1954, p. 12).
21. *Op. cit.* (n. 2, *supra*) p. 343.
22. Spinelli was much helped in this by the socialist Deputy, I. M. Lombardo. See Luigi Vittorio Majocchi and Francesco Rossolillo, *il Parlamento europeo* (Naples: Guida Editori, 1979) pp. 44–9; and Jean-Pierre Gouzy, *Les Pionniers de l'Europe Communautaire* (Lausanne: Centre de Recherches Européennes, 1968) pp. 73, 86–7.
23. For one critique, see Spinelli, 'The Growth of the European Movement since World War II', in C. Grove Haines (ed.), *European Integration* (Baltimore: Johns Hopkins Press, 1957) pp. 58–60.
24. See Gouzy, *op. cit.* (n. 22, *supra*) pp. 89–91.
25. Edouard Herriot, in his key speech in the Assemblée Nationale on 30 August 1954, said the lack of British support was enough to make him reject the treaty. Cited in Uwe Kitzinger, *The European Common Market and Community* (London: Routledge & Kegan Paul, 1967) pp. 61–2.
26. For Federal Union, see n. 20, *supra*. The Liberal Assembly called in 1954 for full British membership of EDC (see Moon, *op. cit.* in n. 8, *supra*) p. 129.
27. See Gouzy, *op. cit.* (n. 22, *supra*) pp. 100–1.
28. *Ibid*, pp. 72, 88–9. Gouzy, who was Secretary-General of the French federalist movement at the time, wrote that 'les partisans de l'Europe acceullissent généralement de manière favorable ou résignée la déclaration du gouvernement français . . . préconisant une armée européenne integrée'.
29. Monnet, *op. cit.* (n. 2, *supra*) pp. 349, 383; and personal knowledge.
30. *Federal News*, no. 227, February/March 1955, pp. 9, 10; and Gouzy, *op. cit.* (n. 22, *supra*) pp. 132–4.
31. Edmondo Paolini, *Altiero Spinelli: Appunti per una biografia* (Bologna: Il Mulino, 1988) pp. 97ff.; Gouzy, *ibid*, pp. 145–7.
32. Gouzy, *ibid*, p. 140.
33. *Federal News*, no. 232, March/April 1956, p. 8.
34. Gouzy, *op. cit.* (n. 22, *supra*) pp. 136–42; and E. G. Thompson tape, 1986.

9 Atlantic Union?

1. See, for example, Lord Plowden, cited in Michael Charlton, *The Price of Victory* (London: BBC, 1983) p. 84.
2. Clarence Streit, *Union Now: a Proposal for a Federal Union of the*

Democracies of the North Atlantic (London and New York: Jonathan Cape and Harper, 1939).
3. National Council Minutes, 6 July 1941.
4. *Federal Union News*, no. 88, June 1942, p. 4.
5. National Council Minutes, 21 January 1950.
6. *Federal News*, May 1951.
7. Douglas Robinson tape, 1980.
8. National Council Minutes, 26 January 1952.
9. *Ibid*, 27 September 1952.
10. Published by Federal Union (not dated; between September 1953 and December 1954).
11. Istram Szent-Miklosy, chapter 3 of thesis entitled *Development of American thinking on an Atlantic Community* (New York: mimeographed at Columbia University, 1962).
12. *Hansard*, 21 July 1953, Col. 328. He had also raised this issue at Strasbourg (Consultative Assembly, *Official Reports*, 5th Session 1953, p. 105).
13. *Hansard*, 17 December 1953, Col. 655.
14. *Freedom and Union* (Washington), November 1951; letter from Livingston Hartley to John Tilney, MP, 10 October 1952.
15. Alastair Kyle to Walden Moore, 16 July 1952; Robinson to Moore, 31 October 1952. The resolution was published in a Dutch newspaper (Declaration of Atlantic Unity papers deposited by Walden Moore in the Columbia University Library, New York).
16. Moore to Robinson, 17 October 1952 (DAU papers).
17. National Council Minutes, 2 October 1954.
18. *Ibid*, 18 July 1953.
19. *Federal News*, no. 229, Summer 1955, p. 7.
20. National Council Minutes, 24 September 1955.
21. *Ibid*, 23 March 1957.
22. *Declaration of Atlantic Unity*, 22 February 1955.
23. Robinson to Moore, 31 October 1952 (DAU papers).
24. *Freedom and Union*, September 1956.
25. 'Atlantic Assembly', *The Economist*, 26 December 1953.
26. Letters from B. D. Barton and David V. Kelly to *The Economist*, 9 January and 23 January 1954.
27. For example, *The Times*, *New Statesman* and *Spectator* make no mention of the idea in 1953–4.
28. *Freedom and Union*, June 1956.
29. *Ibid*, November 1956.
30. *Ibid*, September 1957.
31. Moore to Robinson, 14 March 1955 (DAU papers).
32. Robinson to Clement Davies, 13 January 1955 (DAU papers).
33. Livingston Hartley, 'Towards an Atlantic Assembly', *Atlantic Community Quarterly*, Spring 1966, p. 105.
34. *Freedom and Union*, September 1957.
35. National Council Minutes, 1 January 1959.
36. Barton to Moore, 12 December 1958 (DAU papers).
37. Moore to Barton, 16 December 1958; Lithgow Osborne to Barton, 19

December 1958; Nicholson to Moore, 29 December 1958 (DAU papers).
38. Petition to Atlantic Congress.
39. Programme for 1960 (DAU papers).
40. Barton and Maddan to Rt Hon. Selwyn Lloyd, MP, 8 December 1959 (DAU papers).
41. Note on conference with Christian Herter, 9 December 1959 (DAU papers).
42. Moore to US Sponsors, 5 May 1960 (DAU papers).
43. National Council Minutes, 6 February 1960.
44. Barton to Adler enclosing draft paper to Regional Commission, 8 January 1960.
45. Moore to US Sponsors, 23 November 1960 (DAU papers).
46. *Freedom and Union*, June 1960.
47. *Ibid*, December 1961.
48. *Second Declaration of Atlantic Unity*, April 1962.
49. Moore, European Memorandum No. 3, 17 April 1960; Moore to Monnet, 1 February 1963 (DAU papers).
50. *Freedom and Union*, October 1963.
51. *World Affairs*, March 1963, p. 29.
52. Barton to Maddan, 12 February 1964; Barton to Emery, 1 December 1964; Catlin to Barton, 29 April 1965 (DAU papers).
53. *Freedom and Union*, July–August 1964.
54. See, for example, the editorial, 'The Roads towards World Federation', in *The Federalist* (Pavia), no. 2–3, 1986, p. 77; John Pinder, 'Federal Approaches: The European Experience', *World Federalist News* (Amsterdam), Fall 1986, p. 2.

10 Europe Relaunched

1. Cited in Michael Charlton, *The Price of Victory* (London: BBC, 1983), p. 178.
2. *Ibid*, pp. 194–5.
3. Miriam Camps, *Britain and the European Community, 1955–1963* (London: Oxford University Press, 1964) p. 47.
4. Uwe Kitzinger, *Diplomacy and Persuasion: How Britain Joined the Common Market* (London: Thames & Hudson, 1973) pp. 190–2.
5. Ota Adler tape, 1980.
6. *Federal News*, no. 229, Summer 1955, pp. 13–14; and no. 230, October/November 1955, p. 3.
7. FU Regional Commission Minutes, 10 March 1956. See Chapter 8, pp. 126–7 of the present volume for the EUF Congress of 2–4 March 1956.
8. *World Affairs*, no. 237, January/February 1957, pp. 15–16.
9. Sir Cecil Weir, *The First Step in European Integration: The European Coal and Steel Community* (Federal Trust, 1957); Derek Ezra was closely associated with its drafting. This was followed by the four other pamphlets listed in Ch. 7, n. 10 above.
10. The sponsors from the House of Commons included John Edwards, the Hon. Hugh Fraser, John Hynd, Sir Keith Joseph, Martin Maddan,

Geoffrey Rippon, John Rodgers, Rt Hon. Arthur Woodburn (Regional Commission Minutes, 16 May 1957).

11. *World Affairs*, no. 236, November/December 1957, pp. 15–16.
12. The Fore' ‹ Ministers of the Six agreed in Venice at the end of May 1956 to accept, as the basis for the drafting of the Rome Treaties establishing the EEC and Euratom, the Spaak report, drafted mainly by Pierre Uri, one of Monnet's closest collaborators, for a committee chaired by Paul-Henri Spaak which the six governments had set up following the Messina declaration.
13. Camps, *op. cit.* (n. 3, *supra*) ch. 4.
14. *A European Free Trade Area, United Kingdom Memorandum to the Organisation for European Economic Cooperation*, Cmnd 72 (London: HMSO, February 1957).
15. Regional Commission Minutes, 17 December 1956.
16. Executive Committee Minutes, 11 November 1956.
17. *Op. cit.* (n. 8, *supra*).
18. The Economist Intelligence Unit, *Britain and Europe* (London: EIU, 1957) p. v.
19. Regional Commission Minutes, 17 December 1956; 10 January 1957; 12 February 1957.
20. Regional Commission Minutes, 16 January 1958.
21. *World Affairs*, no. 244, July–August 1958, pp. 48, 60.
22. Regional Commission Minutes, 29 July 1958.
23. Regional Commission Minutes, 28 March, 23 April, 28 November 1957.
24. *World Affairs*, no. 245, Autumn 1958, p. 69.
25. The members of the study group were Derek (now Lord) Ezra, Norman Hart, Jim Hunt, John Pinder and Tommy Thompson (Regional Commission Minutes, 16 January and 6 February 1958).
26. *World Affairs*, no. 238, Spring 1957, pp. 23–5. The conservative MPs were Capt. F. V. Corfield, John Hay, J. E. Leavey, John Rodgers; the Labour MPs, John Edwards, Geoffrey de Freitas, Harry Hynd, Niall MacDermot, Lena Jeger; members of FU Executive and Regional Commission, Ota Adler, David Allen, Caspar Brook, Norman Hart, Tony Morris, John Pinder, Findlay Rea, Tommy Thompson, David Webster.
27. Minutes of FU Executive Sub-Committee on AEF–FU Relations, 31 July 1958; report of FU's 1958 AGM in *World Affairs*, no. 244, July–August 1958, p. 63.
28. *World Affairs*, no. 233, May–June 1956, pp. 3ff.
29. *The Economist*, Christmas number, 1958.
30. E. G. Thompson tape 1986; *World Affairs*, no. 246, spring 1959, pp. 5ff. In addition to Attlee, the delegation included five Labour MPs (Rt Hon. Arthur Bottomley, T. C. Boyd, George Jeger, Roy Jenkins, Niall MacDermot), six Conservative MPs (Martin Maddan, Robert Mathew, Nigel Nicolson, Julian Ridsdale, Geoffrey Rippon, Peter Smithers) and twelve members or associates of the Regional Commission (Ota Adler, Richard Bailey, Caspar Brook, Harry Cowie, Norman Hart, Jim Hunt, Eric Lingeman, Tony Morris, John Pinder,

Findlay Rea, Tommy Thompson, David Webster).
31. *World Affairs*, *loc. cit.*
32. Regional Commission Minutes, 27 April and 27 May 1959, and annexed to the Minutes, a Report of Conference on 'The New Europe, The Overseas Territories and the Commonwealth'.
33. 'The Next Steps', *World Affairs*, no. 250, Summer 1960, p. 59.
34. Kitzinger, *op. cit.* (n. 4, *supra*) p. 190.
35. Regional Commission Minutes, 31 March and 27 April 1959.
36. Regional Commission Minutes, 4 July 1959.
37. Regional Commission Minutes, 4 January 1959; Britain in Europe, Council of Management Minutes, 26 July 1960.
38. The report was printed in *World Affairs*, no. 246, Spring 1959, pp. 3–4, 25–7.
39. Regional Commission Minutes, 3 March 1959.
40. The Economist Intelligence Unit, *The Commonwealth and Europe* (London: EIU, 1960).
41. Britain in Europe, Director's Report to the Council of Management, 5 October 1960, with speech by the Rt Hon. Reginald Maudling annexed.
42. A quantitative analysis of parliamentary debates during the 1961–3 negotiations has shown that 'Commonwealth considerations far outweighed all others'. See Jeremy Moon, *European Integration in British Politics 1950–1963: A Study of Issue Change* (Aldershot: Gower, 1958) p. 156.
43. Lord Windlesham, *Communication and Political Power* (London: Jonathan Cape, 1966) pp. 171–8.
44. Regional Committee Minutes, 6 April, 11 May, 1960; Minutes of Common Market Campaign Sub-Committee, 12 July 1960.
45. Regional Committee Minutes, 8 September 1960.
46. John Pinder, personal recollection.
47. They included David Barton, Colin Beever, John Bowyer, Caspar Brook, Norman Hart, John Leech, John Pinder, Douglas Robinson, Tommy Thompson and Lucy Webster (Britain in Europe, Minutes of Europe House Committee, 27 June, 25 July, 15 November 1960).
48. Lord Gladwyn, 'European Priorities' (based on the address given at Europe House), *World Affairs*, no. 252, Spring 1961, p. 5.
49. Britain in Europe, Minutes of AGM, 2 January 1961.
50. Regional Commission Minutes, 4 January 1961.
51. Regional Commission Minutes, 7 March 1961.
52. Regional Commission Minutes, 4 January, 31 January, 7 March 1961.
53. Regional Commission Minutes, 4 January 1961.
54. The text of the statement and list of signatories are given in Lord Windlesham, *op. cit.* (n. 43, *supra*) pp. 270–3.
55. *Conservative News Letter*, July 1961, cited in Nora Beloff, *The General Says No* (Harmondsworth: Penguin Books, 1963) p. 132.
56. Moon, *op. cit.* (n. 42, *supra*) p. 196.

11 Hopes and Setbacks

1. Lord Windlesham, *Communication and Political Power* (London: Jonathan Cape, 1966) p. 166. Except where otherwise stated, the information about the Common Market Campaign given in the following paragraphs comes from the minutes of the Campaign's Directing Committee from its first meeting, on 19 June 1961, to its last, on 12 March 1963.
2. Reviewed by David Barton in *World Affairs*, no. 257, September 1962, p. 58.
3. R. Colin Beever, *European Unity and the Trade Union Movements* (Leiden: Sythoff, 1960); U. W. Kitzinger, *The Challenge of the Common Market* (Oxford: Blackwell, 1961); Michael Shanks and John Lambert, *Britain and the New Europe: The Future of the Common Market* (London: Chatto & Windus, 1962); R. W. G. Mackay (with a preface by Paul-Henri Spaak), *Towards a United States of Europe: An Analysis of Britain's Role in European Union* (London: Hutchinson, 1961); Richard Mayne, *The Community of Europe* (London: Gollancz, 1962); John Pinder, *Britain and the Common Market* (London: The Cresset Press, 1961); Roy Pryce, *The Political Future of the European Community* (London: Marshbank for the Federal Trust, 1962); Alan Campbell and Dennis Thompson, *Common Market Law: Texts and Commentaries* (London: Stevens, 1962).
4. See, for example, 'A Federal Europe', the editorial for *World Affairs*, no. 255, February 1962. This was the penultimate number edited by Harry Cowie. From September 1962 the editor was Marianne Borman, and Roderick MacFarquhar, subsequently a Labour MP, Trustee of the Federal Trust, and a founder of the Social Democratic Party, was editorial adviser.
5. John Bowyer and John Pomian, report on 'The negotiations between Britain and the Community', see *World Affairs*, no. 258, November 1962, p. 68; Roger Broad and Norman Hart, *Common Sense about the Common Market* (Labour Common Market Committee, 1962); Norman Hart and Anthony Meyer, *Forward Britain into Europe* (Common Market Campaign, 1962).
6. Except where otherwise stated, the information about Britain in Europe and Europe House given in the following paragraphs comes from the minutes of those two organisations and of Federal Union's Regional Commission.
7. Conversation of John Roberts with David Barton, 21 June 1981.
8. Jeremy Moon, *European Integration in British Politics 1950–1963: A Study of Issue Change* (Aldershot: Gower, 1958) pp. 189–93.
9. Regional Commission Minutes, 19 May 1958; 1 September 1958; 3 March 1959.
10. 'The Lawyers and the Community', memorandum by Dennis Thompson, 9 March 1986.
11. A summary report of the conference is to be found in Dennis Thompson, 'European Legal Problems', *World Affairs*, no. 252, Spring 1961, pp. 22–3.

12. *Op. cit.* (n. 3, *supra*).
13. Regional Commission Minutes, 12 March 1962.
14. 'Federal Union Twenty Five', Annual Report, 1963/4.
15. Michael Palmer, 'Cambridge Invites Europe', *World Affairs*, no. 253, Summer 1961, p. 45; and R. J. Jarrett, 'Young Europeans', *World Affairs*, no. 254, Autumn 1961, p. 71.
16. Britain in Europe, Report of Executive Secretary (Jim Hunt), 18 September 1961; and Report of Executive Secretary (Val Schur) to Council of Management, 26 April 1962.
17. Tony Morris, 'Report on Participation of UK Delegates at Rome Congress of European Movement 10–13 June', annexed to Regional Commission Minutes, 1 July 1957.
18. Uwe Kitzinger, *Diplomacy and Persuasion: How Britain Joined the Common Market* (London: Thames & Hudson, 1973) p. 225.
19. The resolution of the AEF's founding assembly in March 1957, calling for a federal pact, is reproduced in Walter Lipgens, *45 Jahre Ringen um die Europäische Verfassung: Dokumente 1939–1984* (Bonn: Europa Union Verlag, 1986) pp. 400–1.
20. J. C. Hunt, 'Report on the Private Study Conference arranged by La Fédération in Paris on March 5 on Problems arising from bringing the European Economic Community into being', 6 March 1958, annexed to Regional Commission Minutes, 13 March 1958; and Minutes of Regional Commission's Sub-Committee on AEF–FU Relations, 31 July 1958.
21. 'Report of Conference on the New Europe, The Overseas Territories and the Commonwealth', held on 18–19 April 1959, annexed to Regional Commission Minutes, 4 April 1959; and 'Study Conference on European–African Relations', *World Affairs*, no. 254, Autumn 1961, pp. 67–70; Regional Commission Minutes, 27 April 1959.
22. Miriam Camps, *Britain and the European Community, 1955–1963* (London: Oxford University Press, 1964) p. 360.
23. Jean-Pierre Gouzy, *Les Pionniers de l'Europe Communautaire* (Lausanne: Centre de Recherches Européennes, 1968) pp. 145–7.
24. 'Democratic Action', *World Affairs*, no. 255, February 1962, pp. 15–18.
25. The conference was reported in Marianne Borman, 'Sovereignty and the Common Market', *World Affairs*, no. 255, February 1962, pp. 9–12.
26. *Op. cit.* (n. 3, *supra*) p. 78.
27. *Op. cit.* (n. 3, *supra*) p. 164.
28. *Op. cit.* (n. 3, *supra*) pp. 13–17, 85–93.
29. Regional Commission Minutes, 22 May 1962.
30. Moon, *op. cit.* (n. 8, *supra*) pp. 206–7; and Kitzinger, *op. cit.* (n. 18, *supra*) p. 417.
31. Directing Committee Minutes, 19 June, 10 July, 31 July 1961.
32. Directing Committee Minutes, 14 September 1961.
33. *Op. cit.* (n. 5, *supra*).
34. Camps, *op. cit.* (n. 22, *supra*) pp. 448–50.
35. Eric Roll, *Crowded Hours* (London: Faber & Faber, 1985) p. 126.

36. Camps, *op. cit.* (n. 22, *supra*) pp. 450–1.
37. For a view of this incident from a Labour European, see George Brown, *In My Way* (London: Gollancz, 1971) pp. 216–19.
38. Moon, *op. cit.* (n. 8, *supra*) p. 207.
39. Lord Windlesham, *op. cit.* (n. 1, *supra*) pp. 158–9; Kitzinger, *op. cit.* (n. 18, *supra*) p. 354.
40. Camps, *op. cit.* (n. 22, *supra*) p. 464.
41. Except where otherwise stated, the information about the Anti-Common Market League comes from Windlesham, *op. cit.* (n. 1, *supra*) pp. 171–8.
42. The *Quiz* is reproduced in Windlesham, *ibid*, p. 274.
43. Moon, *op. cit.* (n. 8, *supra*) pp. 155–8.
44. Windlesham, *op. cit.* (n. 1, *supra*) p. 168, gives the numbers for the Campaign's publications.
45. Moon, *op. cit.* (n. 8, *supra*) pp. 102–4.
46. Camps, *op. cit.* (n. 22, *supra*) p. 513.
47. Roll, *op. cit.* (n. 35, *supra*) pp. 128–31.
48. This and, except where otherwise stated, the following information about de Gaulle's negotiating position is based on Camps, *op. cit.* (n. 22, *supra*) pp. 500ff.
49. Brown, *op. cit.* (n. 37, *supra*) p. 220.
50. Camps notes the severe Continental criticisms of the length and complexity of the negotiations (*op. cit.* in n. 22, *supra*, p. 514).
51. Graphically described in Nora Beloff, *The General Says No* (Harmondsworth: Penguin Books, 1963) pp. 155–6.
52. See Camps, *op. cit.* (n. 22, *supra*) p. 502, and Roll, *op. cit.* (n. 35, *supra*) p. 131.
53. See Kitzinger, *op. cit.* (n. 18, *supra*) ch. 7, particularly p. 207.
54. Directing Committee Minutes of its last meeting, 12 March 1963.
55. Cited from Camps, *op. cit.* (n. 22, *supra*) p. 361.
56. *Hansard* (Lords), 28 July 1971, Col. 473, cited in Kitzinger, *op. cit.* (n. 18, *supra*) p. 279.
57. *Op. cit.* (n. 3, *supra*).

12 Britain into Europe

1. Directing Committee Minutes, 22 January 1963.
2. Directing Committee Minutes, 12 March 1963.
3. Britain in Europe, Annual General Meeting Minutes, 8 April 1963.
4. *Ibid* (President's Address and Policy Statement).
5. *World Affairs*, no. 260, March 1963, p. 17.
6. John Pinder, *Europe Against de Gaulle* (London: Pall Mall Press for the Federal Trust, 1963) pp. 114–18.
7. Jean Monnet, *Memoirs* (London: Collins, 1976) pp. 467–8; and private information.
8. 'Federal Union Twenty-Five', Annual Report 1963/4.
9. Walter Lipgens, *45 Jahre Ringen um die Europäische Verfassung: Dokumente 1939–1984* (Bonn: Europa Union Verlag, 1986) pp. 462–4.
10. 'President's Address' and 'General Secretary's Report on Activities in

1963': Annual General Meeting Minutes, 18 March 1964.
11. 'President's Address', Annual General Meeting Minutes, 24 March 1964.
12. See Uwe Kitzinger, *The Second Try: Labour and the EEC* (Oxford: Pergamon, 1968) pp. 49, 50.
13. Britain and Europe and Campaign for Europe, Annual General Meeting Minutes, 7 December 1967.
14. John Strachey, *Federalism or Socialism?* (London: Gollancz, 1940).
15. The 1950 quotation was cited in Jeremy Moon, *European Integration in British Politics 1950–63: A Study of Issue Change* (Aldershot: Gower, 1985) p. 75; that of 1954 in F. L. Josephy, 'Marking Time at Strasbourg', *Federal News*, no. 223, June–July 1956, p. 5.
16. R. Colin Beever, *Trade Unions and the Common Market* (London: PEP, 1962), and 'Trade Union Re-Thinking', *Journal of Common Market Studies*, vol. 2, no. 2, 1963. The complete list of members of the Labour Committee in Spring 1963 is given in Kitzinger, *op. cit.* (n. 12, *supra*) p. 2. Information about the Committee's activities is given in Federal Union, *op. cit.* (n. 8, *supra*).
17. Britain in Europe, 'Executive Secretary's Report on Activities during 1964', Annual General Meeting Minutes, 24 March 1965.
18. Kitzinger, *op. cit.* (n. 12, *supra*) pp. 14ff. and 49–55.
19. Speech in Strasbourg, 23 January 1967, reproduced in Uwe Kitzinger, *The European Common Market and Community* (London: Routledge & Kegan Paul, 1967) p. 196.
20. Cited in Kitzinger, *op. cit.* (n. 12, *supra*) p. 4.
21. Federal Trust, papers for conference, 12–14 July 1968.
22. Letter dated 13 December 1968, from Altiero Spinelli to George Brown; and note on 'Colloquio con Nenni', attached to letter of 4 December 1968, from Riccardo Perissich to John Pinder.
23. Andrew Wilson, 'Stewart looks both ways on George and Friendly Five', *The Observer*, 10 March 1969.
24. See Uwe Kitzinger, *Diplomacy and Persuasion: How Britain Joined the Common Market* (London: Thames & Hudson, 1973) p. 193.
25. The facts about the Federal Trust's weekend conferences come from the conference documents, and the flavours from John Pinder's participant observations, in the form partly of notes and partly of recollections.
26. In particular, *Britain and the European Community 1955–1963* (London: Oxford University Press, 1964); and *European Unification in the Sixties: from the Veto to the Crisis* (New York: McGraw-Hill, 1966). The quotation is the evocative title of Dean Acheson's book on that remarkable phase of US policy-making: *Present at the Creation* (New York and London: W. W. Norton and Hamish Hamilton, 1969).
27. In particular in *The Political Dynamics of European Economic Integration* (Stanford: Stanford University Press, 1963) and, with Stuart Scheingold, *Europe's Would-Be Polity: Patterns of Change in the European Community* (Englewood Cliffs, New Jersey: Prentice-Hall, 1970).
28. Conference of European Federalists, 31 October to 1 November 1969,

Programme, and 'Summary and Conclusions' (Campaign for Europe, 1969). The European Forum published Nicholas Ridley's contribution.

29. Executive Secretary's Report to the Annual General Meeting, 24 March 1965.
30. David Spanier, *Europe our Europe* (London: Secker & Warburg, 1972) p. 29.
31. Regional Commission Minutes, 12 March 1962.
32. The financial information that follows is to be found in Kitzinger, *op. cit.* (n. 24, *supra*) p. 193.
33. E. G. Thompson tape, 1986.
34. Kitzinger, *op. cit.* (n. 24, *supra*) p. 194. The officers and Committee members of the merged Movement are listed in British Council of the European Movement, Executive Committee Minutes, 22 July 1969.
35. *Ibid*, p. 190.
36. Lord Gladwyn, *De Gaulle's Europe or Why the General Says No* (London: Secker & Warburg, 1969) pp. 150–4.
37. British Council of the European Movement, Executive Committee Minutes, 1 February 1968.
38. British Council of the European Movement, General Purposes Committee, 7 January 1973.
39. British Council of the European Movement, Executive Committee Minutes, 6 February 1973.
40. Kitzinger, *op. cit.* (n. 24, *supra*) pp. 290–2.
41. *Hansard*, 26 June 1950, Cols 1963, 1964, cited in Kitzinger, *ibid*, p. 149.
42. The data in this section on opinion polls comes from a thorough analysis in Kitzinger, *ibid*, pp. 352–70 and 411–21.
43. The information given here about the European Forum comes from Kitzinger, *ibid*, pp. 160–1; Thompson tape, 1986; and a conversation between David Baker and John Pinder in 1987.
44. This is graphically shown in Kitzinger, *ibid*, pp. 354–5.
45. Except where otherwise stated, the information that follows is to be found in Kitzinger, *ibid*, pp. 189–231, and Ernest Wistrich, 'The Federalist struggle in Britain', *The Federalist* (Pavia), no. 3, December 1984, pp. 234–5.
46. Jean Morton-Williams, *Attitudes Towards the European Common Market: Report of an Exploratory Study* (London: Social and Community Planning Research, January 1971); and Barry Hedges and Roger Jowell, *Britain and the EEC: Report on a Survey of Attitudes towards the European Community* (London: SCPR, July 1971).
47. Kitzinger, *op. cit.* (n. 24, *supra*) p. 222.
48. See, for example, Roger Broad and R. J. Jarrett, *Community Europe Today* (London: Oswald Wolff, 1972); Ian Davidson, *Britain and the Making of Europe* (London: Macdonald, 1971); Lord Gladwyn, *De Gaulle's Europe or Why the General Says No* (London: Secker & Warburg, 1969); John Lambert, *Britain in a Federal Europe* (London: Chatto & Windus, 1968); Christopher Layton, with Y. S. Hu and Michael Whitehead, *Industry and Europe: An Introduction to the Industrial Potential of Common Market Membership* (London: PEP,

October 1971); Richard Mayne, *The Recovery of Europe: from devastation to unity* (London: Weidenfeld & Nicolson, 1970), and *The Europeans: Who are we?* (London: Weidenfeld & Nicolson, 1972); Richard Mayne (ed.), *Europe Tomorrow: 16 Europeans look ahead* (London: Fontana, 1972); John Pinder (ed.), *The Economics of Europe: What the Common Market means for Britain* (London: Charles Knight for the Federal Trust, 1971); Ivor Richard, Geoffrey Lee Williams, Alan Lee Williams, Glyn Mathias, *Europe or the Open Sea? The Political and Strategic Implications for Britain in the Common Market* (London: Charles Knight, 1971). Among the numerous pamphlets was Norman Hart and Ernest Wistrich, *Europe out of the Impasse* (London: Fabian Society, 1969).

49. John Pinder, *ibid.*
50. Kitzinger, *op. cit.* (n. 24, *supra*) p. 224. The information that follows is to be found in pp. 224–31.
51. For a brief account of the referendum campaign, see Wistrich, *op. cit.* (n. 45, *supra*) pp. 236–7. In order to ensure all-party support, at a time when there was, following the successful entry campaign, controversy within the Labour Party about the European Movement, Britain in Europe was set up again during this period to campaign and raise funds jointly with the European Movement, and it was then again wound up the day after the referendum.
52. *Loc. cit.*
53. See Wistrich, *ibid*, pp. 237–9.
54. *Eurobarometer*, no. 27 (Brussels: EC Commission, June 1987), table A17; and 'Europe 2000', *Eurobarometer*, special edition (March 1987) table A14.

13 Towards Federation?

1. *Report to the Council and the Commission on the realisation by stages of Economic and Monetary Union in the Community*, the Werner Report, Supplement to Bulletin 11-1970 of the European Communities.
2. Giovanni Magnifico and John Williamson, *European Monetary Integration* (Federal Trust, 1972). The report was reprinted in Giovanni Magnifico, *European Monetary Unification* (London: Macmillan, 1973) pp. 199–222. The conference report was *New Currency Solutions and their Implications for Business* (*Financial Times* in association with the Federal Trust and *Investors Chronicle*, February 1972).
3. Geoffrey Denton (ed.), *Economic and Monetary Union in Europe* (London: Croom Helm for the Federal Trust, 1974); Douglas Dosser and John Pinder, *Economic Union in the EEC* (Croom Helm for the Federal Trust, 1974); William Wallace, 'The Administrative Implications of Economic and Monetary Union within the European Community', report of a study group, *Journal of Common Market Studies*, June 1974.
4. David Lomax, *The Time is Ripe: The European Monetary System, the ECU and British Policy* (Federal Trust, 1984).
5. *The Time is Ripe: Conference Report on the EMS, the ECU and British*

Policy (Federal Trust, 1985). The speakers at the conference included the Viscomte Davignon, the Rt Hon. Roy Jenkins, MP, Christopher Johnson, Alfonso Jozzo, the Rt Hon. Lord Lever, David Lomax, Sir Jeremy Morse, Lord Roll, Tad Rybczynski and Christopher Tugendhat.

6. John Marsh, *A new Agricultural Policy for Europe* (Federal Trust, 1970). The report of a related conference was *Current Agricultural Proposals for Europe* (Federal Trust, 1970).
7. Federal Trust conferences on the CAP were held in February 1973, July 1976, May 1981, September 1982. The Commission presented its proposal for income support in the 'Delors Plan', set out in *Making a Success of the Single Act*, COM(87) 100 final (Brussels: Commission of the EC, 15 February 1987) section IIA.
8. Geoffrey Denton, *The British Problem and the Future of the EEC Budget* (London: Federal Trust and TEPSA, June 1982); and Denton, *The Economy and EEC Membership* (Federal Trust, 1983). See pp. 116–17 above.
9. Stanley Henig, 'The Institutional Structure of the European Communities', report of a study group, *Journal of Common Market Studies*, June 1974. This report, together with the other Federal Trust report by William Wallace (n. 3, *supra*), comprised that special issue of the journal.
10. *The Council of Ministers of the European Community and the President-in-Office* (Federal Trust, 1977). The same authors wrote a preliminary version published in *International Affairs*, October 1976. Geoffrey Edwards was Assistant, then Deputy Director of the Federal Trust from 1975 to 1983.
11. Christopher Irwin, Richard Mayne and the Rt Hon. Michael Stewart, *Electing the European Parliament* (Federal Trust, 1972).
12. Jean Monnet, *Memoirs* (London: Collins, 1978) pp. 512–13.
13. See Luigi Vittorio Majocchi and Francesco Rossolillo, *il Parlamento europeo* (Naples: Guida Editori, 1979) pp. 101–5.
14. See Ernest Wistrich, 'The Federalist Struggle in Britain', *The Federalist* (Pavia), December 1984, p. 237.
15. Geoffrey Edwards, John Fitzmaurice, Anne Stevens and Ann-Margaret Walton, *European Elections: Direct Elections to the European Parliament and their Aftermath* (Federal Trust, 1979).
16. Roy Pryce, *Towards European Union*, New Europe Paper No. 8 (London: European Movement, 1983); Vernon Bogdanor, *Britain and European Union* (Federal Trust and European Centre for Political Studies, 1983); Roy Pryce (ed.), *The Dynamics of European Union* (London: Croom Helm for TEPSA, 1987).
17. John Pinder, *From Luxembourg to European Union* (Federal Trust and TEPSA, duplicated, February 1986).
18. Bernard Burrows and Christopher Irwin, *The Security of Western Europe: Towards a Common Defence Policy* (London: Charles Knight for the Federal Trust, 1972). Christopher Irwin was Assistant, then Deputy Director, from 1969 to 1973, and as such succeeded in interesting Sir Bernard Burrows in the Federal Trust.

19. Bernard Burrows and others, *European Defence Co-operation* (Federal Trust, 1979); Bernard Burrows and Geoffrey Edwards, *The Defence of Western Europe* (London: Butterworth for the Federal Trust, 1982); the report of the conference was published as Bernard Burrows and Andrew Tyrie, *European Defence Co-operation: Prospects and Possibilities* (Federal Trust, 1986).
20. See, for example, Helmut Schmidt, 'Deutsch-französische Zusammenarbeit in der Sicherheitspolitik', *Europa-Archiv*, 10 June 1987; and Alfred Dregger, leader of the CDU/CSU in the Bundestag, reported in *Die Welt*, 19 June 1987.
21. Christopher Layton, *A Step beyond Fear: Building a European Security Community* (Federal Trust, 1989).
22. See, for example, *The Commonwealth and Europe* (Federal Trust, duplicated, 1960); *The Commonwealth*, Common Market Study Paper No. 4 (Federal Trust, 1962). In 1972 Sir Richard Luce chaired a study group on 'Commonwealth Developing Countries and the EC', which led to a conference in September 1972.
23. The paper and the lecture were published by the Federal Trust in 1975 and 1976 respectively.
24. *The European Community and the Developing Countries: A Policy for the Future* (Federal Trust, 1988).
25. Christopher Layton, *One Europe: One World – A first exploration of Europe's potential contribution to world order*, Special Supplement No. 4 to the *Journal of World Trade Law*, 1986; a second edition was published in 1987 by the Federal Trust jointly with the International Institute for Environment and Development, with the main title changed to *Europe and the Global Crisis*. The members of the study group were Patrick Armstrong, Georges Berthoin, John Bowyer, Father Bruno Brinkman, Ian Davidson, Celia Goodhart, Roger Harrison, Ronald Higgins, Richard Holme, Lady Gloria Hooper, Anatole Kaletsky, Roy Pryce, John Roberts, Douglas Sanders, George Wedell and Monica Wingate, and the chairman was John Pinder.
26. On 'Federalism, Federalists and the European Community', in December 1965, when the speakers included John Pinder, Roy Pryce and Dennis Thompson, and on 'Regionalism, European Integration and Federalism', in January 1969, with Max Kohnstamm and John Mackintosh, MP.
27. There was a conference on 'Federalism and Regions of the EEC' in June 1973; and a study group in the late 1970s resulted in a book: Bernard Burrows and Geoffrey Denton, *Devolution or Federalism: Options for a United Kingdom* (London: Macmillan for the Federal Trust, 1980).
28. Vernon Bogdanor (rapporteur), *Against the Over-Mighty State: A future for local government in Britain* (Federal Trust, 1988).
29. Bernard Burrows, Geoffrey Denton and Geoffrey Edwards (eds), *Federal Solutions to European Issues* (London: Macmillan for the Federal Trust, 1978).

Bibliography

The aim of this bibliography is to give a clear impression of the scope of the publications and reports that have been significant in the history of Federal Union. It lists all significant publications of Federal Union itself and of the immediately associated bodies, the Federal Union Research Institute, Federal Trust for Education and Research and Wyndham Place Trust, in chronological order under the name of the organisation where there is no named author, otherwise under the names of the authors, who are listed in alphabetical order, with the organisation given as publisher. Many of the Federal Union documents are to be found in the Federal Union and the F. L. Josephy archives in the library of the London School of Economics.

The bibliography also gives a representative selection of publications by people who were active in Federal Union or related bodies, when these were on the subjects with which the organisations were concerned and at the time they were concerned with them. Thus the intention is to present the *oeuvre* of Federal Union and of those who have been active in or around it and the most closely related bodies, since the gestation period in the 1930s, up to the present. Other works that are significant for British federalism are to be found in the references to each chapter. We hope any errors or omissions will be forgiven.

Aga Khan, Prince Sadruddin, *Islam and the West*, Corbishley Memorial Lecture (Wyndham Place Trust, 1985).

Allen, David (see Federal Union, 1950, below).

Arbuthnott, Hugh and Geoffrey Edwards (eds), *A Common Man's Guide to the Common Market* (London: Macmillan for the Federal Trust, 1979).

Archer, Rt Hon. Peter, MP, *E Pluribus Unum: The Limits of Tolerance*, Corbishley Memorial Lecture (Wyndham Place Trust, 1982).

Armstrong, Patrick, *Cooperate or Perish: The Idea of a World Security Authority* (London: Parliamentary Group for World Government pamphlet, c.1958).

Baker, David and others, *Europe: Power and Responsibilities* (London: Bow Group Memorandum, 1972).

Bareau, Paul, *Europe – the Next Steps Towards a Supermarket* (Federal Trust pamphlet, 1957).

Beever, Colin, *European Unity and the Trade Union Movements* (Leiden: Sythoff, 1960).

Beever, Colin, *Trade Unions and the Common Market* (London: Political and Economic Planning, 1962).

Bentwich, Norman, *The Colonial Problem and the Federal Solution*, Federal Tracts No. 3 (London: Macmillan, 1941), reprinted in Ransome (1943, q.v.) pp. 107–36.

Bentwich, Norman (see Kimber, 1943, below).

Beswick, Frank, MP, *Towards World Government* (London: Co-operative Society, 1961).

Beveridge, Sir William, *Notes on Organisation of Federal Union* (Federal Union, duplicated, 1940) 5 pp.

Beveridge, Sir William, *Peace by Federation?* (Federal Union, 1940), reprinted in Royal Institute of International Affairs, *World Order Papers*, First Series (London: RIIA, 1940).

Beveridge, Sir William, *The Price of Peace* (London: Pilot Press, 1945).

Beveridge, Lord, *For World Government* (London: Crusade for World Government, 1948).

Bogdanor, Vernon, *Britain and European Union* (Federal Trust and European Centre for Political Studies Joint Study Group Report, 1985).

Bogdanor, Vernon, *Against the Overmighty State: A future for local government in Britain* (Federal Trust Study Group Report, 1988).

Bowyer, John (see *Journal of Common Market Studies*, July 1965, below).

Boyd Orr, Sir John, 'Federalism and Science', in Chaning-Pearce (1940, q.v.) pp. 101–6.

Brailsford, H. N., *The Federal Idea* (Federal Union, 1939).

Brinkman, Revd B. R., SJ, *The Good Man and Europe*, Corbishley Memorial Lecture (Wyndham Place Trust, 1981).

Broad, Roger (see Hart, below).

Broad, Roger and R. J. Jarrett, *Community Europe Today* (London: Oswald Wolff, 1972).

Brugmans, Dr H., *Fundamentals of European Federalism* (Federal Union, 1947).

Burgess, Michael, *Modern Federalism: a Select Bibliography* (Federal Trust, 1988).

Burgess, Michael, *Federalism: A Dirty Word? Federalist Ideas and Practice in the British Political Tradition* (Federal Trust Working Paper, 1988).

Burrows, Bernard, 'European Defence', New Federalist Paper, *New Europe*, Winter 1977, reprinted in Burrows, Denton and Edwards (1978, q.v.) pp. 187–97.

Burrows, Bernard, *Turkey and the European Community* (Federal Trust Working Paper, 1987).

Burrows, Bernard and Christopher Irwin, *The Security of Western Europe: Towards a Common Defence Policy* (London: Charles Knight for Federal Trust, 1972).

Burrows, Bernard, Geoffrey Denton and Geoffrey Edwards (eds), *Federal Solutions to European Issues* (London: Macmillan for Federal Trust, 1978), with contributions from Dosser, Wallace (Helen) and authors of New Federalist Papers (q.v.).

Burrows, Bernard and others, *European Defence Co-operation* (Federal Trust Report, 1979).

Burrows, Bernard and Geoffrey Denton, *Devolution or Federalism? Options for a United Kingdom* (London: Macmillan for Federal Trust, 1980).

Burrows, Bernard and Geoffrey Edwards, *The Defence of Western Europe* (London: Butterworth Scientific for Federal Trust, 1982).

Burrows, Bernard and Andrew Tyrie, *European Defence Co-operation: Prospects and Limits* (Federal Trust Conference Report, 1986).

Campbell, Alan and Dennis Thompson, *Common Market Law: Texts and Commentaries* (London: Stevens, 1962).

Camps, Miriam, 'Rethinking Europe's Relations with America', in Federal Trust (1971/2, q.v.) pp. 9–11.

Catlin, George, *One Anglo-American Nation: The Foundation of Anglosaxony as a Nucleus of World Federation: A British Response to Streit* (London: Andrew Dakers, 1941).

Catlin, George, *Anglo-American Union as a Nucleus of World Federation*, Federal Tracts No. 8 (London: Macmillan, 1942), reprinted in Ransome (1943, q.v.) pp. 299–336.

Chaning-Pearce, M. (ed.), *Federal Union: A Symposium* (London: Jonathan Cape, 1940), contributors (q.v.) include Boyd Orr, Curry, Grensted, Jennings, Keeton, R. J. Mackay, Middleton Murry, J. B. Priestley, Ransome, Robbins, Schwarzenberger, Stapledon, Wickham Steed, Duncan Wilson.

Clark, Grenville, *A Plan for Peace* (Dublin, New Hampshire: privately printed, 1950).

Clark, Grenville and Louis B. Sohn, *World Peace through World Law* (Cambridge, Massachusetts: Harvard University Press, 1958).

Corbishley, Revd Fr Thomas, SJ. 'Christians and European Unity', in Wyndham Place Trust (1962, q.v.) pp. 6–10.

Corbishley, Revd Fr Thomas, SJ, 'One World – The Religious Approach' (Federal Trust, appendix to 1964 Annual Report, 1965).

Corbishley Memorial Lectures (from 1977), see Aga Khan, Archer, Brinkman, Eban, Hailsham, Heath, Jakobovits, Marshall, Noël, Ramphal, Ramsey, von Weizsäcker.

Curry, W. B., *The Case for Federal Union* (Harmondsworth: Penguin Special, 1939).

Curry, W. B., 'Federalism and Democracy', in Chaning-Pearce (1940, q.v.) pp. 131–8.

Curtis, Lionel, *Civitas Dei* (London: Allen & Unwin, 3 vols, 1934–7), reprinted in 1938 in one volume as *The Commonwealth of God*, and again as *Civitas Dei*, in a revised edition, in 1950.

Curtis, Lionel, *The Way to Peace* (London: Oxford University Press, 1944).

Curtis, Lionel, *World War: Its Cause and Cure* (London: Oxford University Press, 1945).

Curtis, Lionel, *World Revolution in the Cause of Peace* (Oxford: Blackwell, 1949).

Curtis, Lionel, *The Open Road to Freedom* (Oxford: Blackwell, 1950).

Curtis, Lionel (with others), *Evading a Revolution* (Oxford: Blackwell, 1953) 20pp.

Davies, Lord, *A Federated Europe* (London: Gollancz, 1940).

Deighton, Dr Ann (ed.), *Federalism and the Future of South Africa* (Federal Trust Conference Report and Working Paper, 1988).

Denton, Geoffrey (ed.), *Economic and Monetary Union in Europe* (London: Croom Helm for Federal Trust, 1974).

Denton, Geoffrey, *Financial Assistance to Industry in the UK* (Federal Trust Report, 1976).

Denton, Geoffrey, *Beyond Bullock: Economic Implications of Worker Participation in Control and Ownership of Industry* (Federal Trust Report, 1977).

Denton, Geoffrey, 'Industrial Policy for a Federal Europe', New Federalist

Paper, *New Federalist*, Summer 1977, reprinted together with 'Postscript: The Value of Federalism', in Burrows (1978, q.v.) pp. 108–21, 221–5.
Denton, Geoffrey (see Burrows, 1978 and 1980).
Denton, Geoffrey, *The British Problem and the Future of the EEC Budget* (Federal Trust Study Group Report, 1982).
Denton, Geoffrey, *The Economy and EEC Membership* (Federal Trust Study Group Report, 1983).
Denton, Geoffrey, *Turkey and the European Community* (Federal Trust Study Group Summary Report, 1985).
Denton, Geoffrey and others, *The Economics of Renegotiation* (Federal Trust Study Group Report, 1975).
de Rougement, Denis, *The Way of Federalism: Totalitarianism and Federalism* (Federal Union pamphlet, undated, 1949?).
Dosser, Douglas, 'Taxation', in Pinder (1971, q.v.) pp. 185–211.
Dosser, Douglas, 'A Federal Budget for the Community?', in Burrows (1978, q.v.) pp. 98–107.
Dosser, Douglas and John Pinder, *Economic Union in the EEC*, Federal Trust Study Group Report (London: Croom Helm for Federal Trust, 1974).
Duchêne, François, 'Europe and the Superpowers', New Federalist Paper, *New Europe*, Spring 1978.
Duchêne, François (see *Journal of Common Market Studies*, July 1965, below).
Eban, Abba, *Peace in the Middle East*, Corbishley Memorial Lecture (Wyndham Place Trust, 1986).
Economist Intelligence Unit, *Britain and Europe*, edited by Ann Monroe (London: EIU, 1957).
Economist Intelligence Unit, *The Commonwealth and Europe*, edited by Ann Monroe (London: EIU, 1960).
Edwards, Geoffrey, 'How Large a Community?', New Federalist Paper, *New Europe*, Autumn 1976, reprinted in Burrows (1978, q.v.) pp. 163–73.
Edwards, Geoffrey and William Wallace, *A Wider Community? Issues and Problems of Further Enlargement* (Federal Trust Report, 1976).
Edwards, Geoffrey and Helen Wallace, 'European Community: The Evolving Role of the Presidency of the Council', *International Affairs*, October 1976 (preliminary summary of Federal Trust Study Group).
Edwards, Geoffrey and Helen Wallace, *The Council of Ministers of the European Community and the President in Office* (Federal Trust Report, 1977).
Edwards, Geoffrey and others, *Direct Elections to the European Parliament and their Aftermath* (Federal Trust Report, 1979).
Edwards, Geoffrey (see Arbuthnott, 1979, above).
Edwards, Geoffrey (see Burrows, 1982, above).
Ellis, Tom, MP, 'Why a Federal Britain?', New Federalist Paper, *New Europe*, Winter 1977, reprinted in Burrows (1978, q.v.) pp. 37–50.
Federal Tracts, see Bentwich, Beveridge, Catlin, Joad, Lugard, Robbins, Wheare, Wootton.
Federal Trust for Education and Research (chronological order of publications not listed under author's name):
Annual Reports for 1952–3, 1953–4, 1956, 1958, 1960–1, 1962, 1963–4,

1965–6, 1967–8, 1968–70, 1971, 1972, 1973, 1974, 1975, 1976, 1977, 1978, 1979, 1980, 1981, 1982, 1983, 1984, 1985, 1986, 1987, 1988.
Agriculture and the New European Market (Research Committee pamphlet, 1957).
The Six and the Seven: a comparison of the Common Market and the proposed European Free Trade Association (duplicated report, 1957).
Euratom – A Short Outline (Research Committee pamphlet, 1957).
Europe's Other Market (Scandinavia) (Research Committee pamphlet, 1958).
The Colombo Plan in Perspective (Research Committee pamphlet, 1958).
The Problems of Arab Union (Research Committee pamphlet, 1958).
The Commonwealth and Europe (duplicated report drawing on Economist Intelligence Unit Report under same title listed above, 1960).
Legal Problems of the EEC and the EFTA with British Institute of International and Comparative Law (BIICL) (Conference Report, 1960).
Companies and Taxation in the Common Market with BIICL, see Keenan, below (Conference Report, 1961).
Encouragement and Protection of Investment in Developing Countries with BIICL (Conference Report, 1961).
The Future of the Seven (Conference Report, 1961).
Inside the Common Market? (Conference Report, 1961).
Finance and Investment in the Common Market (Conference Report, 1962).
The Common Market – the second stage (Conference Report, 1962).
The Common Market and Agriculture (Conference Report, 1962).
Europe and America – the Problems of Freeing Trade (Conference Report,1962).
Taxation and the Common Market (Conference Report, 1962).
Transport and the Common Market (Conference Report, 1962).
Common Market – In or Out? (Conference Report, 1962).
Restrictive Practices, Patents and Trade Marks in the Common Market with BIICL (Conference Report, 1962).
Labour Law in the United Kingdom and Continental Europe, Joint Conference with BIICL, Institute for Advanced Legal Studies and the Industrial Law Society, Special Supplement in *International and Comparative Law Quarterly*, October 1962.
Agriculture (Common Market Study Paper 1, 1962).
Sovereignty and the Common Market (Common Market Study Paper 2, 1962).
Economic Aspects (Common Market Study Paper 3, 1962).
The Commonwealth (Common Market Study Paper 4, 1962).
EFTA and the Common Market (Common Market Study Paper 5, 1962).
Industry and the Common Market (Common Market Study Paper 6, 1962).
Britain After Brussels: trading for the future (Conference Report, 1963).
Property in Europe (Conference Report, 1963).
Governments and the Investor (with special reference to Taxation and Exchange Control) (Conference Report, 1964).
International Monetary Problems (Conference Report, 1965).

Problems of Scale in Europe (Conference Report, 1966).
The European Capital Market (Conference Report, 1967).
Sterling – European Monetary Co-operation and World Monetary Reform (Conference Report, 1967).
Industrial Integration in Europe – Practice and Policy (Conference Report, 1967).
Britain, Italy and the European Market (Conference Report, 1967).
Attitudes to European Unity and World Institutions in the 1966 General Election in Britain (Special Study, 1967).
Britain and the European Community (Conference Report, duplicated, 1967).
Ten Years of EEC, Lessons and Prospects for Industry (Conference Report, 1968).
European Monetary Co-operation (Conference Report, 1969).
European Technological Collaboration (Conference Report, 1970).
A New Agricultural Policy for Europe (Study Group Report, 1970).
Current Agricultural Proposals for Europe (Conference Report, 1970).
Britain in Europe Now (Conference Report, 1970).
Industry and the Common Market (Conference Report, 1971).
Europe in the World, Special Edition of *Interstate* 1971/2 (University College of Wales, Report of Federal Trust Conference), contributors (q.v.) include Camps, Spinelli, Younger.
New Currency Solutions and their Implications for Business (Conference Report, 1972).
European Monetary Integration (Study Group Report, 1972, see Magnifico and Williamson).
Patents and the Future (special issue of *Journal of World Trade Law*, 1974).
The Economic and Social Committee (Seminar Report, 1976).
Too Many Parliaments in Europe? (Study Group Report, 1978).
The Time is Ripe: The European Monetary System, the ECU and British Policy (Study Group Report, 1984, see Lomax, below).
The Time is Ripe: Conference Report on the EMS, the ECU and British Policy (Conference Report, 1985).
Europe and World Order (Conference Report and Working Paper, 1987).
Paving the Way: Next Steps for Monetary Co-operation in Europe and the World (Study Group Report, 1987, see Young, below).
The European Community and the Developing Countries: A Policy for the Future (Study Group Report, 1988).
Against the Over-mighty State: A Future for Local Government in Britain (Study Group Report, 1988, see Bogdanor, above).
A Step Beyond Fear: Building a European Security Community (Study Group Report, 1989, see Layton, below).

Federal Union (chronological order of publications not listed under author's name):
Federal Union News (fortnightly then monthly, 1939–February 1944, continued as *Federal News*, then *World Affairs*, q.v.).
Offer Federal Union to the German people and Paralyse Hitler's Armies: A Statement of Peace Policy (leaflet, undated, 1939?).

Europe at the Crossroads (leaflets, produced successively for public meetings 25 January, 18 February, 20 February, 3 April 1940 and for Federal Union week, April 1940).
Federal Union, with a foreword by Sir William Beveridge (pamphlet, 1940).
Federate or Perish (leaflet, 1940).
How We Shall Win (pamphlet, 1940).
Uncommon Sense: The Case for Federation (pamphlet, 1940).
War Aims (leaflet, 1940).
Policy of Federal Union (duplicated, 1941).
'Federation: Peace Aim – War Weapon', *Federal Union News*, no. 88, June 1942, pp. 1–16.
Federal Union Official Policy (pamphlet, 1942).
Federation: Target for Tomorrow! (pamphlet, 1942).
Federation and the Four Freedoms (report of European Committee to the AGM, July 1943).
What is this Federation? (Speakers Notes, undated, 1943?).
Federal News (monthly then bimonthly, March 1944–Oct./Nov. 1955, preceded by *Federal Union News* and continued as *World Affairs*, q.v.).
Federation: Target for Today! (pamphlet, 1944).
Questions and Answers on Federal Union (pamphlet, 1946).
First Things First (leaflet, undated, 1946?).
Peace Bond (leaflet, undated, 1946?).
The Objectives of Peace: Federal Union Plan (pamphlet, undated, 1946?).
Policy Statement (1948).
Draft of a Federal Pact (1949).
Let the Argument Proceed, a reply by Labour members of Federal Union to the policy statement 'European Unity' issued by the National Executive of the British Labour Party (Federal Union pamphlet, 1950; authors David Allen et al.).
Policy Statement (1952).
United Nations Reform: Proposals for a Federal United Nations (report of Joint Commission, Federal Union and Crusade for World Government, 1953).
1955: Year of Decision (leaflet, 1955).
Beyond Power Politics (policy statement, undated, 1956?).
World Affairs (bimonthly then quarterly, Jan./Feb. 1956 to Autumn 1963, preceded by *Federal Union News* and *Federal News*, q.v.).
World Prosperity: Can we build it together? (policy statement, 1956).
Proposals for a Permanent United Nations Force (Federal Union Commission Report, 1957).
PUNF for Peace (shortened version of previous report, 1958).
A Survey of Commonwealth Parliamentary Opinion on British Participation in a Free Trade Area (duplicated report, 1958).
Britain, Europe and the Commonwealth: A Proposal for Economic Union (duplicated report, 1958).
Britain in the Common Market (duplicated report, 1959).
Federal Union's Objects (1959).
Federal Union 21 (Annual Report and review of activities since 1938, 1959).

British Membership of the European Economic Community (duplicated report, undated, 1960?).
Beyond Power Politics (revised policy statement, 1960).
Federal Union (statement of aims, 1962).
A Policy for World Development (Federal Union Economic Commission report, 1964).
Federal Union Twenty-Five (Annual Report 1963–4 with Federal Union policy statement, 1964).

Federal Union Research Institute (FURI) Annual Reports:
First Annual Report 1939–40 (duplicated 142pp., 1940) contains copies of all reports produced for FURI during the period, including reports of three conferences on constitutional aspects of a European Federation, two conferences on relationships with colonies, two conferences (one of them Anglo-French) on economic aspects of the European Federation, and memoranda by authors including Jennings, Kahn-Freund, Lugard, Meade, Robbins, Wilson (J. Harold), Wootton (q.v.).
Second Annual Report 1940–41 (duplicated, 76pp., 1941) contains copies of reports including one by Salvador de Madariaga and Gilbert Murray, on educational functions of a federation.

Fogarty, Michael, 'The New European Enterprise', New Federalist Paper, *New Europe*, Spring 1977, reprinted in Burrows (1978, q.v.) pp. 122–35.

Forman, Nigel, 'The European Movement in Great Britain 1945–1954' (University of Sussex, unpublished thesis, 1966).

Gaitskell, The Rt Hon. Hugh, *An Eight Point Programme for World Government* (London: World Parliament Association, 1962).

Gillett, Hjordis, *Lest Man Perish By His Own Creation* (pamphlet published by author for distribution by Federal Union, 1946).

Gladwyn, Lord, *De Gaulle's Europe or Why the General Says No* (London: Secker & Warburg, 1969).

Goodhart, A. L., 'The Constitution of the United States', in P. Ransome (ed.), *Studies in Federal Planning* (London: Macmillan, 1943) pp. 235–68.

Gordon Walker, Rt Hon. Patrick, MP, *Britain and the Commonwealth: Expanding or Contracting?* (Federal Trust pamphlet, 1958).

Greaves, H. R., *Federal Union in Practice* (London: Allen & Unwin, 1940).

Greaves, H. R., 'Federal States in Europe', in Ransome (1943, q.v.) pp. 201–34.

Grensted, Revd Canon L. W., 'Federalism and Religion', in Chaning-Pearce (1940, q.v.) pp. 75–82.

Hailsham, Lord, *Intellectual Rearmament*, Corbishley Memorial Lecture (Wyndham Place Trust, 1977).

Harris, Simon and Tim Josling, *The CAP and the British Consumer* (Federal Trust Study Group Report, 1975).

Hart, Norman (ed.), *Basis of Federalism: A Symposium*, with contributions by Alexandre Marc, Sir John Boyd Orr, Abbé Groues Pierre and Henry Usborne, MP (Paris: World Student Federalists, 1949).

Hart, Norman (ed.), *Britain in Europe: Viewpoint for the Labour Movement* (Federal Trust pamphlet, 1958).

Hart, Norman with Roger Broad, *Common Sense about the Common Market* (London: Labour Common Market Committee, 1962).

Hart, Norman and Anthony Meyer, *Forward Britain into Europe* (London: Common Market Campaign, 1962).

Hart, Norman and Ernest Wistrich, *Europe out of the Impasse* (London: Fabian Society pamphlet, 1969).

Hayek, F. A. (see von Hayek).

Heath, Rt Hon. Edward, MP, 'A World of Our Making', Federalist Lecture, *New Europe*, Summer 1978.

Heath, Rt Hon, Edward, MP, *The Price of Sovereignty in an Interdependent World*, Corbishley Memorial Lecture (Wyndham Place Trust, 1984).

Heath, Rt Hon. Edward, MP, *European Unity over the Next Ten Years: From Community to Union*, Inaugural Lothian Memorial Lecture, given at Chatham House, 3 November 1987 (London: Lothian Foundation, 1987); also printed in *International Affairs*, Spring 1988, pp. 199–207.

Henig, Stanley, 'The Institutional Structure of the European Communities', *Journal of Common Market Studies*, special issue, 1974 (Federal Trust Study Group Report).

Hennessy, Jossleyn, *Britain in Europe: Viewpoint for Industry* (Federal Trust, 1958).

Holland, Stuart, with Preface by Sir Alec Cairncross, *The Price of Europe: A Reassessment* (London: SGS Associates for Federal Trust, 1971).

Howell, David (see *Journal of Common Market Studies*, July 1965, below).

Hoyland, John S., *The World in Union* (London: Peace Book Co., 1940).

Hoyland, John S., *Federate or Perish* (London: Federal Union, 1944).

Hoyland, John S., *Once More – Federate or Perish* (London: Campaign for World Government, 1947).

Hu, Y. S. (see Layton, 1971, below).

Hunnings, Neville March, 'The Future of Community Law', New Federalist Paper, *New Europe*, Spring 1977, reprinted in Burrows (1978, q.v.) pp. 51–61.

Hunt, James, *Europe and Africa: Can it be Partnership?* (Federal Union Report, undated, 1958?).

Ionescu, Ghita (ed.), *The New Politics of European Integration* (London: Macmillan, 1972).

Ionescu, Ghita, 'The European Social Partners', New Federalist Paper, *New Europe*, Spring 1977, reprinted in Burrows (1978, q.v.) pp. 71–83.

Irwin, Christopher (see Burrows, 1972, above).

Irwin, Christopher, Rt Hon. Michael Stewart and Richard Mayne, *Electing the European Parliament* (Federal Trust Report, 1972).

Jackson, Lady Barbara Ward (see Ward, below).

Jakobovits, Lord Immanuel, Chief Rabbi, *Moral Imperatives in Modern Society*, Corbishley Memorial Lecture (Wyndham Place Trust, 1978).

Jarrett, R. J. (see Broad, 1972, above).

Jenkins, Roy, MP, 'The Next Steps', *World Affairs*, no. 250, Summer 1960, pp. 58–9.

Jennings, W. Ivor, *A Federation for Western Europe* (Cambridge: Cambridge University Press, 1940).

Jennings, W. Ivor, 'Federal Constitutions', in Chaning-Pearce (1940, q.v.) pp. 57–71.

Jennings, W. Ivor, 'Memorandum on Civil Liberties', in Federal Union Research Institute (1940, q.v.).

Jennings, W. Ivor, 'Rough Draft of a Proposed Constitution for a Federation of Western Europe', in Federal Union Research Institute (1940, q.v.).

Jevons, Herbert Stanley, *Why Federation Means Peace* (London: Peace Book Co., *c.* 1940).

Joad, C. E. M., *The Philosophy of Federal Union*, Federal Tracts No. 5 (London: Macmillan, 1941), reprinted in Ransome (1943, q.v.), pp. 39–76.

Joad, C. E. M. (see Kimber, 1943, below).

Joad, C. E. M., *Conditions of Survival* (Federal Union pamphlet, 1946).

Joad, C. E. M., F. L. Josephy, B. H. Liddell Hart, et al., *Exploring Tomorrow* (Federal Union discussion notes, 1946?).

Josephy, F. L. (see Kimber, 1943, below).

Josephy, F. L., *Europe: The Key to Peace* (Federal Union pamphlet, 1944).

Josephy, F. L. (see Joad, 1946?, above).

Josephy, F. L., *The Case for Federation* (Federal Union pamphlet, 1948).

Josling, Tim, 'The Agricultural Burden, a Reappraisal', in Pinder (1971, q.v.) pp. 72–93.

Josling, Tim (see Denton, 1975, above, and Harris, 1945, above).

Josling, Tim, 'Buying Europe's Raw Materials', New Federalist Paper, *New Europe*, Summer 1977, reprinted in Burrows (1978, q.v.) pp. 198–210.

Journal of Common Market Studies, July 1965, a symposium on *The Future of Britain's Relations with Europe*, with contributions by Bowyer, Duchêne, Howell, Lambert, Layton, Mayne, Pinder, Pryce, Salter, Thompson.

Kahn-Freund, Otto, 'Memorandum on the Constitutional Aspects of Federal Union', in Federal Union Research Institute (1940, q.v.).

Keenan, P. B., 'Companies and Taxation in the Common Market: A Conference Report', Joint Conference with BIICL, Institute of Advanced Legal Studies and Industrial Law Society, *International and Comparative Law Quarterly*, July 1961.

Keeton, G. W., 'Federalism and India', in Chaning-Pearce (1940, q.v.) pp. 87–94.

Keeton, G. W., *National Sovereignty and International Order* (London: Peace Book Co., 1939).

Keeton, G. W. (see Kimber, 1943, below).

Kerr, Philip Henry (see Lothian, below).

Kimber, Charles, *Exploring Tomorrow* (Federal Union booklet, 1943 or 1944), with contributions from Bentwich, Joad, Josephy, Keeton, Kimber, Liddell Hart.

Kimber, Sir Charles, 'Federal Union', *The Federalist* (Pavia), December 1984, pp. 199–205.

Kitzinger, Uwe, *The Challenge of the Common Market* (Oxford: Blackwell, 1961).

Kitzinger, Uwe, *Diplomacy and Persuasion: How Britain Joined the Common Market* (London: Thames & Hudson, 1973).

Kitzinger, Uwe, *Europe's Wider Horizons* (Federal Trust pamphlet, 1975).

Kitzinger, Uwe, 'European Ideals: Third World Realities', Federalist Lecture, *New Europe*, Summer, 1976.

Lambert, John (see *Journal of Common Market Studies*, July 1965, above).

Lambert, John, *Great Britain in a Federal Europe* (London: Chatto & Windus, 1968).

Lambert, John and Michael Shanks, *Britain and the New Europe: The Future of the Common Market* (London: Chatto & Windus, 1962).

Law, Richard, MP, *Federal Union and the League of Nations* (Federal Union pamphlet, 1939).

Layton, Christopher (see *Journal of Common Market Studies*, July 1965, above).

Layton, Christopher, *European Advanced Technology: A Programme for Integration* (London: Allen & Unwin for PEP, 1969).

Layton, Christopher, 'The Benefits of Scale for Industry', in Pinder (1971, q.v.) pp. 46–71.

Layton, Christopher, *One Europe: One World: A First Exploration of Europe's Contribution to World Order*, Special Supplement in *Journal of World Trade Law* (Federal Trust Study Group Report, 1986), republished as *Europe and the Global Crisis* (London: Federal Trust and International Institute for Environment and Development, 1987).

Layton, Christopher, *A Step Beyond Fear: Building a European Security Community*, with Foreword by Sir Michael Palliser (Federal Trust Study Group Report, 1989).

Layton, Christopher with Y. S. Hu and Michael Whitehead, *Industry and Europe* (London: PEP, 1971).

Leather, E. M. G., MP, *The Commonwealth, Federation and Atlantic Union* (Federal Union pamphlet, 1953 or 1954).

Leech, John, *Europe and the Commonwealth* (Federal Union pamphlet, undated, 1961).

Liddell Hart, B. H. (see Kimber, 1943 and Joad, 1946?, above).

Lipgens, Walter, *A History of European Integration 1945–1947: The Formation of the European Unity Movement* (Oxford: Clarendon Press, 1982).

Lipgens, Walter (ed.), *Documents on the History of European Integration: Vol. 1, Continental Plans for European Union 1939–1945; Vol. 2. Plans for European Union in Great Britain and in Exile 1939–1945* (Berlin and New York: de Gruyter, 1985, 1986).

Lomax, David, *The Time is Ripe: The European Monetary System, the ECU and British Policy* (Federal Trust Study Group Report, 1984).

Lothian, Lord (Philip Kerr), *Pacifism is not Enough (nor Patriotism Either)* (London: Oxford University Press, 1935), reprinted with a preface by Sir William Beveridge (1941).

Lothian, Lord, *The Ending of Armageddon* (Federal Union pamphlet, 1939), reprinted in Ransome (1943, q.v.) pp. 1–15.

Lugard, Lord, 'Memorandum on the Relations of a Federal Union with the Non-Self-Governing Dependencies', in Federal Union Research Institute (1940, q.v.).

Lugard, Lord, *Federation and the Colonies*, Federal Tracts No. 7 (London: Macmillan, 1941), reprinted in Ransome (1943, q.v.) pp. 137–66.

MacFarquhar, Roderick, 'The Community, the Nation State and the Regions', New Federalist Paper, *New Europe*, Winter 1977, reprinted in Burrows (1978, q.v.) pp. 17–24.

Mackay, R. J., 'Federalism and Sociology', in Chaning-Pearce (1940, q.v.) pp. 139–54.

Mackay, R. W. G., *Federal Europe* (Michael Joseph, 1940), revised and republished as *Peace Aims and the New Order* (London and New York: Michael Joseph, 1941).

Mackay, R. W. G., *Let's Not Make the Same Mistake Twice* (Federal Union pamphlet, 1941).

Mackay, R. W. G., *Britain in Wonderland* (London: Gollancz, 1948).

Mackay, R. W. G., *Western Union in Crisis: Economic Anarchy or Political Union* (Oxford: Blackwell, 1949).

Mackay, R. W. G., *Heads in the Sand: A Criticism of the Labour Party Attitude to European Unity* (Oxford: Blackwell, 1950).

Mackay, R. W. G., *The Economic Aspects of European Federation* (Oxford: Blackwell for Federal Trust, 1952).

Mackay, R. W. G., *Whither Britain?* (Oxford: Blackwell for Federal Trust 1953).

Mackay, R. W. G., *Towards a United States of Europe* (London: Hutchinson, 1961).

Madariaga, Salvador de (see Federal Union Research Institute, 1941, above).

Magnifico, Giovanni, 'European Monetary Integration', New Federalist Paper, *New Europe*, Summer 1977, and in Burrows (1978, q.v.) pp. 87–97.

Magnifico, Giovanni and John Williamson, *European Monetary Integration* (Federal Trust Study Group Report, 1972).

Marquand, David, *Faltering Leviathan: National Sovereignty, the Regions and Europe* (Wyndham Place Trust Commission Report, 1989).

Marsh, John, 'The Changing Structure of Agriculture in the EEC' (see Pinder, 1971, below) pp. 94–116.

Marsh, John, 'European Agricultural Policy', New Federalist Paper, *New Europe*, Winter 1977, reprinted in Burrows (1978, q.v.) pp. 147–60.

Marshall, Rt Revd Michael, *Christianity and Science in Western European Thought: Cold War or Truce?* Corbishley Memorial Lecture (Wyndham Place Trust, 1980).

Mayne, Richard, *The Community of Europe* (London: Gollancz, 1962).

Mayne, Richard (see *Journal of Common Market Studies*, July 1965, above).

Mayne, Richard, *The Recovery of Europe: From Devastation to Unity* (London: Weidenfeld & Nicolson, 1970).

Mayne, Richard, *The Europeans: Who are We?* (London: Weidenfeld & Nicolson, 1972).

Mayne, Richard (ed.), *Europe Tomorrow: 16 Europeans look ahead* (London: Fontana, 1972).

Mayne, Richard, *Postwar: The Dawn of Today's Europe* (London: Thames & Hudson, 1983).

Mayne, Richard (ed.), *Western Europe: a Handbook* (London: Muller, Blond & White, 1986).

Meade, James E., 'Economic Problems of International Government', in Federal Union Research Institute (1940, q.v.).

Meyer, Sir Anthony (see Hart, 1962, above).

Miller, Marcus H., 'Estimates of the Static Balance of Payments and Welfare Costs Compared', in Pinder (1971, q.v.) pp. 117–51.

Miller, Marcus (see Denton, 1975, above).
Monroe, Ann (see Economist Intelligence Unit, 1957 and 1960, above).
Murray, Gilbert (see Federal Union Research Institute, 1941, above).
Murry, J. Middleton, 'Pre-conditions of Federal Union', in Chaning-Pearce (1940, q.v.) pp. 155–63.
New Federalist Papers, 1976–78, authors (q.v.): Burrows, Denton, Duchêne, Edwards, Ellis, Fogarty, Hunnings, Ionescu, Josling, MacFarquhar, Magnifico, Marsh, Pinder, Shanks, Wallace (William), Wistrich.
Noël, Emile, *Peace and Democracy in Europe: The Role of the European Communities*, Corbishley Memorial Lecture (Wyndham Place Trust, 1988).
Palliser, Rt Hon. Sir Michael, 'Foreword', *A Step beyond Fear: Building a European Security Community* (Report of Federal Trust Study Group, 1989).
Parliamentary Group for World Government (chronological order):
The Plan in Outline for World Government 1955, principal author Henry Usborne (London: PGWG, 1947, reprinted by Crusade for World Government, 1948).
Parliamentary Path to Peace (PGWG pamphlet, 1955).
A World Investment Convention (Commission report, 1959, reprinted in *World Affairs*, Summer 1959).
History Syllabuses and a World Perspective (pamphlet, 1962).
Pinder, John, *UN Reform: Proposals for Charter Amendment* (Federal Union pamphlet, 1953).
Pinder, John, *Britain and the Common Market* (London: Cresset Press, 1961).
Pinder, John, *Europe Against de Gaulle* (London: Pall Mall Press for Federal Trust, 1963).
Pinder, John (see *Journal of Common Market Studies*, July 1965, above).
Pinder, John (ed.), *The Economics of Europe* (London: Charles Knight for Federal Trust, 1971).
Pinder, John (see Dosser, 1974, above).
Pinder, John, 'A Federal Community in an Ungoverned World Economy', New Federalist Paper, *New Europe*, Spring 1977, reprinted in Burrows (1978, q.v.) pp. 211–20.
Pinder, John, 'The Political Institutions of the EEC: Functions and Future', in Roy Jenkins (ed.), *Britain and the EEC* (London: Macmillan, 1983) pp. 207–29.
Pinder, John, 'European Union: Steps and Constitution', *The Federalist* (Pavia), December 1985, pp. 161–73.
Pinder, John, 'Federal Union 1939–41', in Lipgens (1986, q.v.) pp. 26–155.
Pinder, John, 'Federalism in Britain and Italy: Radicals and the English Liberal Tradition', in Peter M. R. Stirk (ed.), *European Unity in context: The Interwar Period* (London: Pinter, 1989) pp. 201–23.
Pinder, John and Roy Pryce, *Europe after de Gaulle* (Harmondsworth: Penguin Special, 1969).
Priestley, J. B., 'Federalism and Culture', in Chaning-Pearce (1940, q.v.) pp. 93–9.

Pryce, Roy, *The Political Future of the European Community* (London: John Marshbank for Federal Trust, 1962).
Pryce, Roy (see *Journal of Common Market Studies*, July 1965, above).
Pryce, Roy (see Pinder, 1969, above).
Pryce, Roy, *Towards European Union* (European Movement and Federal Trust Study Group Report, 1983).
Pryce, Roy (ed.), *The Dynamics of European Union* (London: Croom Helm for Trans-European Policy Studies Association, 1987).
Ramphal, Sir Shridath, *Making Human Society a Civilised State*, Corbishley Memorial Lecture (Wyndham Place Trust, 1987).
Ramsey, Dr A. M., Archbishop of Canterbury, *The Nature of Christian Responsibility*, in Wyndham Place Trust (1962, q.v.) pp. 4–6.
Ramsey, Dr A. M., Archbishop of Canterbury, *Christianity and Humanism*, Corbishley Memorial Lecture (Wyndham Place Trust, 1979).
Ransome, Patrick, 'Federal Government', *Fortnightly Review*, October 1939, pp. 416–22.
Ransome, Patrick, 'Federation and International Law', in Chaning-Pearce (1940, q.v.) pp. 239–45.
Ransome, Patrick (ed.), *Studies in Federal Planning* (London: Macmillan, 1943), contributors include Bentwich, Catlin, Goodhart, Greaves, Joad, Lothian, Robbins, Wheare, Wootton, Zilliacus (q.v.).
Reves, Emery, *The Anatomy of Peace* (New York: Harper, 1945; London: Allen & Unwin, 1946; Harmondsworth: Penguin Books, 1947).
Robbins, Lionel, *Economic Planning and International Order* (London: Macmillan, 1937).
Ridley, Nicholas, MP, *Towards a Federal Europe*, Text of a speech delivered at the European Federalist Conference (European Forum, 1969).
Robbins, Lionel, *The Economic Causes of War* (London: Jonathan Cape, 1939), reprinted, with a new preface (New York: Fertig, 1968).
Robbins, Lionel, 'Interim Report on Economic Aspects of the Federal Constitution', in Federal Union Research Institute (1940, q.v.).
Robbins, Lionel, 'Economic Aspects of Federation', in Chaning-Pearce (1940, q.v.) pp. 167–86, reprinted as Federal Tracts No. 2 (London: Macmillan, 1941) and in Ransome (1943, q.v.) pp. 77–106.
Roberts, John C. de V., *Disarmament in Fifteen Years* (Federal Union, 1964).
Roberts, John C. de V., *Disarmament is not Enough* (Association of World Federalists, 1981).
Russell, Bertrand, *Which Way to Peace?* (London: Michael Joseph, 1936).
Salter, Noël (see *Journal of Common Market Studies*, July 1965, above).
Schuman, Frederick L., *The Commonwealth of Man* (London: Robert Hale, 1954).
Schwarzenberger, Georg, 'Federation and the Colonial Problem', in Chaning-Pearce (1940, q.v.) pp. 195–206.
Schwarzenberger, Georg, *Atlantic Union, a Practical Utopia?* (Federal Trust pamphlet, 1957).
Shanks, Michael (see Lambert, 1962).
Shanks, Michael, 'European Social Policy', New Federalist Paper, *New*

Europe, Summer 1976, reprinted in Burrows (1978, q.v.) pp. 136–46.
tiero, 'Democratic Action', *World Affairs*, no. 255, February 1962, pp. 15–18.
Spinelli, Altiero, 'The Enlarged Community and the World', in Federal Trust (1971/2, q.v.) pp. 3–5.
Spinelli, Altiero, 'European Unity and the Left', Federalist Lecture, *New Europe*, Summer 1977.
Stapledon, Olaf, 'Federalism and Socialism', in Chaning-Pearce (1940, q.v.) pp. 115–29.
Steel, Rt Hon. David, 'A Europe Fit for Britain to Live in', Federalist Lecture, *New Europe Paper* (London: European Movement, 1981).
Stewart, Rt Hon. Michael (see Irwin, 1972, above).
Streit, Clarence K., *Union Now: A Proposal for a Federal Union of the Democracies of the North Atlantic* (London and New York: Jonathan Cape and Harper, 1939); first chapter reprinted as *America Speaks* (London: Federal Union pamphlet, 1939).
Thompson, Dennis (see Campbell, 1962, above).
Thompson, Dennis (see *Journal of Common Market Studies*, 1965, above).
Thompson, Dennis, *The International Tropical Timber Organisation and the European Community* (Federal Trust Working Paper, 1988).
Tyrie, Andrew (see Burrows, 1986, above).
Usborne, Henry, *Towards World Government: The Role of Britain, Peace Aims* (London: National Peace Council Pamphlet, 1946).
Usborne, Henry (see Parliamentary Group for World Government, 1947).
Usborne, Henry, *Prescription for Peace: The Case for a Minimal and Neutral Federation of Middle World Nations (Minifed)* (Evesham: Minifed Promotion Group, 1985).
von Hayek, F. A., 'The Economic Conditions of Inter-State Federalism', *New Commonwealth Quarterly*, September 1939, pp. 131–49, reprinted in F. A. Hayek, *Individualism and Economic Order* (London: Routledge & Kegan Paul, 1949) pp. 255–72.
von Weizsäcker, Prof. C. F., *Strategies for Peace*, Corbishley Memorial Lecture (Wyndham Place Trust, 1983).
Wallace, Helen (see Edwards, 1977).
Wallace, Helen, 'Institutions in a Decentralised Community', in Burrows (1978, q.v.) pp. 25–30.
Wallace, William, 'A Common European Foreign Policy: Mirage or Reality?', New Federalist Paper, *New Europe*, Spring 1977, reprinted in Burrows (1978, q.v.) pp. 174–86.
Wallace, William, 'The Administrative Implications of Economic and Monetary Union within the European Community', *Journal of Common Market Studies*, special issue, 1974 (Federal Trust Study Group Report).
Ward, Barbara (Lady Jackson), *Forty Years On: Britain in the Second Half of the Twentieth Century* (Federal Trust pamphlet, 1959).
Weir, Sir Cecil, *The First Step in European Integration – The European Coal and Steel Community* (Federal Trust pamphlet, 1957).
Wheare, K. C., *What Federal Government is*, Federal Tracts No. 4 (London: Macmillan, 1941), reprinted in Ransome (1943, q.v.) pp. 17–38, and by Federal Union (1948).
Wheare, K. C., *Federal Government* (London: Oxford University Press, 1946).

Wickham Steed, H., *Our War Aims* (London: Secker & Warburg, 1939).
Wickham Steed, H., 'Federation and War Policy', in Chaning-Pearce (1940, q.v.) pp. 263–79.
Williams, Rt Hon. Shirley, *Reshaping the Nation State*, speech at Federal Trust's 40th Anniversary Dinner (Federal Trust, 1985).
Williamson, John, 'Trade and Economic Growth', in Pinder (1971, q.v.) pp. 19–45.
Williamson, John (see Magnifico, 1972, above).
Wilson, Duncan and Elizabeth, *Federation and World Order* (London: T. Nelson & Sons, 1939).
Wilson, Duncan, 'The History of Federalism', in Chaning-Pearce (1940, q.v.) pp. 39–56.
Wilson, J. H. (Harold), 'Economic Aspects of Federation', in Federal Union Research Institute (1940, q.v.).
Wingate, M. M., (Monica), *Federation as a political philosophy for the twentieth century Christian* (Federal Union pamphlet, 1952, 1953).
Wingate, Monica, *Christians in a World Society* (Wyndham Place Trust pamphlet, 1959).
1959).
Wistrich, Ernest (see Hart, 1969, above).
Wistrich, Ernest, 'Promoting a European Identity', New Federalist Paper, *New Europe*, Autumn 1976, reprinted in Burrows (1978, q.v.) pp. 62–70.
Wistrich, Ernest, 'the Federalist Struggle in Britain', *The Federalist* (Pavia), December 1984, pp. 230–40.
Wootton, Barbara, 'Report on First Conference: Economic Aspects of Federation', in Federal Union Research Institute (1940, q.v.).
Wootton, Barbara, *Socialism and Federation*, Federal Tracts No. 6 (London: Macmillan, 1941), reprinted in Ransome (1943, q.v.) pp. 269–98.
Wyndham Place Trust (chronological order of publications not listed under author's name):
Christian Responsibility in a World Society (pamphlet containing talks given at a conference at Church House, 1962), contributors Dr A. M. Ramsey, Archbishop of Canterbury (q.v.), Revd Fr Thomas Corbishley, SJ (q.v.), and John Pinder.
Keeping the Peace (Commission Report, 1962).
The Limitations of National Sovereignty (Conference Report, 1966).
Man's Wider Loyalties: Limitations of National Sovereignty (Commission Report, 1970).
Look Outward, Europe (Commission Report, 1971)
Corbishley Memorial Lectures (from 1977, q.v.).
Europe's International Strategy (Commission Report, 1980).
Yassukovich, Stanislas M., 'Capital Flows', in Pinder (1971, q.v.) pp. 152–68.
Young, John, *Paving the Way: Next Steps for Monetary Co-operation in Europe and the World* (Federal Trust Study Group Report, 1987).
Younger, Rt Hon, Kenneth, 'Europe and World Organisation', in Federal Trust (1971/2, q.v.) pp. 5–8.
Zilliacus, Konni, 'World Government and World Peace', in Ransome (1943, q.v.) pp. 337–63.

Members of the Executive Committee, 1939–55

1939–45

Sir Richard Acland
Mr O. Adler
Sir William Beveridge
Mr H. S. Bidmead
Mr W. G. Boys
Major A. M. Braithwaite, MP
Mr R. B. Bucknell
Mr F. A. Campbell
Prof. G. Catlin
Mr W. B. Curry
Sqdn-Ldr P. Edwards
Mr J. W. Fidler
Mr A. E. Farncombe
Mr S. Fox
Mr R. B. Gillett
Dr L. T. M. Gray
Prof. W. J. Gruffydd
Mr L. G. Harris
Mr T. C. Hart
Mr F. Heppenstall
Dr I. Jennings
Prof. C. E. M. Joad
Miss F. L. Josephy
Prof. G. Keeton
Mr C. D. Kimber
Mrs F. G. Knowles
Rev. G. Lang, MP
Mr R. Law, MP
Mr R. W. G. Mackay, MP
Mr G. McAllister, MP
Mr John Parker, MP
Mr E. E. V. de Peyer
Mr P. Ransome
Mr D. L. Rawnsley
Prof. L. C. Robbins
Mr A. Sainsbury
Mr S. F. Sheridan
Sir Drummond Shields
Mr H. C. Usborne
Miss M. M. Wingate
Mrs Barbara Wootton
Mr K. Zilliacus

1945–50

Mr O. Adler
Mr D. G. Allen
Mr S. D. Bailey
Sir Adrian Boult
Mr A. Boyd
Mr R. B. Bucknell
Mr W. E. Catling
Mr V. Collins, MP
Mr J. K. Killby
Mr E. M. King, MP
Cdr Stephen King-Hall
Rev. G. Lang, MP
Mr L. T. Loader
Miss H. M. L. Newlands
Mr J. Pelkman
Mr E. E. V. de Peyer

Mrs M. E. Dru
Mr P. Edwards
Mr J. W. Fidler
Mrs H. Gillett
Mr J. W. Grove
Mr John Haire, MP
Mr Innes Hamilton
Mr L. G. Harris
Mr H. I. D'Arcy Hopkinson
Miss F. L. Josephy
Mr W. J. Proctor, MP
Miss E. Robson
Mr Noël Salter
Mr W. S. Simey
Mrs Stansfield
Mr R. Stevens
Vice-Admiral C. V. Usborne
Mr H. C. Usborne, MP
Miss M. M. Wingate
Mr W. G. Wingate

1951–5

Mr O. Adler
Mr D. G. Allen
Mr B. D. Barton
Sir Adrian Boult
Mrs M. Dru
Mr J. K. Fawcett
Mr D. A. Grant
Mr N. Hart
Prof. C. E. M. Joad
Miss F. L. Josephy
Mr Martin Maddan, MP
Mr J. N. Miskin
Mr J. Pelkman
Mr J. Pinder
Mr E. D. Robinson
Mr D. W. Sanders
Mr E. G. Thompson
Mr C. B. Webb
Mr G. Stuart Whyte
Miss M. M. Wingate
Mr W. G. Wingate

Index